STRIKE FORCE
ORGANIZED CRIME AND THE GOVERNMENT

Previous Books by Clark R. Mollenhoff

Washington Cover-Up

Tentacles of Power

Despoilers of Democracy

The Pentagon

STRIKE FORCE

Organized Crime and the Government

By Clark R. Mollenhoff

PRENTICE-HALL, INC.
Englewood Cliffs, N. J.

Strike Force: Organized Crime and the Government by Clark R. Mollenhoff
Copyright © 1972 by Clark R. Mollenhoff

ISBN: 0-13-852772-5
Library of Congress Catalog Card Number: 79-178137
Printed in the United States of America • 3

Prentice-Hall International, Inc., London
Prentice-Hall of Australia, Pty. Ltd., North Sydney
Prentice-Hall of Canada, Ltd., Toronto
Prentice-Hall of India Private Ltd., New Delhi
Prentice-Hall of Japan, Inc., Tokyo

To Jacquelin Sue Montgomery.

ACKNOWLEDGMENTS

If I were to say a simple "thank you" to all the people who have in some measure helped me to understand the problem of organized crime in America, it would take another book. I will restrict myself to a list of those who have been of some special help in inspiring and packaging *Strike Force*.

First I wish to express my appreciation to my daughter, Gjore Jean Mollenhoff, who suggested the title "Strike Force" and did much of the original research in charting the scope of the project. Without her it is doubtful if this work would have moved off the ground, for she pulled the idea of a book on organized crime down to a manageable size.

This list must include Downey Rice, who was Associate Counsel to the Kefauver Crime Committee when I met him in 1951, a few weeks after I arrived on the Washington scene. He has been the man I have called on in connection with the questions I have had for over 20 years, and I have gone through the many ups and downs which he and his associates had when they first tackled big labor.

It was Walter Sheridan, as Special Assistant to Attorney General Robert F. Kennedy, who directed the day-to-day handling of the all-out drive to incarcerate James R. Hoffa. Hoffa was a formidable foe even for the whole United States government, and the experience of watching that struggle over the years gave me some depth understanding of the problem.

Thomas A. Kennelly, who had been on the "Hoffa Squad," called my attention to the Strike Force operation in Buffalo, New York. It stimulated an interest that has continued to grow even as I have worked on this book and became convinced that the major problem before America today is that of balancing effective enforcement against "the enemy within," but doing it in a way that assures us that there are barriers to arbitrary actions by police, prosecutors, judges, and administrators of local, state, and federal agencies.

This book could not have been written without the work of dozens of committees which have taken on organized crime. The late Senator Estes Kefauver, Representative Clare Hoffman, Senator Paul Douglas, Senator John McClellan, all are major contributors to that record. All will know the contribution made by Robert F. Kennedy as a driving force behind the investigations of the labor racket probes in the 1959 to 1960 period, and that entire staff deserves mention—from Alice Dearborn, who kept the card files, to Jerome Adlerman, Assistant Counsel and later General Counsel. I can single out for special mention Robert Blakey, Carmine Bellino, LaVern Duffy, Phil Morgan, Thomas Nunnally, and Phil Manuel.

At the Justice Department, it was Herbert J. (Jack) Miller, the Assistant Attorney General in charge of the Criminal Division, who provided the firm integrity for the first real start on organized crime. He built a staff in the organized crime field that was even able to make some progress in the face of all of the handicaps which later were placed on the Division by President Johnson and Attorney General Ramsey Clark.

Attorney General John Mitchell, Deputy Attorney General Richard Kleindienst, and Assistant Attorney General Will Wilson gave the Organized Crime and Racketeering Section the approval to use the eavesdropping and wiretapping tools provided by Congress. Also they urged complete cooperation with me by Deputy Attorney General Henry Peterson, who had been head of the Organized Crime Section; William S. Lynch, Chief of the Organized Crime Section, and Edward T. Joyce, his chief deputy. Earlier, I have mentioned Kennelly, but there was the same kind of cooperation from James J. Featherstone, Kurt W. Muellenberg, Philip T. White, and Gerald Shur in their areas.

Commissioner of Internal Revenue Randolph Thrower and Vernon (Mike) Acree, Assistant Commissioner for Inspection, were of special help in getting this book started and in assessing the accomplishments of the eighteen Strike Forces which had been established by the summer of 1971.

In connection with the so-called Bobby Baker case, I owe a special debt of gratitude to former Senator John J. Williams of Delaware who, together with William O. Bittman and Austin Mittler, was responsible for keeping the case moving foward to the final conviction and incarceration. It wouldn't have happened if Senator Carl Curtis and Representative H. R. Gross had been any less courageous in floor speeches, or if Rules Committee Minority Counsel Burkett Van Kirk had been less diligent.

Men of goodwill would have totally different opinions about how to achieve good government and how to eradicate corruption, but in the end it is simply like housekeeping: often a broom will do the job if applied with vigor, but there are other times when a hose, a scrub brush, or a vacuum cleaner is the proper tool.

Twenty years in Washington have convinced me that bigger institutions and bigger budgets have created only bigger problems. We must live with these bigger budgets; but we must find a way to get to the facts and to analyze them periodically to determine the best balanced approach to achieving a stability with justice. We simply cannot insist that all our problems in the slums and all the injustices be ironed out before we take the effective steps to bring order to our society.

It may be good politics to line up with the petty special interest groups that want more and more money allocated to special projects which are sold as some cure-all for what ails America. I am not opposed to any government programs that will work even reasonably well, but I am opposed to piling more and more money into programs without really examining the record to find out how the money has been used.

Good management is the essence of good government, and it starts with a careful analysis of new programs to determine if they can be reasonably well administered by the average man or woman. It must end with a reasonably good possibility that those who are careless or dishonest in the handling of public funds and public authority will be punished—or at least will not be rewarded for their dishonesty.

I believe that most Americans want no more than a reasonable chance for fair play in their dealings with police and with the other agencies of government. All of us will take our tickets with some sense of good grace if we feel it comes from an honest cop; and we will take our punishment if we feel we are sentenced by an honest judge. But if "the fix" is in style in a city, county, state, or federal jurisdiction, there will be bitterness at accepting the consequences of our acts.

I owe a special debt to that group of outstanding investigative reporters who have, for the most part, avoided the ideological hangups that stand in the way of understanding problems and who have kept an eye on the details which are so important. This group includes John Barron, Paul Hope, William Schulz, Ted Link, Wallace Turner, William Lambert, Denny Walsh, Sandy Smith, Robert Green, Harold Brislin, Edward O'Brien, Dan Thomasson, Julian Morrison, George Mills, Ken Clawson, John Herling, Jack Nelson, Robert Jackson, Ron Ostrow, Ben Reece, Montgomery Curtis, Gene Goltz, James Savage, Ronnie Dugger, and Ovid Demaris. Each in his writings or discussions made some contribution of importance in sorting out the facts and getting them into perspective.

C.R.M.

FOREWORD

In recent years such great emphasis was placed upon the Constitutional rights of the criminal that it ofttimes appeared that the Constitutional rights of the innocent had been forgotten. The result has been an accelerated breakdown in law enforcement, an acceleration of the crime rate, and a developing lack of respect—even actual contempt—on the part of the criminal for the law enforcement agencies.

Recognizing this dangerous trend, in 1967 and in 1968 in an effort to combat crime, Congress passed the Omnibus Crime Bill, which established legislation to authorize wiretapping by the Federal Bureau of Investigation and other federal law enforcement agencies.

Clark Mollenhoff in his book *Strike Force* has rendered a great public service in documenting the manner in which legalized wiretapping has contributed toward more effective prosecution of some of the leading members of the underworld, and has pointed out why legalized wiretapping is a "must" if we are effectively to combat the underworld. The failure of the use of this wiretapping authority to contribute more toward better law enforcement in recent years has been not because of inadequacy of the law, but rather because of a lack of sympathy with the law on the part of some of the Justice Department officials whose concern over the rights of the criminal exceeded their concern for the innocent.

I believe

Organized crime has never had any scruples against invading the Constitutional rights of the victim, and certainly society has every right to use the modern technology toward more efficient law enforcement.

Strike Force should be read by every law enforcement officer and every citizen who is interested in better law enforcement.

in agreement

John J. Williams
Former U. S. Senator, Delaware

CONTENTS

1

STRIKE FORCE

"I have served in the office of the District Attorney of New York County for 32 years, the last 25 of them as District Attorney. On the basis of that experience, I believe, as repeatedly I have stated, that telephonic interceptions, pursuant to court order and under proper safeguards, is the single most valuable and effective weapon in the arsenal of law enforcement, particularly in the battle against organized crime. In my judgment, it is an irreplaceable tool and, lacking it, we would find it infinitely more difficult, and in many cases impossible, to penetrate the wall behind which major criminal enterprises flourish." *Frank Hogan, before the Subcommittee of the Judiciary on Criminal Laws and Procedures, July 12, 1967.*

THE term "Strike Force" is meaningful in reference to fighting organized crime only if it stands for action.

Ideally a Strike Force is a small group of highly trained lawyers and investigators from several agencies with authority to cut red tape and go to the top of the Justice Department for the quick decisions necessary to effectively operate against the criminal underworld. If the concept is just another public-relations gimmick, then it does a disservice to the nation.

In 30 years of covering crime in its various forms I have seen hundreds of crime fighters hoist their flags; yet the forces of organized crime continue to baffle and defeat the law-enforcement agencies of local, state, and federal government.

In 1969, 1970, and 1971, the Justice Department under the Nixon Administration achieved significant gains with Strike Forces throughout the country. John Mitchell has made a commendable start in pushing the fight against organized crime. He has been fortunate to follow Ramsey Clark as Attorney General. FBI Director J. Edgar Hoover has called Ramsey Clark the worst Attorney General in history and even liberal Democratic lawyers in the Justice Department agree with Mr. Hoover on that point, though they are at odds with him on many other issues.

When President Richard Nixon took office in January 1969, the public was fed up with crime, whether it involved muggers, militant groups, or the Mafia. In 1968 and 1969, over the objections of President Lyndon Johnson and Attorney General Clark, Congress passed the Omnibus Crime Bill which, among other things, authorized wiretapping by the Federal Bureau of Investigation and other federal enforcement agencies. The President criticized this provision of the bill as "unwise," and the Attorney General ignored it as unnecessary except in cases of national security. As a result, Clark became a sitting duck for Nixon's charge that he was "leading an official retreat" in the war against crime.

"If we are to restore order and respect for law in this country, there's one place where we're going to begin: we're going to have a new Attorney General of the United States of America," Nixon said in accepting the Republican Presidential nomination in Miami.

When John Mitchell took office he had the backing of the majority of the people who wanted the federal government to use all reasonable means to arrest, prosecute, and sentence mobsters. Mitchell considered electronic surveillance an important tool, and assured Congress that his use of it would be consistent with the law and the rights of privacy of the average citizen.

There was an advantage in being a Republican Attorney General.

Traditionally organized crime has been associated with the big machines of the Democratic Party in the major cities; it has also entrenched itself in labor unions, working hand-in-glove with such crooked leaders as James R. Hoffa of the International Brotherhood of Teamsters. Over the years even the highest officials have succumbed to the reality of this association.

In 1947, Attorney General Tom Clark, father of Ramsey Clark, appeared to bend to that reality with orders sharply restricting the Federal Bureau of Investigation in its probe of scandalous vote frauds in Kansas City, Missouri. Few Democrats were willing to challenge this political-criminal nexus directly. One who did was the late Senator Estes Kefauver of Tennessee.

In 1950, Kefauver tackled the big-city Democratic machines in a Senate investigation of organized crime. The hearings he conducted were reminiscent of Theodore Roosevelt's challenge to the corruption in his own party in New York at the turn of the century. Perhaps Teddy's bold example inspired Kefauver to attempt to beat the corrupters rather than join them.

The public support which Kefauver won in his televised crime hearings came close to winning him the Democratic nomination for President in 1952. In the end the big-city bosses and organized crime succeeded in blocking Kefauver's bid and delivered the nomination to Adlai Stevenson, Governor of Illinois. Political figures and underworld characters had lived with Governor Stevenson as a party head in Springfield, and believed they could live with him as President.

Senator Kefauver and his Senate Crime Committee had suggested legalizing the use of eavesdropping and wiretapping by federal officials. They also proposed legislation to provide immunity from prosecution for witnesses whose testimony against underworld figures might possibly be self-incriminating. None of these bills passed. Kefauver failed to capture the Democratic nomination, and organized criminals breathed easier.

In 1956, Senator Kefauver won the Vice-Presidential nomination in a tough fight with Senator John F. Kennedy. Kennedy had the big-city political bosses on his side, along with Southern Democrats who regarded Kefauver as a traitor because of his liberal views on civil rights. All that Kefauver had going for him was his record as a crime fighter. His winning of the nomination convinced Robert Kennedy that a dramatic crusade against crime carried a lot of political kick.

In 1957, Bobby Kennedy, as Chief Counsel for the Select Senate Committee on Labor and Management Relations, commenced the longest sustained drive yet against the alliance of organized crime and dishonest labor officials. He did it with the full knowledge that he would be stepping on the toes of many men important in obtaining the Democratic Presidential nomination for his brother.

The AFL-CIO was totally opposed to the creation of the so-called

Labor Racket Committee, and openly fought its establishment and financing. But before the Committee was finished, Robert Kennedy and Chairman John L. McClellan forced the AFL-CIO to oust the corrupt Teamsters Union. Determined, Kennedy was able to turn a war against labor racketeers and Democratic leaders into a political plus for his brother.

In 1960, John Kennedy was elected President, and appointed his brother Robert as Attorney General. Robert Kennedy continued his attacks on organized crime, even though they hurt Democrats who had been among his brother's strongest supporters. He expanded the Organized Crime Division in the Justice Department, and established a special unit to put Teamsters president, James R. Hoffa, in prison.

The Hoffa unit, operating under Special Assistant Walter Sheridan, showed how a small group of men, using all the facilities of federal investigative agencies, can be most effective in fighting a tough well-financed foe.

Attorney General Kennedy, as brother of the President, forced cooperation between investigative units often inclined to hide their best evidence from other units. The FBI, the Internal Revenue Service, the Narcotics Bureau, and the Securities and Exchange Commission cooperated as never before in the past. Friction arose between Kennedy and J. Edgar Hoover on technical problems; but there was no doubt about who was boss, for none could come between the Attorney General and his brother the President. Major Democratic figures in the city machines were more cautious about making shady overtures which previously would have been regarded simply as "practical politics."

Experience with Hoffa and others convinced Kennedy that legalized wiretapping was "a must" in any crime package. Although there were many areas of disagreement between Robert Kennedy and J. Edgar Hoover, both favored such legislation to amend the Communications Act. Kennedy authorized FBI eavesdropping and wiretapping of Las Vegas casinos. At the same time he endorsed proposals for a law permitting federal agencies to wiretap in cases of national security and organized crime. The law would have placed no limits on state wiretappers.

In 1962, the Kennedy Administration sent Congress a legislative package designed to legalize wiretapping by federal and state authorities under court order, but to outlaw other wiretapping. That legislation was not passed. Nevertheless, other events taking place were more important to the fight against organized crime than any legislation.

On June 22, 1962, Joseph Valachi, a member of the Genovese family of La Cosa Nostra, killed a man in Atlanta Federal Penitentiary. To save his life, Valachi decided to cooperate with the FBI. His subsequent testimony, according to Kennedy, "provided the biggest single breakthrough yet in combating organized crime and racketeering."

Had Robert Kennedy remained as Attorney General with full control to coordinate law-enforcement efforts, some of the later exposure of the Mafia might have come sooner even though it involved important Democratic figures. This was an area in which Kennedy and Republican Herbert J. (Jack) Miller, Assistant Attorney General in charge of the Criminal Division, tended to disregard the political alignment of criminals.

After John Kennedy's assassination in November 1963, Robert Kennedy continued in his job through the summer of 1964. But at first he was too dazed by his brother's death, and then too angry with President Johnson to push forward his campaign against organized crime. He did stay on long enough to see convictions of Hoffa on a jury-tampering charge in Nashville, Tennessee, and a charge in Chicago of conspiracy to commit frauds involving payoffs of some $1 million on more than $20 million in loans from the Central States Southwest Pension and Welfare Fund. These prosecutions, however, were largely carry-overs from past investigations.

The tough crusade had been nipped in the bud.

Cooperation between the FBI and the Criminal Division on the Bobby Baker investigation ended a few days after the assassination. It was only one instance of the deterioration of the drive against organized crime.

Realistic Democratic bosses in the big cities knew that Kennedy's time in office was limited, and they made their contacts with the White

House. President Johnson's good friend, Abe Fortas, had quit as Bobby Baker's lawyer in order to coordinate the investigation of the assassination. The Organized Crime Division weakened under Acting Attorney General Nicholas deB. Katzenbach, and all but expired as Ramsey Clark became the Deputy Attorney General and then Attorney General. Even while Katzenbach held the title of Attorney General, it was recognized that Ramsey Clark was the White House political contact at Justice.

Immediately Johnson put the brakes on the use of eavesdropping and wiretapping, as did Clark.

In 1966 and 1967, the Johnson Administration was under attack for its lack of effectiveness against organized crime. To counter this criticism, Clark established the first Strike Force. But under his direction, the concept, even within the Justice Department, was regarded as little more than a public-relations ploy.

One Strike Force was established in Buffalo in 1966, another in Detroit in 1967. Then, as the Presidential election year of 1968 rolled around, three more were set up: in Philadelphia, Chicago, and Brooklyn. Following Hubert Humphrey's defeat in the election, the Johnson Administration erected the framework for additional Strike Forces in Miami and Newark. However, in all these cases, the investigators were prevented from using the tools so essential: court-approved eavesdropping and wiretapping. As a result, the number of indictments was inconsequential.

In February 1969, only a month after the Nixon Administration came to power, Attorney General John Mitchell authorized the first eavesdropping and wiretapping action against organized crime. In the following order, Strike Forces were established in Boston, New York, Cleveland, Los Angeles, St. Louis, New Orleans, Pittsburgh, Baltimore, San Francisco, and Kansas City up to February 1971. By the summer of that year, the Justice Department had the top mobsters in nearly every city in the United States either convicted or under indictment.

Not surprisingly the haul also included many of the Democratic leaders with whom they had dealt. A few Republicans were also convicted or under indictment for their dealings with organized crime.

But for the most part, the political complexion of underworld business was decidedly Democratic.

Crucial in obtaining leads and gathering evidence in these cases had been the use of eavesdropping and wiretapping. The convictions and indictments in Kansas City, Los Angeles, Newark, or New Orleans, provided stunning proof to counter Clark's contention that eavesdropping and wiretapping were "wasteful and unproductive."

Ramsey Clark was Attorney General for only a couple of inept years. During this time he upset nearly all law-enforcement officials with his questionable decisions bearing indirectly on the Bobby Baker case.

Clark's horror of wiretapping and his often expressed fear that it might turn the United States into a police state may have been sincere views that simply were out of touch with what most crime fighters believed. On the other hand, they might have been simply practical politics.

"Criminal justice has been so long neglected that we come to doubt our principles when it is only their implementation that fails," Ramsey Clark said. "As we build the forces of government to firmly but fairly enforce our laws, we must continue with greater diligence our pursuit of equal justice. Every act of justice makes order surer."

Certainly the prosecution of Bobby Baker dramatized the fact that top political figures are not immune to the law. But Clark, though he was Attorney General at the time, had little to do with this undertaking. It might be justifiably argued that he did nothing to aid the prosecution of Baker, and much to interfere with those assigned to prosecute.

Ramsey Clark's judgment on electronic surveillance was challenged by Congress and men who had real experience in the field. It is doubtful that any incident demonstrated the full value of eavesdropping and wiretapping more than the two authorized surveillances of New Jersey mobsters, which included Samuel Rizzo (Sam the Plumber) DeCavalcante and Ray (the Gyp) DeCarlo.

The DeCarlo-DeCavalcante tapes are classics in the law-enforcement field, for they corroborate and elaborate on the Joe Valachi story.

2

OUT OF THE MOUTHS OF MOBSTERS

"Before the publication of the federal wiretaps from Rhode Island and New Jersey only a few voluntary agencies, such as the citizens' crime commissions . . . have been convinced enough of the portent of organized crime to induce them to do something about it." *Carl M. Loeb, Jr., President of the National Council on Crime and Delinquency, before the Legal and Monetary Affairs Subcommittee of the House Government Operations Committee, August 13, 1970.*

DURING the period when Robert F. Kennedy was Attorney General, the Federal Bureau of Investigation was authorized to install wiretapping devices on the premises of two Mafia bosses in New Jersey—Angelo (Ray the Gyp) DeCarlo, and Simone (Sam the Plumber) DeCavalcante.

The wiretaps were used on Gyp DeCarlo and Sam the Plumber from 1961 until midway into 1965, when President Johnson's views on wiretapping—or his fear of wiretapping—resulted in orders to the FBI to remove the taps. It is not clear just what percentage of the conversations on those wiretaps has been preserved for the record, but a well-rounded picture emerges. Though Sam was aware that he might be tapped, he came through loud and clear for what he was.

The crude and profane manner in which Gyp DeCarlo and his friends spoke about extortion, thievery, and murder left no doubt about their intentions or motives. They pursued a life of crime and violence, and accepted the political fix as part of the game.

Simone Rizzo DeCavalcante has been the Boss of the New Jersey Mafia "family" which bears his name since the death of his predecessor, Nick Delmore, in the early 1960s. It is not one of the largest families—only about 40 members—compared with some of the New York clans of up to 600 members. It is, however, an active family with members engaged in all the popular rackets and actively seeking new gimmicks for the old ones.

From the transcripts of the FBI recordings of conversations at Sam's headquarters, it is possible to draw a frightening, if sometimes ridiculous portrait of a modern Mafia mobster.

During the good old days of Prohibition, business for the mob was uncomplicated. You needed a product—booze, bets, or broads—sawed-off salesmanship, and a concrete method for collecting accounts receivable. Advertising was by word of mouth, and public relations were handled under the table.

Internal Revenue Service computers and sophisticated methods of law enforcement pushed Sam DeCavalcante into new and sometimes more subtle means of operation. He still handled the familiar products—illegal gambling, untaxed liquor, shylock loans, and the redistribution of stolen goods. But he had grown with the times. Sam had diversified. He had moved into "legitimate" fields. His profession was heating and plumbing contracting; but he also used his talents as a labor and management-relations specialist, and considered going into the garbage-removal business.

Sam was a man who had learned new tricks but had been unable to forget the old ways; even in his legal enterprises he could not resist operating outside the law. The same skills stood him in good stead. Sam understood greed, and used it to his advantage to corrupt public officials. Fear of economic ruin brought reluctant businessmen into his circle of business partners. Threats of violence kept disgruntled partners quiet, and tax evasion provided the capital for expansion into new fields.

Sam DeCavalcante's headquarters were in the offices of the Kenworth Corporation, his heating and plumbing business, in the Kenworth Building, Kenilworth, New Jersey. Through his doors came a steady stream of corrupters and corruptibles, from petty hoods seeking Sam's protection to public officials not too particular about the source of their campaign contributions.

Sam's business partner, Laurence Wolfson, had been in business with Nick Delmore, and Sam inherited the partnership when he became Boss of Nick's "family." Because he was Jewish, Wolfson had never been "made" (initiated) as a member of La Cosa Nostra. Membership is restricted to those of Italian descent; but alliances are formed and profits are shared without such petty discriminations.

Larry Wolfson's sister, Harriet Gold, was Sam's confidential secretary. Their relationship was far more than strictly business. Another "regular" at the office—as revealed by the FBI tapes—was Sam's cousin, known to his Kenworth colleagues as Bobby Basile. Bobby ran a separate mob-controlled corporation and Sam's Cosa Nostra errands. He had not been "made" either, but could be if the "books" (membership rolls) are ever formally reopened. While awaiting initiation, he operated in a probationary status.

In late 1964, Sam and his accountant, Jack Kirch, were going over Sam's past tax returns because he had been called in for an IRS audit. Like most Mafia members, Sam habitually understated his income when reporting it to the government. This provided him with additional capital to "invest," and hopefully kept curious public servants from wondering about the sources of his money.

The problem was that Sam liked to live in better style than his reported income would support. Jack Kirch was trying to figure out how Sam could explain his $60,000-home when his tax returns showed an after-taxes income ranging from $10,000 to $13,000 per year. Jack finally decided that "the background doesn't fit the circumstances." The house alone, Jack estimated, ran over $3,000 a year in mortgage payments and such incidentals as heating. College expenses for Sam's two children, age 20 and 22, accounted for another $3,000 a year. Sam had two new cars which cost him about $1,000 a year to operate. Jack could not see how, on what Sam admitted in spendable income, Sam could have handled his $5,000-a-year insurance premiums (he was in a high-risk occupation) and still have any money left to feed and clothe his family. He dreaded thinking about what Mrs. DeCavalcante's checking account would show about the family's life style. He reasoned it as a mathematical impossibility: Net after taxes ... $11,000 ... $10,000 ... $13,000 ... and here Sam showed spending $18,000 ... $19,000.

Sam just wanted Jack's honest, professional opinion: "Would you say there is fraud here?"

Kirch explained that the government had the basis for an excellent "net worth" case against Sam, and simply would not believe that he had borrowed the rest of the money to meet his expenses from his less prosperous relatives. Sam thought he could explain it away by simply telling the IRS that "Italian people are funny people."

Kirch did not share Sam's optimism.

After Kirch left, Sam became a bit more informative about his income. He told Larry and Harriet that since he had joined Kenworth and become respectable his finances had improved tremendously, even his shylocking. From two clients alone he earned more than $34,000 a year in exorbitant interest. Even this, when added to what Sam had reported, barely scratched the surface.

Sam and Larry were in a good business to be used as a base of operations. Construction was booming, and they had figured out all the different ways to make it pay for them. No new units were built without his approval, Sam liked to boast. In fact a substantial number of apartment projects did go up only after arrangements were made with Sam for kickbacks and payoffs. Sam arranged to get the builders coming and going.

For builders who didn't want to use union labor, Sam handled the kickbacks to union officials to ensure peaceful labor relations on the job. In this way a contractor was permitted to use nonunion labor while the union looked the other way. This allowed a favored builder to pay his employees below scale, and gave him a decided advantage in underbidding his competitors. Sam estimated that the use of nonunion labor alone would save more than $1,000 on the price of each apartment unit. Some contractors failed to appreciate the economic advantages of doing business Sam's way and balked at his efforts to save them money. When this happened, Sam could always rely on some of his union partners to help explain the situation.

Carmen DeAngelo, the business agent for a labor union, Local 156, in New Brunswick, New Jersey, was one of those who worked hand-in-builder's-pocket with Sam. He confided about a new project: "Right now the picture is ideal for you, Sam ... I told the guy he's gotta be one hundred percent union ... I told him one hundred percent and that's the way it was left ... I got the pickets ready and everything.

He knows if he doesn't go your way, he's gotta go one hundred percent."

Sam suggested that DeAngelo give the reluctant businessman a call and make the message a little clearer: "Tell him you'll close his job and stop all trucks."

"He didn't start [construction] yet," Carmen explained, adding, "I told him if [he] didn't go union he was gonna have a headache."

At Sam's insistence, Carmen did place a call to the builder. Sam prompted in the background: "Tell him you'll stop all the trucks."

The threat to stop all the trucks was no idle boast. The Teamsters Union served as Sam's enforcement arm in stubborn cases. Tony Provenzano (Tony Pro) of the New York Teamsters could either stop or start a costly strike if Sam needed help. Sam boasted to Bobby Basile and his associates, "Tony called me up the other day . . . anything I want I can have from him . . . in the Teamsters . . . call him direct. I got his private number."

When Tony Pro's boys go out on strike, it is dangerous to cross the picket lines. Although it isn't always fatal, it is definitely unhealthy. There's very little reason to risk the wrath of the Teamsters anyway. A few days without supplies coming in, no deliveries or dumpings going out, means no work can be done on the strike site.

Not only can the Teamsters precipitate a strike against a recalcitrant employer, but the union can break a strike by an unfriendly union against a favored contractor. Tony simply calls off Teamster services to other sites where the offending union has men employed.

When Jerry Graham, partner in a West Orange, New Jersey, nursing home, found himself faced with a strike, he turned for help to Sam to whom he owed $6,000. Sam agreed that it would be easier for Graham to pay the money back if the home continued to operate without interruption. After checking with Tony Pro—to be sure he would call strikes at other hospitals where the striking union had members—Sam offered to mediate the dispute. When the picketing and violence did not cease immediately on his entrance into the negotiations, Sam sent word to the union's international president that if the strike at the nursing home did not end he would "wash the streets with him."

Union officials agreed to negotiate.

Sam's use of force and reliance on the power of the Teamsters was very effective. It was also illegal, but difficult to prove in a society accustomed to charges and countercharges of bad faith by labor, management, and disputing unions. Political figures who decry such tactics risk being labeled as antiunion.

Nick Delmore had split the take on the jobs he set up with the unions so that the officials received 25 percent. Sam considered being more generous, even suggested that he might split 50-50 with his union partners. He was also willing to let Bobby Basile talk him out of his munificent mood. Sam liked to appear generous. He enjoyed telling his colleagues how he had done favors for Jerry Graham and his partners and refused their offer of $2,000 to pay for his time. Sam was touched when, in exchange for his kindness, they presented him with a $2,300-pair of cufflinks. He also liked to include Harriet in the profits on some of his shylock loans.

The construction kickback business was highly profitable. For handling the take on a 100-unit apartment building Sam and Larry could pick up close to $10,000 in nontaxed capital to pump into Sam's other operations. But there was one initial hitch when Sam first took over the operation. Several jobs on which Delmore had made the arrangements were still under construction. Union officials had been paid for some of these jobs by Delmore; Sam, much to the surprise of Joe Richard, whom he described as "that little runt," decided to pay off on the rest.

Following Nick's death, Richard had told Sam, "I guess we have to forget some money." As Sam recalled the conversation: "I said, 'Listen, you jerk. Nick didn't die—only his body is dead. You guys are gonna get paid.' And by Christmas I brought them ten thousand, eight hundred dollars to take care of everything. I got some from the contractors, but I laid the rest out."

Some of Sam's union partners weren't properly appreciative and spotted an opportunity to take advantage of the new Boss. Obviously hoping that Sam wouldn't know the difference, they complained they had received no money before he took over.

Sam met with Bobby Basile and his partners Frank Cocchiaro and Bernie Furst in order to reconstruct the record, contractor by contractor and payment by payment.

Bernie brought the situation up to date. "I was seeing some of these union guys today. Sam, this is what they say they still have coming."

Sam disagreed, and decided how to settle the score. "They didn't get paid? Well, you know what we do? We collect all the money and we don't give them a dime. Now when you hit a job like that—where I paid them myself—these guys are nuts."

On another job Bernie explained: "They [union officers] made the deal themselves."

Sam saw a handy shortcut. "Why don't they do it again, and give you fellows a piece?"

Bobby Basile explained that they had forbidden the union officers to arrange their own kickbacks and payoffs, so it was agreed that Sam and his friends would handle it. Bobby dutifully noted the information in writing, because even the business of shakedowns must be handled in an orderly fashion.

In connection with another deal, Bernie remarked that payment had just been made because Bobby had given union officers their envelope that day. Sam asked Bobby if he had taken anything out of the envelope.

"Nothing," Bobby vowed.

Sam chastised him, "Well, Bob, then you don't listen to me. I told you, 'Here's the envelope, Bobby. Sit down, count yourself in . . .' "

"Now wait a minute, Sam," Bobby protested, "you told me no such thing!"

Frank restored peace. "Sam, it don't matter. They got more money coming." And arrangements were made to deduct Bobby's cut from the next payment.

The next contractor on the list wouldn't play ball, but Bernie had a good suggestion: "Rusty said he would break his back if you want his back broken."

Sam okayed the idea. "Tell him to go ahead."

Bernie double-checked to make sure he had the order straight. "Break his back?"

"Yeah. Tell him, make him holler till he hears the name 'Sam.' "

Frank approved of this solution for straightening out their greedy union partners. "Do you want us to get these guys together and give them a blasting—just for lying?"

The Boss decided it would be more prudent to first get his own records in order and then call a conference with the union boys.

Sam's heating and plumbing operation was also a nice plum. "Owning" a plumbing inspector was a handy way to get advance notice of new construction jobs and approval for substandard work. For this Sam didn't have to entice anyone. Plumbing Inspector Robert Rapp came into his office and offered himself for sale. Sam was out, so Larry handled the arrangements.

When Rapp informed Larry of a new building development for which the plumbing contract had not yet been awarded, he wondered aloud if there were some way they could get together on this.

Larry Wolfson took the direct approach. "We can break their backs—unionwise. They must go union, or else they gotta work with us."

That wasn't quite what Rapp had in mind. "I figure there's a better angle than that. I know what he [the contractor] is doing on the union angle, and its petty larceny. I'm not interested in that . . . I'm figuring a different angle completely. To hell with the union—you don't have to work that way."

Rapp promised he could force a contractor to use a specific plumber, saving Sam and Larry any pretense of making a low bid. Larry quickly saw the advantages and agreed that they would do the plumbing and heating.

For other jobs, Rapp explained what he could contribute to the new partnership. "I know immediately as soon as a building permit is issued. Sometimes I get it before that because in order to demolish a house you have to come to me first. They just passed this ordinance. After I get this information, I could tell you and you could contact the principals." Rapp felt that once he passed on this information it was up to Sam and Larry to "go after the guy and jump right in with strong prices."

Larry envisioned no problem. "If they have to build union, it's gotta cost them a thousand dollars a unit more . . . than nonunion. And if anything gets too tough, I'll turn it over to a couple of our boys and let them go in there and take care of it. They'll break a few heads, and knock them into line." But he promised: "I won't go to extremes unless it's necessary."

"If that's the case, we can make a lot of money," Rapp frankly stated. "I'm not interested in stealing twenty dollars a unit. I want to make a score."

Larry quickly settled any doubts Rapp might have had about the operation. "That's the only way we work!"

Details had to be worked out, and one was the fact that the Plumbing Inspector could not accept checks because the Internal Revenue Service called him in each year to go over his returns. Larry assured Rapp it could be handled, and a new partnership was formed.

Bobby Basile was concerned about the reputation Kenworth Corporation was getting because of the manner in which much of its business was obtained and the damaging effect it had on Sam's good name. He didn't mince words. "You are known as a shakedown artist! You are shaking the contractors down. Do you think anybody [else] would come in here and tell you this, Sam? Do you know that to the outside world your reputation is unbelievable, Sam? That they dread the thought of coming in and talking to you. . ?"

Basile claimed that Larry Wolfson was making unauthorized shakedowns using Sam's name and asked, "How come Larry Wolfson can get a hundred and fifty dollars a unit more than anybody else? You give me the backing—I'll show you how much business I can get."

Bobby counted off a list of builders who would no longer give Kenworth their business, supposedly because of Larry's shakedown efforts. It didn't make sense to Basile that Kenworth could be underbid regularly by other contractors, but Larry still got the business. He wanted to know "what makes Larry such a genius," other than using the pressure of Sam's name.

Sam believed it was because Kenworth's "equipment and jobs are much superior."

"Don't you believe it," Bobby retorted.

Sam and his family weren't satisfied to rely merely on contractors, state inspectors, and crooked union officials. They decided to set up their own union.

Local 242 of the Warehousemen's Industrial Union in New York was under the control of Joseph (Whitey) Danzo, one of Sam's mob associates who was more than willing to cooperate, for a price. He and Gaetano Dominick Vastola (Corky)—a minor-league operator compared with Sam—who dabbled in gambling and stolen goods, had worked out the basic details. Members would be signed up for the existing Local 242 and, after a short period, separated from the parent local and turned over to Corky. Whitey charged $4 a month in dues, but felt that Corky could easily charge $5 a month for his operation. This and the initiation fee, $10 during the "organization drive" and $25 after that, would provide the seed money for the books, stationery, and an office to make the local appear legitimate. After that, these fees would serve as a steady though small regular income for Corky and his partners.

Once assured of Whitey's full cooperation, Sam wanted to know how the profits would be divided. Corky counted heads. He had two men who would be working with him in New Jersey, and Whitey had earned a share for his cooperation and expertise. Corky figured that this made a four-way split, nice and even, 25 percent each. Sam stopped them. "Do you think that's right—to forget *me*?"

Corky and Whitey quickly saw Sam's point and agreed to a five-way division of the profits. Always anxious to be fair, Sam double-checked to make sure that each of his new partners was truly satisfied with this arrangement. They assured him that 20 percent was sufficient for them.

Sam thought they were being small-time and couldn't understand how at only $5 per month from each member they were going to make "a score." Corky revealed his big plans. "Well, I'm gonna make a score this way. When I sit down with the boss [management] I tell him how much its gonna cost him in welfare, hospitalization and all that. Say a plant with two hundred and sixty people will cost him four thousand dollars a month just for hospitalization. So, altogether, I make a package out of it. [I'll say] 'It's gonna cost one hundred thousand dollars a year. Let's cut it in half, and forget about it.' And walk away. I show him first what it's gonna cost—then how much I'm gonna save him by walking away."

It was a classic sweetheart contract worked out for the benefit of management and the union chief with no regard for the membership.

As in the rest of Sam's union deals, no concern was shown for the welfare of the men who made it possible. They were merely convenient hostages from whose work Sam and his Cosa Nostra associates could make "a score."

Sam was not just a "businessman." Simone Rizzo DeCavalcante was a "philanthropist." Like many others whose climb to financial security has been less than exemplary, Sam had discovered a way in which he could buy respectability and possibly enduring affection.

The San Giuseppe Boccone del Poverno Orphanage in Ribera, Sicily, was the recipient of Sam's benevolence for which he sponsored an annual charity ball in Elizabeth, New Jersey. Sam worked on behalf of the orphans. However, some part of his character prevented him from operating even this in an honest manner.

To the gentle Sisters in Ribera, a farming center of nearly 30,000 population, Sam was the rich American gentleman, a retired business-man who had turned to good works to fill his twilight years. His portrait hung in a prominent place over the door in the orphanage.

Between the end of World War II and 1965, mob-dominated donations had paid for half the orphanage expenses and equipment. Now Sam decided that new facilities were needed for the children—a summer camp outside the city. His captains and soldiers were assigned tickets for the ball to purchase and push to their contacts. Sam took great pride in the success of his fund-raising efforts. In addition to turning his strong-arm boys into salesmen, he had hit on a marvelous way to elicit generous gifts from the business community.

Harriet kept all cash donations for the San Giuseppe Orphanage in an envelope in the office safe. When a large enough gift came in, Sam enabled the donor to get a nice tax break on his contribution. He would accept a check made out for the amount which the donor wished to show on his tax return. The difference between what was actually given to the fund and what the record would show was handed back in cash from Harriet's envelope. The Internal Revenue Service would find a gift of $2,000 or more listed with a cancelled check for the receipt. Sam would get, maybe, $1,000 for his fatherless waifs, and the civic-minded contributor would go home with the balance in conveniently untraceable cash.

Sam's system worked. In September 1967, he and members of his orphanage "committee" visited Ribera for the dedication of the new summer camp. His friends there thought that honorary Ribera citizenship would be a fitting tribute to his generosity, but he was deprived of this accolade by the leftist-dominated City Council. The Communist Mayor of Ribera objected more to Sam's American free-enterprise background than to any possible Mafia ties.

When the transcripts of the wiretaps on DeCavalcante's office became part of the public record during his late 1969 appearance before the New Jersey State Investigating Commission, public officials found a haven in Sam's orphanage. In reply to newspaper charges of close familiarity with Sam and his Cosa Nostra *compadres*, it was safe to admit to having met him at the annual charity dinner. The tickets were not expensive, and important members of the Italian community gathered innocently to drink, dine, and dance to Sam's tune. No good politician ignores the ethnic vote if he hopes to stay in office; and no good guest ignores his host. All in the name of charity was the common alibi.

Not only did the FBI learn about Sam's financial and business dealings, but it got an earful about his personal life. In love, as in his other activities, Sam liked to have several options open to him. At one time he had his wife, Mary, at home; Harriet, his confidential secretary, at the office; Audrey, safely tucked away in Trenton; and an out-of-towner who would fly in to visit. They should have been enough to provide a rather full life for any man who claimed that his business and La Cosa Nostra took all his time and energy. But somehow he managed to find enough of each to take Harriet to Philadelphia, Audrey to Florida, Mary to Las Vegas, and to entertain his long-distance love in a New York hotel suite; all in less than three months.

Of course Harriet, as his secretary, knew about his travels with Mary. But when Sam took off for Florida with Audrey, only Bobby was in on the secret. Harriet and her brother Larry were told that Sam was off for parts unknown on Mafia business. Sam hinted that failure could cost him his life. He almost overplayed his part. Larry and Harriet became so fearful for his safety that Larry wanted to go along as his bodyguard. That was not quite the reaction Sam had intended, and he politely tried to discourage him. But Larry insisted, "I want you to know one thing before you say any more, Sam. I've used a piece [gun]. And if anybody's gonna protect you—I want to protect you. I'll do a better job than [Bobby or] anybody else will."

Sam explained he didn't feel it would be necessary because he "always walked with a clean conscience."

"But there are 'meshugana' people in this world, Sam."

"People are crazy," Sam agreed, and patiently continued, "they want to hit me for anything—they got the whole world behind it. . . . Now if it has to happen—you or Bobby or other people, they won't be able to stop it. The only thing is that you guys would go with me. For what? Like I said, I've only done good. The guy that ever does anything to me is the worst SOB in the world."

Larry had no rebuttal for this logic.

Sam was used to obstacles in his attempts to see Audrey. As he told Bobby and Frank Majori, one of his lieutenants, "I go with somebody in Trenton. I parked at her house. As soon as I parked two guys pulled up. . . . They looked like they were headed for trouble. . . . So I got my coat over the pistol [he carried in his car]. And I got the pistol laying out the window. But they just wanted directions! They were lost! See how you can wind up in trouble?"

Bobby was full of admiration for Sam's ability to stay calm when it looked as if his tryst might be cancelled by an attempt on his life.

When Sam took Mary to Las Vegas, he had a wonderful time—though not necessarily with her. His trips West gave him an opportunity to visit many of his Cosa Nostra friends and check out their "investments." Profits went up when Sam was in town. During one trip he gambled away at least $50,000.

Mary did not return from the West Coast with Sam but conveniently stayed more than two weeks longer. This left Sam free to fill his nights as best he could and he lost no time in making arrangements. No sooner did he get back to the office, than he called Harriet to tell her how much he loved her and how miserable he had been without her. He followed this passionate declaration with a quick call to Audrey.

Harriet's vacation, scheduled right after Sam's return, made it possible for him to entertain an out-of-town guest in a suite at New York's Park Sheraton Hotel. Ever courteous, he booked in advance to save his inamorata the bother and embarrassment of checking in. He also made sure she knew that he had registered under his own name and could spell DeCavalcante.

It was not unusual for Sam to let people know what name he was using. Like many members of La Cosa Nostra, he had a handy alias or two ready when needed. In fact, before leaving for a fitting with his tailor, he had to double-check to determine whether he had ordered his suits as Mr. DeCavalcante or as Mr. Rizzo.

Sam's relationship with Harriet was full of contradictions. To Bobby, who disapproved, Sam insisted that his only interest in Harriet was to ensure her complete loyalty and continued silence about his illegal business deals. Bobby argued that her position in the firm was precisely the reason Sam should have maintained a completely businesslike relationship with her. Vito Genovese's wife had blown the whistle on his deals during her battle for a divorce, Bobby reminded his cousin. To him, it was just not prudent to expect a girl friend to be completely reliable when a wife could not be trusted.

Despite Sam's assurances to Bobby, his conversations with Harriet did not indicate a man who was emotionally detached. He might have been an excellent actor, but he was constant in his declarations of love and in coaxing her to tell him how much she loved him. He even wanted her parents to like him and turned on the charm for the older Wolfsons. Whatever his true feelings, he was no more faithful to Harriet than he was to Mary.

Sam told Harriet he was jealous of other men who looked admiringly at her, but went out of his way to try to heal the breach in her marriage. Harriet's husband, Dave, held a minor position in one of Sam's deals.

Sam took Harriet with him on business trips, to the theater, and went home with her for lunch. Even so, he found time to offer his services as a marriage counselor to the couple. He thought that Harriet and Dave should try "to be nice to each other"; he didn't offer any suggestions about when she might find time to do so. On one point there was agreement: Sam and Dave both thought Harriet a sexy woman. They both were in a position to know.

Harriet reciprocated Sam's concern for her well-being. She was terribly upset when her maid, Marie, received an anonymous phone call from a woman who wanted to know if Harriet was "having a good time with Mr. Sam." Sam scoffed, and told her not to worry. She did worry, though, especially when her marriage continued to deteriorate despite Sam's "helpful" efforts.

She warned Sam to "protect" himself because she feared that Dave might seek a divorce and name him as a corespondent. She knew how Sam tried to avoid unfavorable publicity. He was touched by her concern for his reputation and, as a sign, invested some of his own money for her in one of his shylock loans promising her a quick $1,000 as her share of the profits "if everything works out all right."

Sam warned Harriet he couldn't trust anyone completely—"100 percent"—not even her, yet made her privy to the details of his business arrangements. She was trusted to hold in her personal checking account the money which he and Larry siphoned out of Kenworth for nonexistent "business expenses." She had the combination to the office safe where they habitually kept large amounts of loose cash. Except about some of his other women, Harriet knew all the important secrets of his life.

Mary was not so fortunate. The FBI tap did not include Sam's home, so there is no accurate record of his regard for his wife. However, the picture Sam presented to those in his office was not very flattering. The Mary his coworkers saw through his eyes was a mistrustful nag. He was hurt that she thought the trips he arranged for her were just to get her out of the city so he could act the playboy. Harriet wondered how well Mary knew her husband. Sam's griping would indicate that Mary knew him well enough.

There are people who still disbelieve the existence of La Cosa Nostra and the wide-ranging conspiracies of organized crime in which its members participate.

For some, the facts seem to be drawn from movie scripts of the 1930s. Others cannot bring themselves to accept the reality of a force of evil so powerful that it corrupts public officials, imprisons workers in unions supposedly organized for their benefit, and turns formerly honest businessmen to crime through extortion, frustration, or greed. Worse are those who readily admit that organized crime might exist, but simply do not care because they are not directly involved and, therefore, feel that it doesn't affect them. These blind citizens ignore the fact that flourishing illegal gambling spawns a disregard for the law which carries over to other areas. They discount the disproportionate tax burden they must bear because of the billions of dollars in untaxed profits to the underworld. They watch municipal taxes rise and the quality of public services deteriorate without associating these problems with grafters who fill their pockets from the public purse through kickbacks and illegally granted public contracts.

Sam DeCavalcante believes in La Cosa Nostra. He is a member, the Boss of his own family. He has his own lieutenants and soldiers. He follows the directions of the "Commission." Sam even plays office politics, for La Cosa Nostra, like any other large organization, experiences the same jockeying for position to be on the winning side after every upheaval. In the Mafia past, the winning side often meant the surviving side.

During the mid-1960s, the Mafia was afflicted by one of its periodic power struggles. Joseph (Joe Bananas) Bonanno, the head of his own large Mafia family and a member of the nine-man Commission, had lost his status with the other eight commissioners. It is the responsibility of the Commission to oversee the internal affairs of La Cosa Nostra, to ensure that the families whose territories often overlap "respect" each other's spheres of interest. The Commission also acts as a supreme court with the power of death over any member who threatens the security of the organization.

Not only had Bonanno dared to ignore Commission rulings, but he had defied the Commission by refusing to come before the members to present his side of the story. In retaliation, the Commission had "put him on the shelf" (ordered him ostracized by the entire Cosa Nostra). Members of his family were divided in their loyalties. Some accepted the decree and waited for a decision on the future of the family, while others, including Sam's good friend "Joe Bayonne" Zicarelli, remained loyal to Bonanno. Unless a solution could be arranged, the underworld was threatened with war.

The situation had reached a crisis when one Bonanno family member informed the Commission that Bonanno tried to arrange for him to kill Commission members Carlo Gambino and Thomas (Three Fingers Brown) Luchese. The informant subsequently died, and his death had all the appearance of a Bonanno poisoning.

Bonanno had already been accused of trying to move into California and wrest control of that area for one of his sons, and of "making" new members when the books had been ordered closed. The Mafia encourages its families to expand their operations, but not when it endangers the organization as a whole. Called in to answer the charges against him, Joe Bonanno refused to go.

Sam, aware of the dangers this created, offered his services as an intermediary. He knew that an all-out war would be "all the government would want . . . it would be like World War III." He was able to contact Bonanno and tried to convince him that he should come in peacefully. He told Joe: "I didn't make the rules. You made them. You and the Commission made them, and you know them."

Bonanno let Sam know in no uncertain terms that as far as he was concerned, the whole matter was strictly an internal family squabble and none of the Commission's business. Not only did he reject Sam's offer to help, but Joe Bonanno disappeared. Nobody would admit knowing his whereabouts. There was speculation that the Commission had finally found him and taken him into custody. It was also considered possible that the FBI or some other law-enforcement agency had arrested the Mafia maverick. Rumors were rampant, but evidence was scarce.

Joe Bayonne confided to Sam that although he wanted to abide by the rules of the Commission, his first loyalty was to his boss. "Right or wrong, if he calls me, I'm going. If I'm gonna get hit—the hell with it! I get hit and that's the end of it."

Joe was not alone. Even after the story became widespread that Bonanno had arranged to have his own people kidnap him to avoid being found by the Commission, many of his soldiers remained loyal.

The longer it took to settle the problem, the more restive the lieutenants became. They smelled power. Gaspar De Gregorio, who had fallen out with Bonanno, was favored by the Commission to replace him. Members of the family who considered him a catalyst in the whole affair refused to ponder the idea. Sam did not have the power in his own family to guarantee the safety of all parties, and wanted to keep his family insulated from any adverse repercussions. Through his friendship with Jerry Catena and Carlo Gambino, he tried to arrange for a parley between the Commission and the fractious lieutenants.

The Bonanno family could not be left without a boss; but everyone was not agreed that Joe Bonanno was permanently out. The Commission had been forced to issue contracts (orders to kill) on several of the more troublesome dissidents, but peace was restored before widespread bloodshed broke out. The final settlement saw Bonanno stripped of most of his power and banished to Arizona while De Gregorio, with the support of Buffalo Boss Steve Magaddino, moved into the front-running spot to take his place.

Adding to the tension throughout the affair was the fact that members of the mob were becoming aware of leaks within their organization, leaks they could not locate. Members were being picked up for questioning, and the questions were too close to the point not to be the result of some break in the code of *omerta* which demanded silence to the death from members of La Cosa Nostra.

The FBI men were everywhere: at meetings Sam set up between the Commission and members of the Bonanno family; at restaurants the mob frequented, such as the Copacabana; and they had even discovered that Sam "Rizzo" had taken Nick Delmore's place and were asking about him. They also asked about a good many other members, and it was impossible to be sure just who they were after.

As for the leaks, Sam wasn't too worried. He had the office checked for "bugs," and took the basic precautions to hamper eavesdroppers.

He tried to conduct important conversations only when they would be obscured by a radio. He even sent confederates out to make phone calls for him from a nearby pay station. But Sam was not consistent; he constantly had to be reminded to turn up the radio or to speak more softly. He never succeeded in finding the listening equipment which the FBI had planted in his office.

It has always been the policy of Mafia leaders to insulate themselves from the actual day-to-day street operations of the mob. Sam had slightly modified this tradition. Although he still dealt primarily through Frank Majori and Bobby, he often met with the members of his family to provide advice and assistance. Sam liked to be reminded that things were a great deal different from Delmore's rule, when everyone simply took orders without the opportunity to discuss them. He prided himself on running a more democratic ship, so much so that he risked losing the respect of the Commission for working too hard on behalf of his men. As a result, Sam was vulnerable to being fingered by any of his soldiers who might decide to cooperate with federal officers.

Sam got one such scare when, in late 1964, John LaMelo was questioned at length about his Mafia connections. As Bobby related the story: "They asked him about La Cosa Nostra." When John pleaded ignorance, he was asked if he knew what the words meant. John had replied, "Sure, [it means] this belongs to me—it's one of my things." Bobby was sure that John's heavy Italian accent had convinced the officers that John was simple and honest. He didn't like the idea of federal officers calling on "the whole family." They were, he felt sure, piecing things together and had a pretty good fix on Sam's position in the overall structure.

This also bothered Sam. He did not like his enemies to know that he frequently used the name "Rizzo," and he decided that to protect both his family and himself he should stay more in the background. Bobby was instructed to "be the contact man, my messenger," and to pass the word "to all the guys that I don't want nobody here no more [sic]."

It was impossible for him to separate himself completely from his members. He had to call in two of his *capos* to settle a feud between them. John Riggi complained that Joe Sterra was not showing him the proper respect, but Sam refused to listen until both men appeared together to straighten out the matter.

Respect is important in the Mafia. It is the protocol which keeps disputes from erupting into uncontrolled violence.

John resented that "as an *amica nos* and a *caporegima,* I'm not getting the respect that I should from Joe." Every time he tried to get some small favor for one of his men, if Joe was involved, it had to be taken to Sam or Frank Majori before there was any action. Members of the same family were supposed to look after each other's welfare. John felt it was unfair that "as an *amica nos* . . . I can't go to my friend and get a favor for one of my soldiers. Even as a *caporegima,* I can't do nothing. I want to know why."

Joe defended himself by claiming that John never gave him time to act before going over his head. Sam agreed that John was not forceful enough in exercising his position as a *capo* and turned to his superiors for help too quickly. The squabble was resolving itself nicely when Joe forgot himself and challenged John's authority as a *capo.* Sam exploded. He reminded them that discipline and respect allowed their organization to survive. Joe was warned he must never again be so foolish as to question the power of another Mafia member.

Sam ordered the two to shake hands and apologize. He did not dare permit his family's security to be threatened at a time when he was desperately trying to prevent a war. If his men caused him to lose respect by their disagreements, he would stand little chance of succeeding.

When John and Joe failed to respond immediately to Sam's order, he bellowed, "What are you guys—deaf? Joe—John, get up! Both of you get up." They promptly obeyed and agreed to Sam's demand that the story of their feud go no further lest they both lose the respect of their men.

They knew enough to heed Sam's warning. He was explicit in describing how he dealt with those who did not.

Sammy Sheritola had made the mistake of not coming when Sam called for him after one of their deals went wrong and the police became involved. That, Sam claimed, "was against his principles." He had gone after the truant. Corky, taken along to handle the dirty work, administered a sound professional beating while Sam elicited Sammy's promise that it would never happen again.

Of the nearly 60 men in the next room during the beating, not one moved to help Sammy.

Sam DeCavalcante did not believe in the harsh methods of Nick Delmore and wanted to give his men more freedom, but he used whatever physical force was necessary to remind them he was indeed the Boss. Minor indiscretions brought a warning. Anyone who forgot himself could expect to be whipped back into line—literally.

With his family affairs in order, Sam was free to study another problem—namely the disposal of bodies. The solution in the old days had been for the Mafioso to dispose of their victims in a specially constructed double-deck coffin provided by an *amica nos* who ran a mortuary as his legitimate front. Enough strong Mafia pallbearers could handle the double weight without the mourners ever noticing the difference. The system had worked well for years, but the only foolproof one would be no body at all. "Richie the Boot" Boiardo reputedly had an incinerator on his estate which took care of all but the larger bones. Sam wanted something better, something that left no remains.

There were several possibilities. One reliable method was a machine used to smash up old automobiles and convert them into neat metal cubes ready for disposal or recycling. It was commonly considered the best thing then on the market. Sam had heard about another machine being developed that would convert a human body into "a meatball." That still meant getting rid of the leftovers. Sam was most interested in machines for pulverizing garbage. Since he was planning to expand into the garbage removal business, this kind of device would fit right in. If he were able to get his garbage dump, it would mean having a place in which to keep this type of equipment without arousing suspicions, and its legitimate use would be a profit-making enterprise. Working models were not available; but Sam's need was not immediate. The boys were ordered to stay abreast of technological advances and keep him informed.

Sometimes, however, the Mafia wanted a body to be found as a warning. Sam and Angelo (Ray, or "The Gyp") DeCarlo had discussed such a case. A fellow Mafioso had been murdered as a warning to others, but they were appalled because it had been done without proper "respect" for the man's family. Ray explained how he would have handled the job. "Now like you got four—five guys in the room. You know they're goin' to kill you. They say, 'Tony Boy wants to shoot you in the head and leave you in the street, or would you rather we [give you a drug overdose and] put you behind your wheel. We don't have to embarrass your family or nothing!' " He concluded, "That man never should have been disgraced like that."

"Respect" for the victim was not always desired. Pure sadism was revealed in one conversation the FBI picked up between two Chicago hoodlums.

James Torello: "[William] Jackson was hung up on that meat hook. He was so heavy he bent it. He was on that thing three days before he croaked."

Fiore Buccieri: (giggling) "Jackie, you shoulda seen the guy. Like an elephant he was, and when Jimmy hit him with that electric prod. . . ."

Torello: "He was floppin' around that hook, Jackie. We tossed water on him to give the prod a better charge, and he's screamin'. . . ."

Now and then members nostalgically reflected on past murders, as in a conversation at DeCarlo's headquarters, The Barn, in Mountainside, New Jersey.

Tony Boy Boiardo reminded Ray: "How about the time we hit the little Jew?"

Ray: "As little as they are, they struggle."

Tony: "The Boot [his father] hit him with a hammer. The guy goes down and he comes up. So I got a crowbar this big, Ray. Eight shots in the head. What do you think he finally did to me? He spit at me and said, 'You——.' "

DeCarlo's violence finally caught up with him. He was convicted of extortion against Louis D. Saperstein, deceased.

When Saperstein, a mortgage broker, died on November 26, 1968, the cause was listed as gastric upset. His death would have gone unremarked outside his circle of friends and relatives except for one detail: the day before, he had written to the FBI telling why he feared that his life was in danger.

Saperstein was known as a labor racketeer who had been convicted in 1959 of conspiring to embezzle more than $900,000 from the welfare funds of the International Laundry Workers Union.

Prompted by his letters, an autopsy was ordered. Saperstein's body was found to contain enough arsenic "to kill a mule." The case went to the Essex County grand jury. Although the grand jury did not find sufficient evidence to bring a murder charge, four members of the mob were indicted for conspiracy and extortion. The quartet, arrested on August 28, 1969, included Angelo DeCarlo, tavern owners Daniel (Red) Cecere and Peter (Peter the Bull) Landusco, and Joseph (Indian Joe) Polverino.

In his opening statement in January 1970, Prosecuting Attorney Frederick Lacey outlined his case. Saperstein was in debt to the defendants for $400,000, including interest payments of $5,000 a week. The racketeer had used the money, Lacey explained, to finance illegal speculations in foreign securities. When federal agents investigating his operations froze his Swiss-banked funds, he was unable to make the interest payments. The defendants, in an effort to collect, had savagely beaten Saperstein and ordered him to pay up by December 13, 1968, or be murdered.

As part of the trial record, Saperstein's letters to the FBI were a damning accusation against the defendants. "Cecere, DeCarlo, and Polverino also stated many times that my wife and son would be maimed or killed." The convicted embezzler pleaded with the authorities, "Please protect my family. I am sure they mean to carry out their threat."

One letter described how he had made interest payments to "Red" Cecere at his Berkley Bar in Orange, New Jersey, every Thursday. His second letter detailed "another shylock deal" with DeCarlo and "Peter Landesco [sic] —owner of the Living Room [bar and restaurant] in East Orange." Payments for this loan were also due on Thursdays and were paid to Peter (the Bull) Landusco at the Living Room.

Louis Saperstein's letters made it clear that he didn't hold out much hope for himself, but "maybe others can be helped by my plight."

The prosecution's first witness was Gerald Martin Zelmanowitz, a self-proclaimed financial expert and partner in Saperstein's speculatory investments who constantly irritated Cecere's attorney, Michael Querques, with his eagerness to tell the whole story.

Zelmanowitz was hardly an upstanding businessman doing his civic duty. The 32-year-old investor had been arrested twice in 1968 by the FBI for the sale of stolen bonds, was under indictment in New York County for forgery and grand larceny, and was suing the federal government for dismissal of a $140,000 tax lien.

During cross-examination by Querques, Zelmanowitz brashly admitted that in the preceding five years he had made $1 million on which he had paid no income taxes. He blithely acknowledged that he was unable to tell how much had been earned honestly and how much by breaking the law. He even destroyed his own suit against the government by testifying that it was based on an illegal document.

Querques was indignant that anyone would have the gall to sue the government after defrauding it of taxes. In pursuing this attack against the integrity of the witness, he demanded: "Who was your lawyer in that case?" Obviously he had not expected the answer he received. Zelmanowitz identified one counsel as Norman Schiff (a defendant in the Addonizio trial) and the second as "Sam Foosaner, whom you recommended."

Even the prosecuting attorneys, well aware of Zelmanowitz's unsavory history, began taking hasty notes when he admitted his role in the sale of stolen securities. He identified "the other ... thieves," including Raymond Patriarcha, Boss of the New England Cosa Nostra family, Anthony (Fat Tony, or Tony Fat) Salerno, a top gambling figure and a lieutenant in the Tommy Three Fingers Brown-Luchese mob, and Gil Beckley, a big-time bookie from Miami.

Zelmanowitz described a fall (1967) meeting he and Saperstein had had with DeCarlo at The Barn. When Saperstein asked for a "loan" of $100,000, it was explained to him how profits could be made by "arbitrage"—the practice of buying and selling securities simultaneously in different countries to take advantage of differences in the currency. Although arbitrage can be legal, Zelmanowitz conceded it was not—as he practiced it. Saperstein was referred to "Red" Cecere who DeCarlo said would "handle the financial end of things."

Under the agreement between Saperstein and Zelmanowitz a numbered Swiss account was opened to handle their dealings in securities. The partners barely got their scheme off the ground before suspicious Internal Revenue Service officials froze their assets, putting Saperstein in a perilous position early in 1968.

In April of that year, Zelmanowitz and Saperstein, with Cecere along to protect his investment, flew to Geneva where they withdrew $100,000 from the numbered account. Cecere promptly deposited the money in another numbered Swiss account and returned home. The $100,000 then surfaced from sources in this country and was distributed among Saperstein's creditors.

Unable to continue meeting his payments, Saperstein went into hiding in a New York City hotel. He apparently hoped that his silent partners would think he had fled the country. Zelmanowitz testified that Saperstein tried to borrow the money from him, but he did not give it to him.

Saperstein came out of hiding in mid-September and contacted Zelmanowitz, insisting they meet. The witness related how he notified Red Cecere, who decided to accompany him to his apartment.

At noon on September 13, 1968, when Saperstein arrived in the lobby of the New York Hilton for the meeting and saw Cecere and his sidekick, Lennie, he tried to flee. Lennie and Cecere restrained the terrified investor, and calmed him with reassurances that it was safe for him to return with them to New Jersey. To appease his creditors, Saperstein promised he would take out a $100,000 insurance policy "and jump out of a window if you don't hurt my family. I'll make you the beneficiary."

Zelmanowitz took his own car, joining the trio at DeCarlo's Barn. By the time he arrived, Saperstein, already savagely beaten, was "lying on the floor, purple, bloody, tongue hanging out, spit all over him. I thought he was dead. He was being kicked by Mr. Polverino and Mr. Cecere. He was lifted up off the floor, placed in a chair, hit again, knocked off the chair, picked up and hit again."

When DeCarlo entered he was outraged that The Barn had been used for the beating. The witness quoted Gyp DeCarlo: " 'You've messed him up, he's bloody, and maybe the place is bugged. Take him out.' "

Outside, Cecere tried to continue the beating but was stopped by DeCarlo who told Saperstein to make $5,000 weekly payments every Thursday and to repay the total loan and vigorish (exorbitant) interest by December 13, "or you'll be dead."

DeCarlo's attorney, Michael P. Direnzo, created nationwide publicity for his client's trial when he demanded that the defense be given copies of any wiretapping at The Barn. It was his contention that the government's case was based on illegal eavesdropping, which, if true, would have been the basis for a motion to dismiss the charges. Federal Judge Robert Shaw, following precedent, agreed and went one step further by making the transcripts a part of the public record of the trial.

The 1,200 pages of transcripts covered four years of conversations at The Barn between 1961 and 1965. Because the bug had been removed two years before the Saperstein affair, Direnzo had revealed his client's underworld life without gaining his freedom from prosecution.

The DeCarlo tapes contained everything from the preferred way to handle a Mafia murder to the personnel problems of running a gambling office. What really worried the gang at The Barn, though, was the amount of information which the FBI obtained on La Cosa Nostra. As DeCarlo put it, "They know who we're with, and who we ain't with, who the mobs are, and everything else." But he remained optimistic: "As long as they can't prove nothing, I don't care."

The FBI, in turn, was concerned how the Mafia learned so much about its own business.

Defense Attorney Direnzo requested Judge Shaw to declare a mistrial because of the publicity surrounding the tapes. The Judge, explaining he had sequestered the jury during the trial to avoid the effects of any publicity, refused to grant Direnzo's motion. The seven men and five women hearing the case may have been the only people in New Jersey who had not heard of the DeCarlo tapes.

By the time the case went to the jury, only DeCarlo and Cecere were still on trial. Polverino, ill with a kidney ailment, and Landusco, a diabetic, were granted severances and postponement of their trials by Judge Shaw on January 14. After deliberating less than four hours, the jury brought back verdicts of guilty on all six counts against both DeCarlo and Cecere.

Reaction of the New Jersey officials whose names frequently appeared on the tapes varied. Some admitted to being acquainted with mob members, but claimed no knowledge of their illegal activities. Others, denying any acquaintanceship, blasted the release of the tapes and maintained they were the innocent victims of unprincipled braggarts and name-droppers.

Several denounced it all as a Nixon Administration plot to destroy the New Jersey Democratic Party whose leaders were discussed or referred to with alarming frequency and familiarity by DeCarlo and his intimates.

3

LESSONS FROM LUIGI FRATTO

"Evidence from other individuals and documents can sometimes be used to persuade a reluctant witness to cooperate. Nevertheless, experience has shown that over the long run the best way to persuade the type of individual most often found in organized crime investigations to cooperate is to confront him with the sound of his own voice. The point was made by Senator Robert F. Kennedy, when he was Chief Counsel for the McClellan Committee, in reference to a witness [Hoffa] who appeared before the Committee: 'The kind of proof makes a difference. He can say very forcefully someone's a liar—that's easy. But we have his own voice on tapes. He couldn't deny it.' " *American Bar Association Project on Minimum Standards for Criminal Justice. Standards Relating to Electronic Surveillance, pp. 73-74.*

THERE is only one way to learn about organized crime: follow the footsteps of a member of the organization over a period of years. Trailing an able, slippery fellow, one finds out where he goes and with whom he associates—but seldom catches him in the act. He will always have an explanation for everything he has said or done; and a totally brazen operator will look you straight in the eye and tell you he did not do what you saw him do. He will swear under oath that he did not say what you heard him say; the only thing he really fears is a recording device that can prove what he said and precisely how he said it.

If he is a clever criminal, he will never be near the scene of the crime. It would be foolish, when he could set things in motion by making a long-distance telephone call from a pay booth.

One man was primarily responsible for showing me the ropes. Lew Farrell took me through the ABC's of organized crime and gave me a healthy respect for the ability of the organization man to deceive the "good people" in society and corrupt the unwary who believe that somehow they cannot fall under the compromising spell of the underworld.

My early lessons from Lew Farrell started back in 1941 and 1942 when I was a police reporter on the *Des Moines Register.* Lew Farrell was not a master criminal. He was no more than a second or third operator from the lower ranks of the Capone mob in Chicago.

He was born Luigi Thomas Fratto, and around the Chicago police station was known as "Cockeyed Louey." His brothers, Rudolph and Frank (One-eared Frank) Fratto, were also well known in police circles. Lew was on the lam from Chicago and the mob sent him to Des Moines to cool off, as he told friends when he arrived in 1939.

Yet between 1941 and 1951 I saw him move into the Des Moines area. He hobnobbed with detectives and other higher ranking police, made friends with the judges in municipal court and district courts, won favor with the Polk County Sheriff, and in 1945 was awarded an honorary lifetime membership in the Des Moines Junior Chamber of Commerce. Praised by the clergy for his fine civic works, Lew Farrell was generous with his money and time. No church dinner or party was too expensive for him to buy a few tickets.

At least one Polk County District Judge attended his wedding; and, when he was in trouble a few years later, the same judge wrote a letter stating what a fine man Lew Farrell was.

When the *Des Moines Register* started to expose his background at the time of his indictment in connection with a local gambling raid, many said that "Lew isn't a bad guy" and deplored the fact that the newspaper was "getting on his back." I knew a good deal more than I was able to write because some of the editors feared that Farrell might sue us, or that our pursuit of Farrell might make it appear we were persecuting him.

Whenever he was charged with a crime, some kindly judge or prosecutor would always let him off on a technicality.

To obtain a federal beer wholesaler's permit he simply hired a lawyer who was the Iowa Democratic Committeeman. As a result, the Washington office of the Bureau of Internal Revenue overruled the local and regional officials opposed to his receiving the license.

I knew Farrell was lying under oath about his background and arrest record, but the hearing took place in a closed session of the Federal Alcohol Tax Unit. The orders opposing his request were secret. The hearing of the Alcohol Tax Unit in Washington—where his politically acceptable lawyer concocted one of the most tortuously reasoned opinions in the history of the ATU—was also secret. (I hope it was not the normal functioning of that agency.)

The evidence that Lew Farrell had committed perjury was buried for six years in the secret hearings of the Alcohol Tax Unit because this second-rate mobster had the political punch and the money to hire a well-connected lawyer.

Justice was for sale at the Bureau of Internal Revenue in Washington. The mysterious power of Lew Farrell and his associates could reverse well-founded agency decisions at the highest levels, and then bury the whole record under a lot of gibberish about Farrell's "right" not to be held up to ridicule.

The record also spelled out Farrell's Des Moines background more clearly than anything before. The Junior Chamber of Commerce would not have awarded him an honorary lifetime membership if the public had known his record. Neither is it likely that police, judges, and prosecutors would have been seeing him in public, and that one state judge would have written a letter in support of Farrell had they feared that that record would eventually be disclosed.

The full story of Lew Farrell did not emerge until March 1951, when the little Des Moines beer distributor appeared on television before the Kefauver Crime Committee. Senator Estes Kefauver (Dem., Tenn.) and his staff of lawyers, accountants, and former agents of the FBI did the job that few local or state investigative bodies could or would do. They called for the documents from the secret federal, state, and local hearings, and put local law enforcement officials under oath to testify as to what they knew about organized crime. They also subpoenaed men identified with organized crime and gave them the opportunity to deny the records, or to explain their actions and associations with police, sheriffs' deputies, and other city, county, state, and federal government officials. Associate Counsel Downey Rice did this highly effective work in a matter of days, and I saw for the first time the full value of congressional hearings.

In one hour before the Kefauver Committee, Downey Rice uncovered more information on Lew Farrell than we had printed in his ten years in Des Moines. Newspapers are always skittish about libel, as they should be, and public officials are cautious about making public comments critical of one with the power and money which Lew Farrell was reputed to have.

By becoming part of the record of the Kefauver hearings, the record of the Alcohol Tax Unit was freed for use in newspaper accounts of Farrell's background. For the first time we could name names and put the man's activities in perspective. It was not a pretty picture.

Farrell arrived in Des Moines in 1939 to replace Charles (Cherry Nose) Gioe, who for unexplained reasons was giving up his role as the Capone mob's ambassador to Iowa.

I first became acquainted with Cockeyed Louey in early 1942 while working as a cub reporter. He was a police character of considerable mystery, and I was working the police beat. I saw him around with the Italian tavern operators Alphonse (Babe) Bisignano and Johnnie Critelli. Babe's restaurant provided illegal liquor and slot machines on Sixth Avenue, and Johnnie Critelli ran an all-night bar and gambling joint on Harding Road. Farrell followed what I came to recognize as a typical pattern as he insinuated himself into the fringe of Des Moines and Polk

County politics, avoiding direct public confrontations with public officials. Farrell's operation at that time was low key compared with Babe Bisignano's. Babe's brazenness resulted in his arrest and jailing on illegal liquor charges. He was also jailed for contempt of court for his manhandling of Municipal Judge Harry B. Grund (for what Bisignano regarded as unfair treatment in a criminal case) at a local YMCA.

Critelli regarded himself above the laws prohibiting sale of liquor in places where beer was sold, and ran for Safety Commissioner. His ludicrous campaign slogan was: "Be Honest with Yourself. Vote for Johnnie Critelli."

He had convinced himself that most Des Moines citizens supported the illegal sale of liquor and were not at all concerned if fellows like himself and Bisignano played politics to permit their places to operate in total disregard for the law.

Thousands of dollars were poured into the Safety Commissioner campaigns each year while other city campaigns were virtually ignored. This post did not pay much money, but it controlled the police and fire departments. The Safety Commissioner and his team controlled the naming of the Chief of Police, the Chief of Detectives, the head of the Vice Squad, and promotions within those units. No one was really much concerned about who served as Fire Chief, or who headed the Traffic Division of the Police Department.

Johnnie Critelli decided it was time to put in charge of the police department a gambler or bootlegger who would give the people what they wanted. He spent thousands of dollars on billboard advertisements and staged a free dance at the old Tromar Ballroom. A huge crowd attended, but most of them were teen-agers, and Critelli racked up only 800 votes in the city election. Thus he proved to many political observers that although voters favored changing the liquor laws, they did not want a convicted bootlegger in charge of law enforcement.

It is understandable why Des Moines liquor runners and gamblers were unhappy with the way the city operated in those days. There was no guarantee that a Safety Commissioner who was "bought" would stay bought. The local liquor places had to have direct lines to "friends" in the police department, and there was an added charge for tipoffs whenever a raid was coming.

Pete and Gladys Rand (the name had been Randa) operated with less trouble at the Mainliner nightclub just outside the city and under the jurisdiction of the Polk County Sheriff's office. The club was across the road from the airport and only a short distance from Fort Des Moines, one of the first posts of the Women's Army Corps (WAC).

Dave Fidler, a former boxer, also found the Sheriff's office jurisdiction better for his Club 100 where he combined liquor, gambling, and Hollywood-name floor shows. In addition Dave operated a little place around the corner from the Register and Tribune Building, and it was a favorite hangout for editors, reporters, copy editors, and photographers. Illegal operators always try to compromise newspaper editors and reporters to keep trouble at a minimum and provide sources for tipoffs.

On the surface, Dave, Babe, Lew, and Johnnie were "wonderful guys" with a fondness for newsmen and police, and had a special interest in college athletes and sports writers. Lew even offered to pick up the tab for me for a weekend "you won't forget" in St. Louis or Chicago. I am sure now that I never would have forgotten that weekend; I wouldn't have been permitted to do so. But at the time it seemed like a generous offer made by a nice fellow who was misunderstood by the Chicago police.

Initially I was unaware how Farrell fit into the Des Moines underworld picture; but in a short time, the night Police Inspector, Jack Brophy, and the night Police Captain, John Gill, hinted at his mysterious power with political figures including prosecutors and judges of the Des Moines Municipal Court and the Polk County District Court. And as time went by, chatting with police on the 6 P.M. to 2 A.M. shift, I heard more sinister things about Farrell. Brophy had seen Farrell's arrest sheet, which included some 20 arrests and convictions. At least one or two charges involved either possession of a gun or threats with a gun.

Either Brophy or Gill told me that Farrell's real name was Luigi Fratto, and that he had two brothers in Chicago who still went by that name. Both had police records, and were regarded as strong-arm men in the lower ranks of the Capone mob.

On September 13, 1939, in his first days in Des Moines, a team of detectives called on Farrell at the old Chamberlain Hotel and took him to the police station for questioning. He was photographed and fingerprinted, but the "street-smart" Chicago man insisted that the police agree to destroy the picture and fingerprints if they brought no charge against him.

Although some of Farrell's pictures and prints were destroyed by the detectives, Brophy, a former Chief of Detectives, made sure that a copy went to the Bureau of Criminal Investigations, and another copy was retained in the Des Moines Police Department file. Farrell was infuriated when later, at the hearing on his wholesale beer permit, he discovered that Des Moines police and the Iowa Bureau of Criminal Investigations still had copies of the photographs and fingerprints identifying him as Louis Thomas Fratto of the Chicago police courts.

Des Moines was small enough to devote considerable time to following the progress and connections of a man like Farrell. Within a few years after his arrival he struck up a close friendship with Paul Castelline, later named as Chief of Detectives. Both were bachelors and they became close friends, frequently going off on weekend jaunts to St. Louis, Chicago, Kansas City, and other points. Farrell also became well acquainted with other policemen, from patrolmen up to inspector, and employed on them the same flattery so useful with local judges and political leaders.

By the time I met Farrell I had been conditioned by the police gossip; but I was to hear more as I went along. Farrell was a pleasant fellow with a perpetual smile, a constant line of flattery, and an alert and observing eye. The slight deviation in his eye alignment that resulted in the nickname "Cockeyed Louey" made him just a bit self-conscious about looking directly at you; but he managed to scrutinize you indirectly just as well.

He would have been in his late thirties at the time of our first meeting. His hair was a wavy coal-black, and he kept up a flow of questions as he sized you up—all the while beaming that seemingly warm smile.

I was naively excited about being a reporter on the *Des Moines*

Register and the prospects of meeting and talking with real live gangsters. I had read *The Autobiography of Lincoln Steffens* only two years earlier, and had come to the conclusion that Steffens had exposed all there was to know of corruption in city, county, state, and federal government. Secretly I bemoaned the fact that Steffens had wised up the world to the existence of police corruption and deals between public officials and criminals. It seemed he had left too few worlds to conquer.

Although I have never lost my optimism about saving lost sheep, I realize how organized crime preys on our desire to forgive. My experiences with Farrell and others have taught me how easy it is for the criminal or his lawyer to urge forgiveness when the evidence is clear. But society tends to forget once the crisis is over. It is essential to be realistic about the whole business of "rehabilitation," and try to distinguish between those who are genuinely interested in living within the law and those who have simply learned new tricks to avoid capture and conviction.

From the time I met him until his death 25 years later, Lew Farrell was never rehabilitated. When he died of cancer on November 23, 1967, Farrell was under indictment in Chicago on a charge of "counterfeiting and forging a $52,500 check in a swindle scheme." He was one of five indicted, and the overall conspiracy was alleged to include Chicago crime syndicate terrorist Felix (Milwaukee Phil) Alderisio, a cousin of the Fratto brothers who had controlled prostitution in Milwaukee.

At the time of his death, Farrell was still proclaiming himself "absolutely innocent" and contending that "for years someone has been trying to frame me."

"I'm the only man in the world who has appeared before three U.S. Senate investigating committees [Kefauver, Capehart, and McClellan] and I've never been convicted," Farrell complained with an injured air.

The standard procedure of mobsters appearing before the Senate Crime Committees headed by Senator Estes Kefauver (Dem., Tenn.); or Senator John McClellan (Dem., Ark.); or before the federal and state grand juries which have periodically tried to clean up organized crime is to deny any action not photographed, any conversation not recorded. They try to get photographs or recordings excluded from the evidence, admit only those facts which can't be disproved, and insist there was no criminal intent on their part. Farrell exemplified the pattern.

In my early naivety I could hardly believe some of the things I was told about Farrell. How could a character from the Chicago underworld be living openly in Des Moines and associating with public figures?

Over the next few years I watched the tentacles of Lew Farrell reach into the Des Moines Police Department to promote his friends; into the Sheriff's Office for a gun permit; into the Prosecutor's Office to kill a criminal indictment; into the local courts to manipulate decisions on evidence; and into the state political arena. I could see what was done to help Farrell and his friends, but usually it was impossible to learn how it was accomplished.

Rarely could newsmen pin on Farrell anything solid enough to print; and occasionally when we did have something, he would simply deny any involvement, threaten to sue the newspaper if anything was printed and, from time to time, was such a convincing liar that he actually persuaded the editors and me that we might be wrong.

In 1942, Farrell became the subject of a District Court injunction when it was alleged he had pulled a gun on Pete and Gladys Rand to force them to pay him money. The injunction was granted because Farrell failed to show up in court to fight it, but we could run only one brief story. Since the charge that Farrell demanded a 25 percent cut of the Mainliner profits was not made part of the court record, we were unable to get in print with it at the time.

Much of the story was spelled out a few years later when agents for the Alcohol Tax Unit took action to bar Farrell from obtaining a federal wholesale permit to distribute Canadian Ace beer in Iowa. Those agents, J. J. Ingals and James D. Smith, were amazed that Farrell was permitted to operate as a beer wholesaler in Iowa for the old Manhattan Brewing Company. They had access to his record with the Chicago police, and had interviewed Peter and Gladys Rand and others in Des Moines.

Lew Farrell's background plus his activities in Des Moines were not such that Ingals and Smith believed he would be likely to operate within the law in wholesaling beer. The work they put into the case convinced ATU District Supervisor A. L. Durkin of St. Paul that Farrell was not a proper man for a federal beer permit.

But the agents were amazed to see the mysterious power of Lew Farrell and his associates reach the federal agencies in Washington. Deputy Commissioner of Internal Revenue Stewart Berkshire ordered the beer permit granted despite a record showing that Farrell had committed perjury by denying his Chicago police record and that he had ever had a gun in his hand.

I was told that Farrell had lied before the hearing examiner, and that the examiner had ruled against him because of his criminal record in Chicago and his attempt to shakedown the Rands for 25 percent of the Mainliner. But since it was a secret hearing, although there was no justification for secrecy, I could not get my hands on the record.

In Washington, Farrell was represented by Frank Comfort, a Des Moines lawyer who had served as Democratic State Chairman; A. J. Myers, another Des Moines lawyer; and Washington lawyer Frank Ludwick. It is impossible to determine whether it was Frank Comfort's political clout alone that upset the ruling against Farrell, or whether additional pressure was exerted by the well-connected Capone organization in Chicago.

Although the work of the Internal Revenue investigators was futile in blocking the permit, in the end it gave the Kefauver Committee investigators the reason for going into the case. As Kefauver's Associate Counsel Downey Rice examined the documents in late 1950, it became apparent that it was indeed a strange record.

Farrell had made his initial application for a beer permit with two Chicago partners, Morris Greenberg and Mrs. Sylvia Zevin.

ATU Hearing Examiner Robert C. Nash had concluded that Farrell had given false testimony:

"You are familiar with the testimony of the applicant denying he was involved in the Chicago cases [twenty-one arrests]. His testimony in this regard is deemed false, and along with the rest of the evidence established that he is not likely to maintain operations in conformity with the Federal Alcohol Administration Act."

The record revealed that Farrell had been hauled into the Chicago police station more than once a year over a period of nearly 20 years on charges including larceny, carrying concealed weapons, and violation of the federal postal laws.

In Des Moines, Farrell had taken over operations of the Manhattan Brewing Company and was linked with the operation of at least two downtown gambling operations—the old Sports Arcade, at 612½ Grand Avenue, and the Downtown Businessmen's Club, at 415½ Locust Street.

The record called attention to Farrell's friendship with Chief of Detectives Paul Castelline, District Judge C. Edwin Moore, and former Safety Commissioner Myron J. Bennett. It also mentioned Farrell's activities in civic drives and his honorary lifetime membership in the Des Moines Junior Chamber of Commerce.

The pattern was familiar to Downey Rice, a former FBI agent considerably experienced in organized crime problems.

Farrell had even received a boost from Lieutenant Commander Truman Jones, former head of the Navy Officer Recruiting Office in Des Moines. In a letter, Commander Jones stated he was satisfied that Farrell had the proper background and business experience to make an excellent officer, but that an eye injury disqualified him on physical grounds. Jones lauded Farrell's outstanding service as "a civilian recruiter for the Navy." "He has brought to us 75 to 100 men of his acquaintance who have joined the Navy," the Commander stated.

Farrell told the ATU Hearing Examiner that he had headed a War Bond Drive which sold "more than a million dollars' worth of war bonds," and pointed out that he had received a framed award for "outstanding service" for "accomplishments in civic welfare in behalf of Italian-Americans in the City of Des Moines."

Carl Caciatore, of Des Moines, former President of the Iowa Junior Chamber of Commerce, told the hearing examiner of Farrell's contributions to Des Moines including his leadership in arranging the 1945 May Day Frolic of the Junior Chamber.

Farrell himself said, "I have been chairman of about seven different benefit organizations this year. I was chairman of the May Day Frolic. That was the greatest May Day Frolic they have ever had in the history of Des Moines." He said the Junior Chamber of Commerce "gave me a plaque" for "outstanding service" to the community.

At Farrell's request, Reverend Cornelius Lalley, of St. Anthony's Catholic Church, testified that "since the time Lew came to Des Moines he has been noted for his charity and kindness to every cause. I think he's donated a lot of money for the city and mankind."

Father Lalley said he had made the customary investigation of Farrell at the time of his marriage at St. Anthony's, and had received a letter from Farrell's pastor in Chicago "testifying he was free to marry, that he was a good Christian and citizen, and there was no objection registered against him." The technical question of how Farrell's early marriage and divorce were handled was not raised and apparently hadn't been called to Father Lalley's attention. Farrell had married a Chicago girl, Evelyn Glasser, in 1929, and according to birth records introduced at the hearing he was the father of a child born to her that year.

The only information on the dissolution of that marriage came in affidavits from Farrell's father, Tommaso Fratto, and his brother Rudolph. His father said the marriage had "broken up." Rudolph said that Lew and Evelyn were divorced at about the time Farrell went to Des Moines; but the Polk County Clerk's Office record indicated that Farrell had neglected to reveal an earlier marriage when he applied for a license to marry a Des Moines girl.

Farrell had obtained dozens of affidavits from businessmen in support of his application for a beer permit. Those who went on record on his behalf included two Des Moines sports writers, department store officers, a hotel public relations man, several bankers, and even one judge.

Most of those who filed affidavits or wrote letters stated they knew nothing bad about Farrell. The clothing-store executive said he was a good customer and paid his bills promptly. The sports writers said they knew him as an enthusiastic sports fan. A number of other beer distributors said he was "a clean" competitor.

Walter Brick, Chief Clerk of the Municipal Court, said he knew of Farrell's arrest in 1939, but had heard nothing bad about him since. He said he didn't know anything about his Chicago background.

The sole elective official to go to bat for Farrell was District Judge C. Edwin Moore. Having known Farrell well enough to be a guest at his

Des Moines wedding, Judge Moore assured ATU Supervisor Durkin that granting a permit would cause him no embarrassment. Moore wrote:

"I am informed that Mr. Lew Farrell of the Manhattan Brewing Company of Chicago, Ill., has filed an application with your department for a basic permit to sell and distribute malt beverages in the State of Iowa. I wish to take this opportunity to pass on to you my recommendations of this man.

"Mr. Farrell has lived in this city during the past few years, and has been very active in Junior Chamber of Commerce work, bond drives, and various civic and church affairs. In my opinion this man has conducted himself as a good citizen, and I know of no reason why he should not be granted this permit.

"Mr. Farrell recently married one of our fine young ladies who had lived in this city all her life, and I feel he will continue his fine activities in the community and any business carried on under this permit will be strictly according to all the laws, rules, and regulations, and you need not fear any embarrassment or violation if this permit is granted." The letter was signed: "C. Edwin Moore, Judge of the Ninth Judicial District of Iowa." (Moore has since become Chief Judge of the Iowa Supreme Court.)

The field investigation by the ATU had convinced Supervisor Durkin that Farrell should not have a permit. Most of the business people Farrell had given as references said they knew little or nothing about him.

The notice of contemplated denial was sent to Farrell on May 14, 1945, and Farrell requested a hearing, which was set for June 24 and July 27.

Attorney A. J. Myers represented him. Under questioning by Myers, Farrell denied he had ever been arrested. It was at this time he termed the gun-pulling incident at the Mainliner as "a misunderstanding" and denied ever having carried a gun.

On cross-examination, Farrell was presented with the records of the Chicago police and federal courts. Farrell still denied he had ever been arrested, and contended that the testimony should not be allowed on the grounds that Louis Thomas Fratto was not the same man as Lew Farrell.

Farrell admitted he had obtained a gun permit from former Sheriff Vane B. Overtuff, but denied he had ever had any use for it or ever had a gun in his possession. This testimony was in direct conflict with that of Gladys and Pete Rand, who had obtained the injunctions following the fuss at the Mainliner three years earlier. The Rands were buying Farrell's beer, and said he was almost a nightly customer at the county night spot.

"For some reason or other Mr. Farrell thought he should have twenty-five percent of the Mainliner," Gladys Rand told Hearing Examiner Durkin. She said there had been some telephone conversations to that effect from Farrell.

"When Mr. Farrell came to the Mainliner, I was standing in the big barroom and he came rushing through. I went through the entranceway from the barroom to the Casino. He was behind me. He asked me where Pete was at. I told him he had left. I asked if he would not please leave too before there was any trouble. I don't remember his exact words at the time. He didn't leave."

Gladys said she was at the front end of the nightclub when Pete's car pulled in.

"Mr. Farrell and Louis Mays were outside. Pete got out of his car, and Lew pulled a pistol on Pete. Pete's brother took the pistol away from Lew."

Mrs. Rand said neither she nor Pete owed Farrell any money. Rand gave substantially the same account. He said he had dashed into the Mainliner and obtained a gun, but by the time he got out Farrell had been disarmed and had gone away.

Sheriff's records showed personal service on Farrell when the injunction suit was filed; yet Farrell denied he had any knowledge of the injunction until he read about it in the newspapers.

"Did you have a permit to carry a revolver at that time?" the government attorney asked.

"Yes, I did, but I never carried a revolver in my life," Farrell answered.

"Was that permit cancelled?" Farrell was asked.

"Not that I know of," he said. "I never carried one [a gun] anyway so it didn't make any difference."

The record of the hearings indicated that Farrell had stayed clear of the courts from that time until he was indicted in 1948 in connection with horse gambling at the Sports Arcade.

One bit of testimony indicated that Farrell was associating with Sam Saratella, a bootlegger convicted in Chicago in 1941. Gus May, a tax investigator, said he saw Farrell with Saratella in Chicago in May 1944, at the corner of South Wentworth and Thirty-fifth Street. May had been doing some surveillance on Saratella in connection with the transportation of liquor on which the federal tax had not been paid.

The testimony on Farrell and Saratella was introduced to show Farrell's continued association with known violators of federal liquor laws.

In August 1945, Supervisior Durkin stated he was denying the federal permit after concluding that Farrell had "testified falsely as to his arrest record and had made a false statement relative to matters within the jurisdiction of the department."

Attorney Myers claimed it was an "arbitary" act. He charged that Durkin erred in "relying on incompetent evidence" which included "unauthenticated alleged records" from "certain purported public officials in Chicago relating to offenses charged against one Louis Fratto who is now claimed to be the same as Lew Farrell."

Durkin then set aside his own denial and ordered new hearings for the introduction of new evidence. Frank Comfort, then a prominent Democratic Party official, was engaged as one of Farrell's attorneys and he appeared with Myers at the second hearing from October 31 to November 2, 1945.

Farrell did not testify at this hearing, but an affidavit from him offered an explanation of his statement that he had never been arrested. He stated he never thought of his trips to the police station as "arrests" but only as "pickups."

His affidavit stated:

"At one or possibly two places in my testimony I was asked the questions whether I had ever been arrested. My answer was no. After discussing this matter with my counsel, I now find I was mistaken because I am advised that whenever I was taken to the police station or taken into the custody of an officer, I had been arrested.

"I believed that in order to be arrested I had to be charged with some criminal offense and be tried for said offense. I always called those trips to the station pickups. I was asked on one occasion by two policemen to go to the police station when I was residing at the Hotel Chamberlain in 1939. I regarded that as a pickup.

"That was one of the occasions that I gave my fingerprints to the city police department. . . .I was promised at the time that the fingerprints would be destroyed and my photograph would be destroyed if and when they decided they did not have any charge or could prove no charge against me."

Farrell said he was not aware of having been on trial or being on probation at any time. He never remembered paying any fines in Chicago.

The difficulty encountered in dealing with such a brazen liar as Farrell was emphasized to me. Government attorneys met Farrell's affidavit with photostatic copies of the Chicago police records, and testimony from Internal Revenue agents who had examined the record. Those investigators linked Farrell with several convictions and with several arrests despite his flat lies.

The Louis Fratto arrested in Chicago was the same age as Farrell and had given his address as 825 S. Leavitt Street, the address of Farrell's parents. On several occasions when bond was posted, the collateral had included the home at 825 S. Leavitt Street. On January 29, 1926, a Louis T. Fratto had been charged with stealing a $14 overcoat. The $500 penal bond was signed by Louis T. Fratto of 825 S. Leavitt Street. Fratto was put on probation for one year by the court.

Nevertheless, Farrell's attorneys continually objected that the records might not be authentic.

The amounts of money and types of crimes were not as important as establishing that this was the same Louis T. Fratto who had a police record as long as his arm, who had been found guilty, had been on probation, and who obviously was lying about his record. He was lying because he believed he could get away with it, and because Chicago officials either had not taken his fingerprints or had lost them. This was why he had tried to make a deal with Des Moines police to destroy his fingerprints and picture; he did not want any possible link between Lew Farrell of Des Moines and Cockeyed Louey Fratto of Chicago.

To establish that Farrell and Fratto were the same person, investigators put still more records together.

On February 25, 1929, Louis Fratto was charged with disorderly conduct and fined $15 and $6.50 costs. He was released to the chief probation officer.

Another disorderly conduct charge was filed against Fratto on June 13, 1930, and he was fined $1 and costs.

In June 1931, Fratto, then age 24, was charged with carrying "a loaded pistol." He was tried and found guilty, according to the investigators. Farrell was linked to this case by the fact that Tommaso Fratto, of 825 S. Leavitt Street, was surety on the $1,000 bond.

Investigators testified that the application for probation, signed by Louis T. Fratto, indicated he was Lew Farrell. In that application, Fratto stated that he lived at 1813 West Washburn Street, was married, and had a two-year-old daughter named Delores. An affidavit from Farrell's father, Tommaso Fratto, and also city birth records, showed Farrell to be the father of a two-year-old daughter of the same name and address.

At this point Examiner Nash stated: "The court record indicates that a party of a similar name has been under the jurisdiction of the court at Chicago to a degree beyond that which may be described as only 'picked up.'

"If we want to get at the truth of the matter, I would like to hear the views of counsel as to the suitability of placing him [Farrell] under oath on this matter."

Attorney Frank Comfort said he wished to try the case in his own way. Farrell never was recalled to testify under oath, despite more testimony on later arrests.

On March 29, 1933, Louis Fratto was arrested on a charge of defrauding an innkeeper, and investigators testified that "from March 1933 to October 1939, Fratto was arrested nine times by Chicago police."

Over the objection of Lawyer Comfort, Fratto was identified by fingerprints and by police photographs as the Lew Farrell who was arrested at the Chamberlain Hotel in 1939.

Investigator Lloyd Walker testified that the records of the U.S. District Court for the Northern District (Eastern Division) of Illinois showed Louis Fratto had been indicted with one Samuel Levich and others on September 27, 1933, for violating the federal postal laws. There was no testimony on the details of the indictments or on the way the cases were disposed of.

Nash and Durkin concurred that Farrell should not be granted a permit, and on February 1, 1946, following notice of appeal to Washington, Durkin wrote to Deputy Commissioner of Internal Revenue Berkshire:

"Only arrests of Lew Farrell leading to conviction were put in evidence, although the inspector's report showed he was arrested 21 times, including once in federal court."

Farrell's case was taken up by Deputy Commissioner Berkshire in the quiet confines of his office. Farrell went to Washington, but did not attend the hearing on advice of Washington counsel Frank Ludwick. It was effective strategy. In some way Farrell's attorneys convinced Berkshire that an injustice had been done. Emphasis was placed on the fact that so many fine citizens of Des Moines were fronting for him, including a District Court Judge.

On April 16, 1946, Berkshire reversed the decision of his field office and granted Farrell the federal wholesale permit. The letter was a masterpiece of contradiction. Berkshire said that the Rand incident was the only evidence to indicate Farrell had been in trouble in Des Moines, or might engage in "illegal activity" or "high-pressure methods." "Although there is no doubt in my mind but that Farrell was the defendant in the Chicago criminal proceedings, the crimes in themselves are of such a minor nature I do not feel that they evidence a present intention not to operate his business in conformity with law," Berkshire wrote. "I do not believe that, considering Farrell's background, his failure to disclose his record in Chicago and his attempt to avoid being connected with his past, evidence such an attitude of mind to act without regard for law as to justify our denial of his application for a permit."

Berkshire stated, in fact, that there was no doubt Farrell had lied, but that false statements under oath on a material matter dealing with arrests should not be held against him. The tortured reasoning claimed it was understandable why a fellow with such a bad past would want to cover it up. Perjury in a hearing was not evidence of a disregard for law and order, Berkshire maintained in a decision that he intended to keep secret.

Such lack of judgment and bending of political pressures by the ATU caused the Kefauver Committee to comment a few years later:

"The Committee fails to understand how the Alcohol Tax Unit could grant a wholesaler's permit to hoodlums such as Joe DiGiovanni [Kansas City mobster] and Lew Farrell." The Kefauver report identified Farrell as "an alleged Capone syndicate hoodlum with a considerable criminal record," and added: "In spite of Farrell's record and an adverse report on him by field supervisors, the ATU gave him a license to distribute beer."

Farrell did not limit his activities to the beer business after he received the permit. Although there were periodic reports of his involvement in gambling, he was a quiet operator. He had apparently patched up his differences with Pete and Gladys Rand, and entered into a joint gambling venture.

Only once more did Farrell get into actual trouble with the law. On April 26, 1948, Polk County Deputy Sheriffs walked into the Sports Arcade, a basement gambling joint at 612½ Grand Avenue, arrested two employees, and seized a variety of gambling equipment. I was along on that raid, and ascertained that the deputies made note of a retail sales tax permit naming the operators as Hymie Wiseman, a boxing promoter, and Lew Farrell. County Attorney Carroll O. Switzer filed the charge that Farrell, Wiseman, and Al Cramm, an employee, were engaged in a conspiracy to violate the gambling laws.

Farrell denied any connection with the operation. Several months later, Wiseman and Cramm entered pleas of guilty to a charge of keeping a gambling house and were fined $300 by District Judge C. Edwin Moore. Judge Moore, who a few months earlier had been a character witness for Farrell, dismissed the charge against him.

The Sports Arcade was not Farrell's only interest in gambling, for during this same period he was reporting income as one of 13 partners in the Downtown Businessmen's Club. But this did not end Farrell's false statements under oath, which he continued to make even before the Kefauver Committee, as Associate Counsel Downey Rice cited the income Farrell had reported and the business deductions he had taken for "horse [wire] service" and "deterioration of dice tables."

Lew Farrell was typical of the second tier of hoodlums from the Capone mob. The code was to deny everything, to admit nothing until confronted with the evidence, and then claim a "misunderstanding" on the questions.

The only way to deal with a man like Lew Farrell was to put him under oath in a public forum, confront him with records contradicting his testimony, and then question him about his relations with public officials and others. Such a forum was created in 1950 when the Senate established the Kefauver Crime Committee, and Chairman Estes Kefauver started exposing the links between politics and crime in a dozen different cities.

In almost every area of the country, the Kefauver investigators worked with local crime reporters who knew much of the story and knew what it meant.

Following the career of Luigi Fratto in later years was no less rewarding from a standpoint of learning of the brazen lies he could and would tell and the political schemes he could concoct. Fratto was the same whether it was racketeering in aluminum siding contracts—as exposed by Senator Homer Capehart (Rep., Ind.) in 1954—or his dealing with James R. Hoffa and other Teamsters hoodlums, as exposed by Senator John McClellan (Dem., Ark.) and Robert F. Kennedy in the period from 1956 to 1960.

To follow Fratto was to follow the network of Teamsters racket figures from coast to coast: Anthony (Tony Ducks) Corallo, an associate of Democratic political boss Carmine DeSapio in New York; Joey Glimco, the associate of the Democratic machine in Cook County, Illinois; or Anthony (Tony Pro) Provenzano, out of the morass of Cosa Nostra politics in northern New Jersey.

One of Fratto's closest associates was the colorful 300-pound Robert B. (Barney) Baker, a versatile labor goon, who ranged from New York's waterfront to Miami, to the Kansas City and Omaha area. He gave friendly tips on how to turn Teamsters power into garbage monopoly rackets. Baker, a close associate of Hoffa, worked for W. Averell Harriman in 1956, when the then New York Governor was seeking the Democratic Presidential nomination. Baker later married the daughter of one of Iowa's most prominent Democratic political figures.

Fratto and Baker never quite put together the winning team the Mafia used to exploit union power and politics in northern New Jersey, but no one could say that Fratto wasn't working at the job up to his death in 1969.

Fratto was never able to overcome the exposure by the Kefauver Committee in 1951. Many cities, large and small, owed their escape from Mafia-dominated politics to the hearings by Senator Estes Kefauver in 1950 and 1951, which outraged the big-city Democrats in so many areas.

However, as the Kefauver Committee started its work in 1950, there was only slight hope of an in-depth investigation of the links between organized crime and politics. Just a few months earlier there had been a disappointing experience in efforts to get a real depth-probe of the Kansas City vote frauds by Attorney General Tom Clark. That investigation was an important part of the problem of getting effective action against organized crime.

4

KANSAS CITY VOTE FRAUDS

"The war on organized crime is inseparable from a war on political corruption. . . . In this fact may lie hidden the reason why it is so difficult for political leadership to wage a comprehensive war on

organized crime—for to do so would risk severe political consequences." *From the statement of 23 House Republicans in a
criticism of President Johnson in August 1967, for the lagging war
on crime.*

POLITICAL chicanery frustrated the investigation of the
vote frauds in Kansas City in 1947 and clearly demonstrated how
brazen political acts are not beyond Cabinet officials. Kansas City was
not the only city plagued by vote frauds. Chicago, New York,
Cleveland, Philadelphia, and Newark have suffered from the same
political acquisitiveness. However, the Kansas City investigation, or lack
of it, was the direct responsibility of Tom Clark, father of Ramsey
Clark, who himself would later hamper Congress in the fight against
organized crime. Organized crime puts first things first, and the election
of men who do their bidding is a first thing.

We do not know Tom Clark's motivation; we can only speculate why
he would be so negligent as to restrict the FBI in a vote-fraud
investigation in President Truman's hometown. Clark said it was
because of his great concern for the civil rights of those who might be
accused of vote-stealing.

The Kansas City *Star* assigned two reporters to the job of running
down evidence of vote frauds. With the help of 32 ex-GI's, the *Star*
reporters interviewed and took affidavits from more than 1,000
registered voters and election officials in Kansas City. It was a great
start, but also a frustrating experience before it was all over.

On May 20, 1947, Senator James P. Kem (Rep., Mo.) introduced a
resolution calling for an investigation into Attorney General Tom
Clark's handling of vote-fraud charges in the Kansas City primary
election the preceding August.

The Democratic primary battle for the Fifth Congressional District
nomination attracted nationwide attention. Roger Slaughter, the
Democratic incumbent, was not supported by President Harry Truman
because of his outspoken opposition to the Truman policies. The
Truman-backed candidate, Enos Axtell, was being given the full support
of the revived Pendergast machine. Putting new life in the old alliance
was Tom's nephew, Jim Pendergast, who had been convicted of tax

violations in the wake of a 1936 election-fraud investigation which resulted in 278 convictions. Many of the old gang had completed their sentences or received clemency and were ready to stage a comeback.

Senator Kem, following the course of a postprimary investigation into allegations of fraud conducted by the Kansas City *Star,* had seen nearly 100 indictments handed down for state law violations, and repeatedly tried to find out why there had been no similar action on the federal level.

Attorney General Clark had assured him that his Department had conducted a thorough investigation and concluded there was no basis for digging further, and that any violations were, at most, of state law. Kem questioned his reasoning and wondered how, if there had been so many indictments for state law violations, the federal laws could not be applied since federal candidates were on the same ballots.

Even when the Republican candidate, Albert L. Reeves, Jr., defeated Axtell in the general election, Kem was not satisfied to let the matter drop but assigned two members of his own staff to investigate and report what they were able to find out. Their work formed the basis for Kem's resolution for a full Senate inquiry into the Kansas City vote fraud and its handling by Tom Clark.

The resolution directed the Judiciary Subcommittee to work with a "view to ascertaining whether the Attorney General and the officers of the Department of Justice have properly performed their duties with respect to the investigation and prosecution of any violations of law which may have occurred in connection with [the August 6, 1946] Primary election [in Kansas City]."

In the fall of 1946, when the Kansas City *Star* began publishing the results of its own investigation, it had become impossible for the Justice Department to ignore the situation. The Federal Bureau of Investigation was directed to conduct an investigation under strict limitations which permitted it to question only the *Star* reporters and investigators, and the four members of the elections board who claimed that violations had been called to their attention.

To obtain a federal indictment for election-law violations at that time there had to be a conspiracy either to prevent a voter from casting his ballot, or incorrectly count his vote, or to dilute his vote (ballot-box stuffing). And the conspiracy had to affect candidates for federal office.

Between October 12 and 24, the FBI conducted a preliminary investigation and compiled a 355-page report. Copies were forwarded from Kansas City to Washington FBI headquarters, and to Sam Wear, United States Attorney in Kansas City, all in line with the instructions of the Attorney General.

Sam Wear prepared his own synopsis of the report, presented it to three federal judges of the Western District of Missouri and asked them if, based on his synopsis, they saw any need to impanel a special grand jury to investigate further. They did not.

In the meantime a House Committee investigating election campaign expenditures failed to uncover any violations of the federal campaign expenditures law. This law, however, did not apply to primaries. Subsequently (in January 1947) the Criminal Division of the Department of Justice ordered the FBI to close its investigation of the Kansas City charges.

When a state grand jury was impaneled to investigate the primary, the FBI was notified to keep the Department advised of any results of the probe which might indicate violations of federal law. It was not, however, authorized to reopen the investigation.

On May 27, 1947, the day before the Ferguson Subcommittee began its investigation, the Kansas City grand jury returned its findings, based primarily on an examination and recount of ballots in some precincts. The grand jury concluded that the primary had been stolen from Slaughter and several other nonmachine candidates. It returned 81 indictments against 71 persons, and recommended a complete recount of all the ballots. It also advised the presiding judge that the FBI, with fingerprint, handwriting, and document experts, should be asked to continue the investigation.

As a result of this decision—which publicly raised the suspicion that the Attorney General had attempted to whitewash the case—Clark appeared before the Ferguson Subcommittee to defend his reputation. Shortly after the Subcommittee began to interrogate him on May 28, Kem was notified that the vault in the Kansas City Election Board office had been blown open and the ballots which had been examined by the grand jury had been stolen.

In the face of this, Clark finally ordered the FBI back on the case.

The major point of disagreement between the Senators and Attorney General Clark had to do with the completeness of the FBI investigation. Clark characterized the investigation as the most thorough he could remember in his years with the Justice Department. In a letter to Senator Kem on February 10, 1947, he had stated: "As I previously advised you, the Federal Bureau of Investigation, at my insistence, conducted a full investigation into the charges of fraud in this primary."

Committee questioning of FBI Director, J. Edgar Hoover, revealed a slightly different story.

"On August 12, 1946," according to Hoover, "our Kansas City office received an anonymous telephone call alleging that there were flagrant vote frauds in the primary election at Kansas City. This information was furnished by the Kansas City office of the FBI to our headquarters, and under date of August 14, 1946, I transmitted that to the Assistant Attorney General in charge of the Criminal Division, Mr. Caudle. On September 5, 1946, Mr. Caudle advised that the Criminal Division did not feel that the anonymous information to the Kansas City office warranted any investigation.

"Now, under date of September 9, 1946, a letter was received from our Kansas City office, advising that the reporters for the Kansas City *Star* were conducting an investigation of the alleged election ir-regularities in Kansas City.

"On September 27, this information was furnished to the Criminal Division, to Mr. Caudle, and on October 2, 1946, Mr. Caudle advised that the United States Attorney, Mr. Wear of Kansas City, had furnished to the Criminal Division investigative reports of the Kansas City *Star* indicating irregularities in four election precincts during August 6 primary.

"On October 11, 1946, the Attorney General advised the Federal Bureau of Investigation that he had received copies of the investigative reports prepared by the reporters of the Kansas City *Star* and he re-quested that the Bureau conduct a preliminary investigation."

The Attorney General issued the following instructions in con-nection with this "preliminary" investigation:

"While many of the irregularities charged amount at most to violations of the state law, such as assistance by election officials to voters in marking ballots without filling in the necessary oaths of assistance, improper selection of election officials, improper methods of tallying and counting ballots in the absence of a showing of actual miscounting, nevertheless, reports of the investigators indicate that persons, first, are officially listed as having voted while claiming that they did not vote; or, second, are officially listed as not having voted while claiming that they did vote; or, three, appeared at the polling place and found that their names had already been voted. These latter irregularities indicate a violation of Section 51, for if the charge can be substantiated, that would have amounted to a conspiracy to deny to qualified voters their federally secured right to vote for a candidate for federal office, to have that vote counted as cast, and to have all legitimate ballots honestly and accurately counted free of dilution or falsification or fictitious ballots.

"Possible violations of Section 52, Title 18, U.S.C. are indicated if officials acting under color of law in officiating at primary elections which are an integral part of the state electoral processes either alone or with others perpetrated denial of the rights mentioned above.

"It is therefore requested that the following persons be interviewed and such information elicited from them as will determine, first, the identity of federal voters who were deprived of the right to vote for a federal candidate; and, second, the identity of persons, with their official positions, if any, who stuffed ballot boxes with false or fictitious ballots or failed to count ballots for federal candidates honestly or accurately together with all circumstances surrounding the violations:

"(1) Ludwig Graves, Richard S. Jansen, William Davis, Joseph R. Stewart, members of the Board of Election Commissioners, Jackson County Court House, Kansas City, Missouri; (2) Ira B. McCarty and John P. Swift, reporters for the Kansas City *Star*, who have written articles on the above described matters, and such other *Star* employees as participated in the *Star* investigation.

"Please give the investigation your special attention and submit reports to me as promptly as possible. Please conduct your investigation in cooperation with the United States Attorney at Kansas City, Missouri, and furnish him copies of your report."

The report to U.S. Attorney Sam Wear was accompanied by a cover letter from FBI Agent Dwight Brantley calling attention to the limited scope of the Bureau's investigation.

When questioned about Brantley's letter, Hoover replied: "Well, I think that the differentiation and the idea in the mind of Mr. Brantley, as it was in my mind when I transmitted the report to the Attorney General in my cover memorandum, was that this was a preliminary investigation, specifically directed by the Department, contra to what we would call a full investigation.

"In other words, we were instructed by the Department to obtain information from six specific people, and no one else. We were also instructed by the Department to submit the report to the United States Attorney. Then we would await either instructions from the United States Attorney as to any further investigation he might desire, or any further investigation that the Criminal Division might desire. . . . I concluded the memorandum [October 25] with this statement: 'You will note that only the specific investigation requested in your memorandum has been conducted, and I shall appreciate your advising me as soon as possible whether any further investigation is desired.' "

Hoover's Assistant Director, D. M. Ladd, also testified that Brantley's letter had been meant "to prevent the possibility of our reports being cited as the result of investigation proving that further investigation or prosecution is not justified."

Senator Ferguson asked Hoover if he had written on one page: "Were we so restricted by Department orders?"

Hoover: "That is correct."

Kem: "You thought they [the report] might be so used by the United States Attorney?"

Hoover: "That is correct."

Hoover admitted that eventually he did receive a reply from the Department of Justice to his request for further instructions: "On January 6, 1947, I received a reply from Assistant Attorney General Caudle, who advised that the investigation conducted by the Bureau was thorough and the Criminal Division had concluded that there was no certain basis for the prosecution of anyone under Section 51, Title 18, U.S. Code, for election-fraud violation."

Kem: "Did you say that the investigation by the FBI was described as thorough?"

Hoover: "Yes. I can refer to the original memorandum."

Kem: "That was somewhat inaccurate, was it not, Mr. Hoover?"

Hoover: "It was thorough insofar as the instructions received from the Criminal Division were concerned. We complied thoroughly with those."

Kem: "That is not what he said. He said the Bureau was thorough. Would you be good enough to read that?"

Hoover: "The investigation in this case was thorough and we concluded—"

Ferguson: "But, Mr. Hoover, as a matter of fact, there had not been an investigation by the FBI."

At this point the Attorney General interrupted the questioning to explain his definition of "thorough." "It does not say that. It says the investigation was thorough. We had one from the *Star,* and we had one from the [House] Committee."

Ferguson: "The question is, Mr. Clark, whether or not the Attorney General is going to substitute, for an investigation by the FBI, the investigation of two newspaper reporters in Kansas City and the statements of four men who are involved in the particular conduct. Now do you want to tell this committee that that is what you want to do? You want to substitute the [Kansas City] *Star's* investigation for your own investigation?"

Clark: "I want to say this, Mr. Chairman—that the *Star* had thirty-four people who were out working on this case, thirty-two of whom were ex-GIs, and two of whom were experienced reporters of many years."

Ferguson: "But, Mr. Clark, I will take my hat off to the GIs in certain fields—but did you have any evidence that anyone of these GIs, or either of the two newspapermen, knew anything about the federal law and could therefore properly investigate and question witnesses in relation to federal crimes?"

Hoover explained that all FBI agents must be lawyers, accountants, or take special courses in languages, and receive more than four months of special training before they are sent into the field to conduct investigations. In addition, agents return to Washington at regular intervals for further training and refresher courses.

Ferguson: "In other words, your Department, with due respect to newspapermen, is never willing to go out and take a newspaperman's story as an investigation?"

Hoover: "That would not be a full investigation in any sense of the word."

Ferguson: "It is merely information."

Hoover: "That is correct."

Ferguson: "And the so-called statements by the Election Commission, not taken by your men, would be merely information; is that correct?"

Hoover: "That is correct."

Ferguson: "So you [the FBI via Brantley's cover letter] were flagging the District Attorney [sic] Sam Wear to the fact that this was not an investigation at all: it was merely submitting to him two reports that you had your men pick up, one from the Kansas City *Star* reporters and one from the Election Commission.

Hoover: "That is correct."

Ferguson: "That is all it amounted to."

Hoover: "Yes."

Kem: "You did not mean to place the authority of the FBI back of those reports?"

Hoover: "No."

Although Attorney General Clark finally admitted that this was a "preliminary" investigation, he still insisted to the Committee: "I would not agree ... that no investigation was made, Senator. For a preliminary investigation, I think it was the most thorough preliminary investigation that I have seen in my ten years in the Department of Justice."

Ferguson: "Where they did not go out and do any investigating themselves, but merely took reports? You claim that is one of the most thorough investigations you have seen?"

Clark: The *Star* reporters had thirty-two people working for them. . . . On top of that, we had the House Investigating Committee report. . . ."

However, Assistant Attorney General Caudle had written in one of his memoranda on the case: "The [House] Committee investigators directed much of their attention to the question of campaign expenditures which entailed no violation of the Federal Corrupt Practices Act, since that act specifically excludes primaries from its operation."

Returning to Clark's letter to Senator Kem, in which he had stated that the Federal Bureau of Investigation had "conducted a full investigation into the charges of fraud in this primary," the Committee Chairman asked the Attorney General: "Now was there a full investigation by the FBI?"

Clark: "There was a preliminary investigation."

Ferguson: "So the word 'full,' then, is not a correct description as to what happened?"

Clark finally conceded: "The FBI conducted a preliminary investigation."

Senator Kem, furious over the Attorney General's attempt to pass this limited investigation off as thorough, recalled the fine work of the FBI in the 1936 vote-fraud case in Kansas City: "I would like to say that the only distinction, so far as I know, between the vote-fraud cases in 1936, which resulted in two hundred and seventy-eight convictions, based upon prosecutions in which every person . . . either pleaded guilty or was convicted by a Missouri jury—and the present case, is that in 1936 the FBI immediately made a thorough investigation."

Asked why in 1946 his Bureau failed to follow through in the same way, Hoover blamed the restrictions against investigating vote frauds that were added in 1941 to previous restrictions in the areas of antitrust, labor, and civil rights.

Ferguson: "So during the first vote frauds in Kansas City you were in a position to go in and make your investigation without any restraint and any special instructions from the Attorney General?"

Hoover: "That is correct."

Attorney General Clark repeatedly insisted that the FBI report had shown no evidence of a conspiracy, a requirement for indictments under the federal law. But the Committee was curious how hard he and his department had worked to find any such evidence.

Ferguson: "Did you ever follow up this preliminary investigation, as you call it here in the letter [memorandum to FBI of October 11, 1946]?"

Clark: "Well, after we got the preliminary investigation, and it showed that as far as federal voting was concerned, that there were only two wards in which there was [sic] any discrepancies at all and that would involve only, I believe, seven votes in one and fifteen in another, why we presented the matter to the three U.S. District Judges there, with a view to getting a grand jury."

Clark repeatedly insisted: "It was an investigation to investigate, to interrogate those complainants [the reporters and election officials who claimed to have evidence of fraud] and then, if anything showed up that the District Attorney [Sam Wear] thought should be investigated, they would investigate further. That is what it was."

Ferguson: "Now did the message [instructions] here to the FBI permit the District Attorney out in Missouri to limit this investigation, or was the FBI fully authorized to make a complete investigation on it [the charges] to ascertain if there was a conspiracy to miscount, to dilute or to deny the right to vote or any combination or parts of those?"

Clark: "On this preliminary investigation, the FBI was to interrogate the complainants that were set out in the FBI memorandum there [from Clark], and report back to the United States Attorney and to the Department. Then, if the Department and the United States Attorney felt that there was additional investigation needed, that indicated a violation of federal statutes, why then they would have to have a complete investigation. . . ."

Kem indicated that under the Attorney General's instructions it would have been almost impossible to find any direct evidence of a conspiracy. As he pointed out: "No one of those witnesses would be a witness to any fact. No one of them was a party or present at the time the alleged conspiracy took place."

Ferguson: "You mean of the actual counting [of ballots]?"

Kem: "Yes, no one of them."

Clark: "Two of them [the witnesses] were *Star* reporters who had statements."

Ferguson: "That would be hearsay."

Clark: "In an investigation we are not bound by that."

Kem: "You would go to the *Star* reporters to get the facts. Is that the way you investigate to get—"

Clark: "We would get leads."

Kem: "Did you follow up the leads?"

Clark: "No."

Ferguson: "Do I understand that none of these witnesses were men who actually worked in the [voting] booths and would be part of the conspiracy?"

Kem: "No one of them, Mr. Chairman, no one of them could possibly be a witness to the overt act."

Ferguson: "The actual overt act of conspiracy."

Kem: "To the conspiracy."

Kem: "Now do you want the Committee to understand that the FBI, after investigating or interviewing the witnesses set out in your letter, obtained no information that would indicate that a further investigation was in order?"

Clark: "If there was a conspiracy between the judges [election judges] there, you would have a case. However, I want to say that the *Star* took affidavits, lengthy ones, some eight or nine pages, from every judge, and in no instance was there any evidence of that type."

This was too much for the Chairman. He could not let that go unchallenged.

Ferguson: "Oh, General, you do not expect them to go out and ask the judges, 'Did you have a conspiracy?' And have them tell you, 'Yes, we did have a conspiracy.' "

Clark: "Well, if you have two Democratic judges, two Republican judges, two Democratic clerks and two Republican clerks—"

Ferguson: "Have you never heard of Republicans and Democrats both getting into conspiracies, in the same bed, for that matter?"

Clark: " . . . If there was anything like that, I am satisfied somebody would have said something."

Ferguson speculated about the possible effect on the investigation of a letter addressed to the Attorney General and received by the Justice Department before October 30, 1946, complaining about the political consequences a full investigation would have in Missouri. It was a "Dear Tom" letter and signed only with initials, but the Attorney General claimed he did not know who it was from and considered it as just an anonymous letter:

"The trick of the *Star* is to get enough of these [complaints] to get you to order the (ballot) boxes opened," said the writer. "Some discrepancies will no doubt be found in some few precincts. It won't affect the election, but it would be a discredit to Truman and the Party and that is all they want. They blame the bulk for the few. You can go into any election and find irregularities in some places, but there isn't any use of ruining the Democratic Party because of a few. This was a local fight anyway, and in no way affects the nomination of the congressional candidate at all. If the ballots were opened and the FBI conducted the investigations though, of course they would find some irregularities. But no one would be ruined except the Democratic Party."

Ferguson, addressing Clark, concluded: "And you are one of them. This was a family affair."

Attorney General Clark defended his handling of the case on grounds that he could find no evidence of "conspiracy." *Star* reporters had found otherwise. Among other things, they had obtained affidavits from citizens who claimed they had showed up at the polls only to be told they had already voted. One man stated that the records showed his wife had voted despite the fact she had died a month before. Other "voters" were discovered to have moved from the district prior to the election; still others listed vacant lots as residences.

Election judges, clerks, and even one policeman told of voters who arrived at the polls, couldn't remember their names, went outside the polling places and shortly returned with memories refreshed. Frequently voters were not even given ballots, and looked on helplessly as election officials deposited premarked ballots in the boxes for them. Large numbers of voters who asked for the Democratic ballot and assistance were never asked for whom they wished to vote and never required to complete the necessary assistance forms. Ballots were counted by precinct captains and others who were in the polling places illegally.

Nevertheless, despite the *Star's* evidence of wholesale miscounts, Attorney General Clark maintained that "in all of those statements that were compiled and sent to me by the FBI, there are only ten votes in a Congressional election that are shown to have been erroneously or in some way miscounted. . . ."

Senator Kem insisted there was ample cause for a full investigation.

Clark: "Do you have any evidence of conspiracy, Senator?"

Kem: "Plenty of evidence."

Clark: "You have not furnished me with any."

Ferguson continued the questioning: "General, if you have a conspiracy to allow a certain official to count certain ballots, and then count and find that those officials made a miscount of sixty votes out of two hundred-something, do you not think that there is circumstantial evidence of a conspiracy to violate this section?"

Clark: "We do not have that. All the evidence indicates this [the alleged irregularities in counting reported in numerous precincts] is a matter of convenience, that it was a convenient way of doing it."

Ferguson: "Yes, but the people who counted them and made a mistake of sixty, a variation of sixty—is that not evidence of a conspiracy?"

Clark: "Not of itself."

Ferguson was also concerned that the Attorney General had not ordered a full investigation of the alleged irregularities until the day after the ballots had been stolen.

Ferguson: "Mr. Hoover, this is a fact, is it not, that if you had made a thorough investigation prior to the time that the ballots were stolen, you would expect a better measure of success than you will be able to obtain now, when the ballots are not in existence."

Hoover: "Well, there is no question now that the ballots, or some of them at least, have been stolen, that our investigation will be seriously handicapped, and it will probably require much longer time to conclude and will not be as complete as it would have been if we could have had the examination of the ballots for our investigation."

Ferguson: "In other words, the ballots themselves, if certain things were done in certain booths, in various booths, at the same time, would be at least circumstantial evidence that there was a conspiracy to defraud."

Hoover: "It would be certainly assistance in proving that."

Ferguson: "And without the ballots you will be greatly handicapped in your investigation along that line."

Hoover: "That is correct. We will be handicapped."

Anxious to be of help, Clark interjected: "We can use, Senator, the testimony before the state grand jury and the counting of the ballots there even if we do not recover the ballots."

Clark tried to convince the Ferguson Committee that he had not really waited until after the theft of the ballots, but had forwarded newspaper clippings on the Jackson County grand jury investigation to the FBI in case "they thought further investigation along that line should be made which, evidently they did not." However, the Committee realized that the FBI had been told the case was closed and was powerless to act unless directed to do so by the Attorney General. Clark presented no memorandum or other evidence to prove that he had asked the FBI for an opinion on reopening the investigation or any documentation of any finding by the Bureau indicating that in its view no further investigation was warranted. All he could produce was the fact that in April he had told Caudle to inform the FBI to "watch the proceedings [of the Jackson County Grand Jury] and get any federal violations."

Ferguson and Kem were not impressed. They wondered why the Justice Department would rely for evidence of federal crimes on the work of a county grand jury concerned solely with violations of state law rather than on the experience and expertise of the FBI. To back up their contention that the Justice Department had still not been interested in a "full" investigation until after the theft of the ballots, they introduced into the record a letter to Caudle from Sam L. Smith of the Justice Department. "I asked Mr. Wear to direct the agents in this new inquiry in such a way as to avoid any possible criticism of the federal investigation into what now appears to be entirely a state matter," Smith had written. This was hardly what they considered an encouragement to the FBI.

Mindful of the Attorney General's explanation that federal law required the showing of a conspiracy to deny the right to vote or to dilute or miscount votes, the Committee took a long look at some of the evidence available to Clark.

Alden A. Stockard, research assistant to Senator Kem and an attorney from Missouri, went to the Justice Department to go through the information gathered by *Star* reporters. Only a small number of the affidavits and statements were made available to him, because the rest had either been returned to Kansas City or were included in the FBI report which was considered "confidential."

Although the Attorney General had been unable to find any evidence of a conspiracy, Stockard found repeated patterns of violations of state law which caused him to suspect that a conspiracy or multiple conspiracies had existed.

In the Justice Department file on the Tenth Precinct of the First Ward, Stockard had come across the following notation:

"This file contains good proof that at least twenty-two votes were cast by impersonators who claimed to be voters who in fact did not cast a vote on election day. About six of the voters complained to the board of elections and were permitted to cast their own vote."

This, Stockard explained, affected both the right to vote and the right to have that vote undiluted by improperly cast ballots. "There is no indication in the file that the original votes cast for those six were ever taken out," he told the Committee. "The result was that you had two votes cast for these six persons in that precinct and, of course, [that] would knock off the count for those six. Then for the remaining sixteen, you would have ballots cast for people who never showed up."

Clark: "You did not find any conspiracy with reference to that, did you, in our files?"

Stockard: "Well, I was noticing that in your statement to the FBI, that it states that if the charge [of preventing voting or of diluting the count] can be substantiated that would have amounted to a conspiracy to deny the qualified voters their federally secured right to vote."

Clark did not want to be held to his earlier statement on what it took to prove a conspiracy, but stuck to only one point: "You have to have a conspiracy. You agree with me?"

Stockard: "In the file in your office, we took this [lack of any admission of a conspiracy] into consideration, that we did not expect to find in those files any affidavits from any individual wherein he stated 'I am guilty of a conspiracy.'"

Clark pressed: "You did not find any."

Stockard: "So far as I know, a conspiracy can be proved either by a confession, which we did not expect to find in your files, or it can be proved by a statement against interest, which we felt would be rare, if at all in your files, or it can be proved by circumstantial evidence."

Kem: "Of which you found a great abundance."

Stockard: "Yes, of which we found a great abundance."

Ferguson, struck by the number of times voters had been told they "had been voted" by someone else, decided to clear up any question about the legality of such a practice in Missouri. He asked Stockard, "Can you vote in Missouri by proxy, that is, to authorize the captain to vote you?"

Stockard: "I have had occasion several times to look into the election laws of Missouri, but I never yet have found that authority."

Kem: "You would risk your reputation as a Missouri lawyer to say that it is not permitted under Missouri law?"

Stockard: "I will risk my reputation on that."

The young attorney went on to explain how premarked ballots were used in many precincts: "In the first case the person went in and asked for the ballot. He was handed the ballot. It was already marked. It was folded and put in the ballot box."

Attorney General Clark saw nothing wrong in that. "Maybe that is the way he wanted to vote. You do not deprive him of the personal right to vote. Maybe that is the way he wanted to vote."

Stockard countered, "I am glad you mentioned that, because the second situation was that people went in and asked for a ballot. They were handed a ballot already marked, and they protested, but the ballot, in spite of their protest, was put in the ballot box. In view of the fact that they voiced a protest in the presence of all of the election officials, it is beyond me to see how that could have been accomplished without the concurrence and the conspiracy and the agreement of the election officials in that precinct voting place."

Martha Aldrich, a Republican Judge in the Fifth Precinct of the First Ward had told *Star* investigators this story:

"A man came in and said he was Tom Skains, 1015 Paseo, who is my brother-in-law. I objected and said, 'That is not my brother-in-law.' He asked for a Democratic ballot, and the judge marked it. The Democratic challenger said, 'I made a mistake. His name is Kanns.' But I know he does not live at 1015 Paseo. . . . I saw Jack, the Democratic Precinct Captain, pay quite a few people. I saw this through the window. Jack gave me four dollars in one-dollar bills. He refused to tell me what it was for, but I know it was to keep me quiet. He quit paying four dollars at about six o'clock, and started paying only one dollar."

Clark asked, "Is that a federal violation?"

"You mean to cut the price?" quipped Stockard.

Bribery, Clark explained, was not a federal offense and, therefore, Mrs. Aldrich's charges involved state law at most. He ignored the question of fraudulent voting being permitted by at least two Democratic election officials and bribery of a Republican election official. Although the Supreme Court had decided that bribing a voter did not infringe on his rights, the bribery of an election official was a different matter. Under the ground rules laid down by the Attorney General, the FBI was restricted from talking with Mrs. Aldrich about her statement.

The files Stockard studied also contained the statement of probationary Detective William H. Banks who had been assigned to election duty. Banks had witnessed election officials looking over the shoulder of voters while the latter marked their ballots. He had seen Republican ballots put into a pile with Democratic ballots when they were sorted for counting. After the counting, which, he stated, was not in accordance with state election laws, he followed one of the election officials, Joe Tigerman, from the polling place to a telephone where he heard Tigerman place a call to Tim Moran, a Pendergast-machine member, to give him the tally. According to the detective, Tigerman asked how many votes one of the candidates should receive for that precinct, and accordingly lowered the number of votes before reporting the "official" results to the election board. The FBI had been precluded from following up this excellent material.

Stockard wondered how these violations could have been accomplished without a conspiracy.

When Clark's explanations failed to impress the Committee, he launched an attack on Stockard's qualifications. He demanded: "Have you ever tried a civil rights case in your life? . . . How long have you been practicing law? Have you ever tried a civil rights case in your life?"

Kem defended his staff member, and explained that the man had been a member of the bar for ten years and had graduated from law school at the head of his class. He also made it clear that in his opinion, as a result of the 1936 vote-fraud case in Missouri, the attorneys in his home state were probably more familiar with state and federal election laws than lawyers in any other part of the country.

Clark retreated slightly. "I am just questioning his experience in a very technical field, for civil rights is a very technical field, one that Mr. Smith here [from the Justice Department] has devoted years of his life to. . . ."

Even Subcommittee Chairman Ferguson was not exempt from Clark's criticism: "You are a fine lawyer, but at the same time you are not versed in civil rights—and these boys here are."

"I am not going to take a lesson from you from what I have heard in this case," replied the Senator.

Clark continued, "You can take a lesson from the boys that got it up. . . ."

"I have had some experience in conspiracy cases," Ferguson said, adding, "We got convictions."

"We get them when we get the evidence," Clark said.

Ferguson refused to let that pass. "When you get the evidence. You did not get the evidence in this case. You did not even try to get it." He continued, "I am glad to hear that this is such a technical statute and that they were using these amateurs [former servicemen] to collect the evidence of a violation, of a conspiracy of such a technical law that only the real experts know about it. Not even the Senators know anything about this."

Stockard related how, at one polling place, two party officials had allegedly remained during the vote counting in violation of the law. The Attorney General thought that this merely indicated "they may have been interested in the state election."

Stockard suggested another possibility which seemed to have escaped Clark: "They may have been interested in the Congressional one."

Attorney General Clark did not claim that the FBI investigation alone was responsible for his department's decision to close the case. He relied greatly on the opinion of three federal judges in Missouri that the FBI investigation had uncovered no evidence to warrant calling a grand jury. This decision in itself was unusual, since as a rule a federal judge is not asked whether a grand jury should be convened but merely requested to impanel one.

Kem: "Do you want the Committee to understand that as Attorney General you requested a grand jury to be called and the United States judges for the Western District of Missouri declined and refused to do it?"

Clark: "I will tell the Committee this, that the District Attorney called—informed me that he conferred with the three judges . . . with a view to talking with them about the grand jury, and that they all three unanimously stated to him that they did not think there was sufficient evidence to call a grand jury or to impound these ballots."

Ferguson: "You could get a grand jury and compel [reluctant witnesses] to answer."

Clark: "We asked for that."

Ferguson: "So you claim that you did ask for a grand jury?"

Kem: "Did he [Wear] ask the judges to call a grand jury. . . . What do you mean by your statement that he asked for a grand jury?"

Clark: "I mean he talked it over with them. He filed no papers asking for the grand jury."

Clark admitted that when his decision to close the investigation was made he had not even seen the FBI report "at that particular time."

Kem: "Had you seen it at the particular time you wrote me the letter saying you had examined it?"

Clark: "Oh, yes, I had looked through it."

Kem: "We will satisfy you that there was an abundance of . . . evidence."

Clark: "You did not satisfy the Department because they have gone over this for months and they did not think there was, and three federal judges did not."

Kem: "Their judgment was no better than their information."

Clark: "They had good information. They had the FBI information."

Kem: "That will come out . . . as to what information they had."

Clark made much of the fact that the three judges had been provided with copies of the full 355-page FBI report. As later testimony from the judges was to reveal, they had in fact received only the synopsis (prepared by United States Attorney Wear) which was far from complete or objective, as testimony also proved.

Whereas the FBI reports do not form opinions on the collected information, the synopsis was not so shy. Wear presented an outline of the various charges by precinct and ward. Each section contained a final legal conclusion to the effect that there was "absolutely no evidence of a conspiracy." It was on this summary that the three federal judges were asked to make their decision, and it was on the basis of that decision that the FBI was ordered to close the case.

One of the three judges, Albert J. Reeves, Sr., was questioned. Reeves—coincidentally the father of the Republican Congressman who had defeated Axtell in the general election—testified he had only received a copy of the synopsis, though he added, in all fairness, that Wear had told him the FBI report was available if he cared to see it.

Ferguson: "You did not have before you these affidavits that were read this morning?"

Judge Reeves: "No, sir."

Ferguson: "I will ask you whether or not there was anything in what was read here this morning that would have changed your mind in relation to this matter."

Reeves: "Well, Senator, probably I would have suggested further investigation, that is, if I had been called upon to give advice on that matter. The only thing submitted to me was whether or not, from this report [the Wear synopsis] we would be justified in calling a grand jury."

Ferguson: ". . . you were never consulted on the proposition as to whether or not there should be a further investigation?"

Reeves acknowledged that this was correct. Asked if he had seen a copy of Brantley's letter advising the District Attorney of the limited nature of the FBI report, Judge Reeves answered in the negative.

Ferguson pressed the point. "Did you understand that this was a real synopsis of a genuine investigation by the FBI?"

Reeves: "Yes, sir, I thought it was."

Ferguson: "Was it your understanding that the FBI had made a thorough investigation, and that this was a synopsis of that?"

Reeves: "Senator, I thought that at the time."

Ferguson wanted to know: "Had you been consulted by Mr. Wear in any other cases as to whether or not he had sufficient facts for you to call a grand jury?"

Reeves: "I do not recall [any such] discussion. The habit and practice has been for the District Attorney to say to the Court that they have matters they want to present to the grand jury and ask one of the judges to call a grand jury."

Ferguson: "In other words, this is the only occasion, then, as I understand it, where Mr. Wear came to you and submitted facts and asked your advice on whether or not to call a grand jury."

Judge Reeves said that to his knowledge this was so.

Had the judges known in advance that their opinion would be cited as a basis for closing the case?

The jurist assured the Committee they had not.

Attorney General Clark had stated that the reason the ballot boxes had not been impounded in Kansas City was that the judges had said it was unnecessary. The Committee Chairman asked Judge Reeves whether he was "ever asked about impounding the ballots."

Reeves said he had not been. Neither had he known about the 1941 order precluding the FBI from investigating election frauds unless specifically so directed by the Attorney General.

That Reeves was the father of the Republican candidate may have raised the specter of political bias had his testimony not been generally corroborated by his two colleagues, Judge Albert A. Ridge and Judge

John Caskie Collet. The only minor disagreement was one of degree. Collet felt that the affidavits were sufficient justification for further inquiry, and Ridge said that the affidavits alone would not have induced him to call a grand jury.

U.S. Attorney Wear admitted that the reason he asked for the opinion of the judges—a highly unusual move—was because, as a Democrat, he was sensitive to the political implications of the case and did not wish to make the final decision on his own.

The Republican members of the Committee couldn't help speculating that possibly this "political sensitivity" was the basis for the misleading synopsis which Wear presented to the judges. It still remained to try the indictments that had been returned by the Jackson County grand jury.

When the theft of the ballots was announced, Hugh C. Moore, foreman of the jury, stated it looked "like a brazen admission of guilt on the part of someone."

He was concerned over the effect of the theft: "It might mean the result of eight weeks' work by the jury is destroyed. The evidence was carefully sifted, and the indictments were built on what we believed to be strong cases. I hope this doesn't knock out the prosecution."

Beginning in January 1948, a federal grand jury returned indictments against nearly 40 individuals for the violation of the federal election laws in the 1946 primary.

In both the state and federal cases the theft of the ballots was the basis for dismissal of the indictments. Of the more than 100 persons indicted by the two grand juries, only three avoided complete escape. One defendant pleaded guilty; a second entered a plea of no contest; and the third, found guilty, was granted a new trial.

Judge Richard M. Duncan sustained a defense motion for a directed acquittal in another trial on the grounds of insufficient evidence. As a direct result, the federal government requested the dismissal of the remaining charges. Richard M. Phelps, Special Assistant U.S. Attorney General, admitted that Judge Duncan's ruling against permitting the former grand jurors to testify in the absence of the ballots had made any further attempt to prosecute "a futile gesture."

In ordering the dismissal, Judge Duncan stated that he believed there had been irregularities and fraud, but that without the missing evidence the federal law did not effectively cover vote-fraud conspiracy cases.

Under the Missouri state law, Circuit Judge James W. Broaddus ruled that the grand jurors could testify as to the results of their recount of the lost ballots only in the face of perjury. The County Prosecutor James S. Kimbrell had little choice but to dismiss the indictments.

The 1946 Kansas City vote-frauds case clearly demonstrated the problems of obtaining aggressive law enforcement, especially where politics are concerned. An attempt had been made to use the reputations of the FBI and three federal judges to convince Congress and the public that not only had there been no "whitewash" as Senator Kem had charged, but that meticulous attention had been given to the case.

A month after the government moved to dismiss the last federal indictments in Kansas City, Tom Clark was nominated to the Supreme Court by President Truman.

5

KEFAUVER TAKES ON THE MOB-POLITICAL ALLIANCE

"Organized crime does exist. . . . The doubts which originally existed in the minds of many intelligent and careful persons as to whether crime is organized in the United States was in a great measure deliberately planted there. It was created by criminals who have vast resources and incalculable power. They have amassed and hoarded tremendous wealth out of the proceeds of their criminal activities and with it they have sought to purchase respectability so that the true nature of their operations could not become known. They have insidiously cultivated the association of persons whose integrity and character are unquestionable. They have sought membership in social clubs and other organizations where they might acquire the status of respectability in their respective communities. They have been lavish in their gifts to charity and they have publicly promoted philanthropies, all in an effort to hide the crimes behind the shielding cloak of respectability." *Kefauver Committee, Second Interim Report No. 141, page 2, February 28, 1951.*

THE Special Crime Committee to Investigate Organized Crime in Interstate Commerce opened its hearings in Miami, Florida, on May 26, 1950. But Kansas City—home town of President Harry Truman—was the scene of the second full-scale hearings into the web of organized crime and politics. Before Chairman Estes Kefauver and his five-man Committee ended their work a year later, they had traveled more than 52,000 miles and had conducted hearings in 15 cities.

In Florida, Senator Kefauver stepped all over the political toes of Democratic Governor Fuller Warren for lack of effective action, and put him on the spot by offering him the opportunity to testify on the evidence of a political-crime alliance. In every city visited, the Tennessee Democrat and his staff put the finger on at least a few pieces of the jigsaw-puzzle alliance between the criminal underworld and the Democratic Party—Miami, Tampa, New Orleans, Kansas City, Cleveland, St. Louis, Detroit, Los Angeles, San Francisco, Las Vegas, Philadelphia, Washington, Chicago, and New York.

Estes Kefauver and his Bible-quoting colleague, Senator Charles W. Tobey, a balding New Hampshire Republican, were hailed as great crusaders against the criminal underworld. Their investigation received the plaudits of the press for its nonpartisan handling of the crime probe in every area. Kefauver rankled Democratic Party leaders in New York and Chicago, but in no place did he foment more resentment than in Kansas City—home base of the man in the White House. Those hearings exposed the mobster-political combine that dominated Kansas City in the late 1940s, recalled the Kansas City vote-fraud scandals, and dredged into the open for closer scrutiny the political events which had preceded the slaying of Democratic political boss Charles Binaggio.

On April 5, 1950, only a few weeks before the hearings, Binaggio and a political crony, Charles (Mad Dog) Gargotta, were slain in a Democratic political clubhouse. Binaggio was the successor to Pendergast as the political power in Kansas City, and Gargotta was a Mafia-connected hoodlum with a record of 39 arrests on charges ranging from burglary to murder.

Understandably, Senator Kefauver might want to focus attention on Kansas City if he wished to move Mr. Truman out of the way for the 1952 election. Understandably, President Truman never forgave Kefauver for spotlighting the political favoritism and the modus operandi of Democratic Missouri politics in that period of time.

The Kefauver Committee pinpointed the manner in which Charles Gargotta was able to corrupt various aspects of local and state government from the police station to the Missouri Pardon Board. A venal police officer had tampered with the evidence by changing identification tags on the murder weapon in an incident in which Gargotta had killed a man in cold blood on the streets of Kansas City. The police officer was eventually sent to the penitentiary for his role, but only because a persistent former Sheriff pressed a felonious assault charge years later and won a conviction.

The case against Charles Gargotta had more than 25 postponements before it finally went to trial. He won an early release from his three-year sentence because the Missouri Pardon Board, against the objections of the Kansas City Police Department, recommended a pardon that was approved by Republican Governor Forrest Donnell.

The group known as the "Five Iron Men" in Kansas City consisted of Binaggio, Gargotta, Jim Balestrere, Tony Gizzo, and Tano Lococo. Functioning in the shadow of this group were Morris (Snag) Klein and Edward P. Osadchey, the latter also known as "Eddie Spitz." The Kefauver investigation stated that jointly these men had controlled most of the important gambling in the Kansas City area, with their tentacles reaching into Nebraska, Iowa, and Kansas.

Out of the testimony in Kansas City came the most direct disclosure of the power of the racket network and its efficacy in controlling local and state government. Jim Balestrere, a Sicilian-born Mafia leader, revealed to the Kefauver Committee how the late Tom Pendergast had arranged for him to be dealt in on a keno gambling game run by Kansas City racket figures.

Later, Charlie Binaggio emerged as the leader of the First Ward Democratic Club to replace Pendergast, and pulled strings to make arrangements for the protective network of political figures needed by the mob at all levels in order to function. Roy McKittrick, of St. Louis, a former State Senator who was Attorney General in Missouri at the time of the Kefauver hearings, provided direct testimony on the manner in which Binaggio maneuvered in Missouri politics.

Binaggio had urged McKittrick to get into the 1948 political race as a candidate for governor against Forrest Smith because "he just had to have a governor" to keep his gambling places running. Later, Binaggio told him to get out of the race; McKittrick finally agreed to run for Attorney General on a ticket with Smith.

"He [Binaggio] is the balance of power," McKittrick said. "He had a lot of friends and supporters in St. Louis, and he was the controlling factor in Kansas City. He had good alliances at St. Joe. He was very active. He was well supplied with money to operate with."

McKittrick said he had some discussions with Binaggio about slot machines and bookmaking places, and they couldn't agree. Later, Binaggio announced that he was going with Smith. McKittrick related that he was offered as much as $50,000 to bow out of the gubernatorial race, and finally ran for Attorney General on an agreement pledging support to him in a U.S. Senate try in 1952.

Testifying before the Kefauver Committee, McKittrick recalled asking Binaggio why he wanted him to run for Attorney General. He said Binaggio replied:

"Well, to be just frank about it, there is some discussion about how much heat Smith will take. . . . We figure that if you are there you could brace him up and make him take more heat than he would otherwise. . . . You know he is kind of slippery at times."

In the end, Governor Smith did not give Binaggio and his team the green light they wanted in St. Louis. In fact, when Governor Smith appointed an independent lumberman, Colonel William L. Holzhausen, as President of the St. Louis Board of Police Commissioners, trouble began to develop for Binaggio. Problems in the control of the Kansas City Police Board also occurred in the period just prior to the slaying of Binaggio and Charles Gargotta on April 5, 1950.

The Binaggio-Gargotta slaying hurled Kansas City into an unwelcome limelight, and Governor Smith reacted in the only manner possible in the face of a Chamber of Commerce demand for a cleanup.

He asked for the resignation of all members of the Kansas City Police Board. Although the precise relationship between Binaggio and Governor Smith was confusing, the Kefauver Committee report stated:

"It is abundantly clear that Binaggio did support Forrest Smith, and that his organization was active in the Governor's campaign. . . . But whatever Binaggio's expectation may have been as a result of his efforts in the campaign for Governor Smith, there is no substantial evidence that Governor Smith made any kind of commitment to Binaggio, or that Binaggio was successful in opening up the town.

"On the other hand, it is inconceivable that Governor Smith, being an experienced politician, could have failed to know of Binaggio's background, or that Binaggio expected a quid pro quo for his support. Smith's assertion under oath that he did not discuss politics with Binaggio, or discuss Binaggio's expectations, are simply not credible."

President Truman was adamantly opposed to Kefauver thereafter for focusing national attention on his home state of Missouri, and on the kind of Mafia characters playing such an influential role in electing Democratic candidates. He did not want to be reminded of the 1948 vote frauds in the congressional race between Roger C. Slaughter and the Pendergast-backed Enos Axtel that created nationwide interest in the theft of ballots from the Jackson County courthouse, and the belated and lax handling of the whole matter by Attorney General Tom Clark.

Still other developments demonstrated links between the Mafia hoodlums in Kansas City politics and in other areas including Chicago, Omaha, and Des Moines.

What the Kefauver Crime Committee did in unveiling the links between politics and the crime world in Kansas City and in Iowa represented only a sample of what was done in exploring syndicate operations in other areas.

Older and more senior senators were cool to Senator Kefauver; and certainly Senator Lyndon B. Johnson, then a Junior Senator from Texas, did not applaud what Kefauver was doing.

In the first place, Lyndon Johnson was not about to commend a liberal Southern Democrat who might be the toughest opposition he would have in his obvious White House ambitions. In addition, the Kefauver investigation reflected unfavorably on Tom Clark, a fellow Texan who was a hindering influence in the 1948 vote-fraud investigations.

Kefauver did not take his crime probe into Texas, but he was not building popularity with those from the Lone Star State who followed the dictum of House Speaker Sam Rayburn:

"If you want to get along, you got to go along," was the Rayburn slogan. He repeated it over and over to young Democratic representatives in the House, and in those years his wise words were quoted in the Senate by Lyndon B. Johnson and his protégé, Robert G. (Bobby) Baker. Speaker Rayburn detested Kefauver, and he didn't bother to cover it up much of the time.

Another Texan who also did not appreciate what Estes Kefauver was doing to the Democratic Party in New York, Illinois, Florida, and a dozen other places, was Senator Tom Connally. He was one of the last of the Old-School senators that included the late Senator Walter George (Dem., Ga.) who took part in the effort to discredit Senator Kefauver as a serious candidate for President and to downgrade him as a useful member of the United States Senate.

On a radio show, Senator Connally commented that Senator Kefauver was absent from the Senate Foreign Relations Committee because he was apparently "off chasing crapshooters." It was initially regarded as an effort to put Kefauver in his place, but the irate public reaction to the comment was hardly what Senator Connally would have expected. He wrote to Senator Kefauver to explain that "no discourtesy" or "lack of appreciation" of Senator Kefauver's investigation of crime was intended. He said that the comment was "merely an attempt at facetiousness."

This reaction did not pull the rug out from under the dissenters, but it did demonstrate that those who opposed the Kefauver crime probe had to do it with an understanding that the tall Tennessean had in a few months been able to rally the sentiment of America against the criminal underworld. From this point on, most of his opposition had to take place along complicated lines calculated not to reveal the antagonism to Senator Kefauver as resentment of his attacks on the big-city machines of the Democrats.

The Kefauver Crime Committee went far beyond what anyone could have anticipated in bringing the problem of organized crime to the attention of the public, and in outlining the alliances with Democratic political figures. Occasionally Republicans were involved, but from a practical standpoint the criminal underworld had tended to put most of its money on the big powerful machines of the Democrats.

In 1950 television had just emerged, and there is no question that the Kefauver Crime Committee made the biggest impact ever made on the American television viewer up to that time. An estimated 20 million viewers saw the parade of underworld figures from Kansas City, Chicago, New York, Miami, Las Vegas, New Orleans, Detroit, Cleveland, Los Angeles, Philadelphia, and even Washington, D.C.

On the television screen the officials came across in a way they had never come through before. They could answer the questions in a frank and open manner; they could refuse to answer; or they could equivocate. To public officials just becoming familiar with television, it was a surprise to discover that they came across on the television screen in a manner that was unflattering unless they were willing to come out firmly against some of the political forces that had been their allies for years.

Senator Kefauver and his Committee members and staff made it clear to the audience that some of the officials had been condoning criminal activity that was vicious and corruptive of the entire Democratic process. Many of the political figures whose acts were examined had probably never thought of their relationship with some of the Mafia members in any more than a casual way. Some had.

Politically, it had been unwise to make too deep an inquiry into the state of law enforcement, and usually it was just as well that a gambling figure from Chicago, Las Vegas, or New York be treated as a respectable businessman. The racketeer's version of the racketeer's past was frequently the most that it was wise to know, because otherwise it might create an obligation that would necessitate questioning the source of the biggest and most consistent campaign contributions.

Those who watched the televised hearings as well as those who actually attended the hearings in the hearing room were probably better informed about the background of the gangster than the Governor, Sheriff, or policeman had been a few hours before taking the witness stand. Frequently the public officials actually didn't know what had taken place in their jurisdiction, or they didn't know enough of the facts to become too concerned about the lack of law enforcement and the almost total disregard for the law.

In Florida, Chairman Kefauver called attention to the actions and lack of action on the part of Democratic Governor Fuller Warren. At the same time he was calling attention to the large political contributions made to Warren's campaign by friends and associates of the Mafia mobsters who were establishing themselves in the Florida playground.

The Kefauver investigators exposed the political protection that the S and G syndicate enjoyed from local sheriffs, and identified Florida as the stamping ground for the gambling enterprises of Joe Adonis, Meyer Lansky, Jack Lansky, Frank Erickson, and Vincent (Jimmy Blue Eyes) Alo, all from the New York and New Jersey area. An assortment of Mafia gambling figures from Chicago, Detroit, Cleveland, and St. Louis had settled in the Florida sunshine to enjoy the pattern of leisurely law enforcement.

Governor Warren submitted an affidavit stating the total contributions to his campaign as $8,825. He omitted from his list the names and donations of three major contributors—Louis E. Wolfson, C.V. Griffin, and William H. Johnston, "principal operator of four Florida dog tracks and an Illinois race track, and an old-time associate of Al Capone's legatees."

"The total contributions of these three alone was in excess of four hundred thousand dollars," the Kefauver report said.

"Johnston and his tracks seem to enjoy immunity from state-level inquiry," the Kefauver Committee report stated. That report linked Johnston with a number of Chicago-gangster types, including Tony (the Enforcer) Accardo and other equally prominent gangland figures.

Governor Warren's name frequently cropped up in connection with questionable activity on the part of state agencies, and on the part of the Governor himself in the manner in which he took action against sheriffs in various areas where the evidence of payoffs was great.

On three separate occasions, the Kefauver Committee offered Governor Warren the opportunity to appear before the Committee to answer the allegations made against him. After Warren refused to appear voluntarily, the Committee, on July 9, 1951, issued a subpoena requesting his appearance. Governor Warren refused, basing his objections on state sovereignty. Later he said he would have a conference with the Kefauver Committee, but would not take an oath.

"In other words, the Governor took the unusual position that while he would talk to the Senate Committee, he would not swear that his statements were true," the report said. "Such unsworn statements could not be the basis of perjury charges if they were found untrue."

The Committee terminated its efforts to obtain Governor Warren's testimony, and in the summer of 1951 concluded that despite the most commendable efforts of certain groups and organizations in Florida—such as the Crime Commissions of Greater Miami and Tampa—"illegitimate activities, such as gambling, continue to exist on an extensive scale."

"This gambling is controlled by interstate syndicates and unsavory associates of some men in high office," the report stated. Needless to say, the Kefauver hearings in 1950 and 1951 did not win Kefauver the political support of Governor Warren or other Democratic political figures allied with the Warren political organization.

The Kefauver Committee amassed enough information to be able to determine, in May 1951, that "there are two major crime syndicates in this country." Those two major syndicates were identified as "the Accardo-Guzik-Fischetti syndicate, whose headquarters are Chicago, and the Costello-Adonis-Lansky syndicate based in New York."

That finding was made before FBI Director J. Edgar Hoover was willing to publicly state that there was a nationwide crime syndicate. Of course, that was before the McClellan Labor Rackets Committee had laid out much of the structure in the labor racket hearings in the 1956-1960 period. It was nearly a dozen years before Joe Valachi told his story about life inside the Cosa Nostra, and years before the government made the Rhode Island and New Jersey wiretaps available for full examination.

The Kefauver reports stated that the operations of the Accardo-Guzik-Fischetti syndicate were apparent in places such as Chicago, Kansas City, Dallas, Miami, Las Vegas, Minneapolis, Des Moines, and West Coast points such as Los Angeles. The Costello-Adonis-Lansky operations were found in New York City, Saratoga, Bergen County in New Jersey, New Orleans, Las Vegas, Miami, Tampa, and, again, on the West Coast. It appeared at that time that they had the territories fairly well allocated except that Florida, Nevada, and the West Coast were apparently open territory with some kind of working arrangements.

"There is a sinister criminal organization known as the Mafia operating throughout the country with ties in other nations, in the opinion of the Committee," the report stated. "The Mafia is the direct descendant of a criminal organization of the same name originating on the island of Sicily. . . . The Mafia is a loose-knit organization specializing in the sale and distribution of narcotics, the conduct of various gambling enterprises, prostitution, and other rackets based on extortion and violence. The Mafia is the binder which ties together the two major criminal syndicates as well as numerous other criminal groups throughout the country. The power of the Mafia is based on a ruthless enforcement of its edicts and its own law of vengeance, to which have been creditably attributed literally hundreds of murders throughout the country."

The Justice Department was still denying the existence of a criminal syndicate when that report came out with its recommendations for a National Crime Commission.

The Kefauver Committee stated that "despite known arrest records and well-documented criminal reputation, the leading hoodlums in the country remain, for the most part, immune from prosecution and punishment although underlings in their gangs may, on occasion, be prosecuted and punished.

"This quasi-immunity of top-level mobsters can be ascribed to what is popularly known as the 'fix,' " the report stated bluntly. "The fix is not always the direct payment of money to law-enforcement officials, although the Committee has run across considerable evidence of such bribery. The fix may also come about through the acquisition of political power by contributions to political organizations or otherwise, by creating economic ties with apparently respectable and reputable businessmen and lawyers, and by buying public good will through charitable contributions and press relations."

The major focal point of the spotlight in Chicago fell on Police Captain Dan (Tubbo) Gilbert, who became famous in the hearings as "the world's richest cop." He had been Chief Investigator for the Office of State's Attorney for Cook County. There was laxity in every area, but the Kefauver Committee found "neglect of official duty and shocking indifference to violations of the law."

At the Kefauver hearings, the Chicago newspapers were grabbing at every new bit of information about the mobsters who were usually so difficult to deal with in print. When all was over, the impact on the 1950 election had knocked out the Democratic Senator, Scott W. Lucas. He was first elected to the United States Senate in November 1938, and was completing the second six-year term in 1950 when the Kefauver Crime Committee knocked him out.

Senator Lucas was serving as Majority Leader in the Senate at that time, and was a driving force in Illinois politics. He never forgave Senator Kefauver for ending his Washington political career with the spotlight on the Democratic machine in Illinois.

The politics of the mob has always been quite bipartisan in the Chicago area, but there is not much doubt that the Democratic side dominates. The Kefauver Committee took substantial testimony that some members of the Illinois legislature, particularly those living in districts most heavily infested by racketeers, have voted against legislation to curb gangster activities and freely associated with their gangster constituents.

It was not necessary for anyone to spell out the pattern for Virgil Peterson, the former FBI agent who had been the vigorous Director of the Chicago Crime Commission for so many years. Peterson had seen the long arm of the syndicate reach into the Justice Department and into the Parole Board when Tom Clark was Attorney General. He had seen the springing of gangsters barely eligible for parole.

When Peterson and the Chicago Crime Commission proposed reform legislation they were not surprised to find the opposition spearheaded by Roland Libonati, the then Democratic State Senator and a close associate of the Capone group. James J. Adducci, a Republican member of the legislature, was cited by the Kefauver Committee as a member of "the bipartisan coalition against reform." Adducci had been arrested a number of times with Capone mobsters and he admitted accepting campaign contributions from Lawrence Mangano, a well-known figure in the Capone hierarchy. He claimed it was necessary to accept such contributions from any kind of business. John Rosselli, once a Capone henchman, frankly testified that the wire service, the handbook, the slot machines, and other Chicago rackets depended on political corruption.

George E. Browne, business agent for the International Alliance of Theatrical Stage Employees and Motion Picture Operators, and Willie Bioff, a Capone mob figure who at the time specialized in labor racketeering, cooperated in an effort to extort $1 million from the major movie studios, Loew's, 20th Century-Fox, and Warner Brothers. When Browne and Bioff were convicted, so too were some of the top people in the Capone organization.

The use of wiretapping evidence under the New York state law provided the intelligence background to break this most important gangster-union case in the early 1940s. Frank Nitti committed suicide in 1943 while under indictment, and half a dozen of his associates were convicted of a conspiracy to extort millions of dollars from the movie industry through their domination of the Motion Picture Operators Union. Others convicted were Louis (Little New York) Campagna, Paul (the Waiter) Ricci, Charles (Cherry Nose) Gioe, Phil D'Andrea, Nick Circella, and John Rosselli, all of whom had been close to Capone.

The Kefauver Committee said that these cases "marked a milestone in the governmental ability to cope with union infiltration by gangsters and the use of unions by gangsters to shake down business enterprises."

But the Kefauver Committee expressed grave concern over the implications of two developments. It was established that Tony (the Enforcer) Accardo had visited three of the Chicago mobsters in Fort Leavenworth prison. He had used the name of a lawyer as he accompanied lawyer Eugene Bernstein when he visited Ricca, Campagna, and Gioe at the federal prison.

More shocking to the Kefauver Committee was the fact that "the three mobsters [Ricci, Campagna, and Gioe] were released on parole after serving a minimum period of imprisonment although they were known to be vicious gangsters."

"A prominent member of the Missouri bar presented their parole applications to the parole board, which granted the parole against the recommendations of the prosecuting attorney and the judge who presided at their trial," Kefauver commented critically even when President Truman was in the White House, and Tom C. Clark was in the Justice Department. "In the opinion of this committee, this early release from imprisonment of three dangerous mobsters is a shocking abuse of parole power."

In New York the hearing focused attention on Frank Costello, the reputed king of the underworld. He refused to have his face on television as he answered the questions for the Committee, and denied any role or influence in the selection of New York mayoralty candidates in the face of the strongest evidence to the contrary.

Ambassador to Mexico William O'Dwyer, a former Mayor of New York, admitted visiting with Costello in his apartment in 1942 when he was an officer in the Army. He claimed it was to obtain information about military contract funds.

O'Dwyer, an Ambassador appointed by President Truman, admitted he had appointed persons with underworld connections to high offices, including one judgeship. O'Dwyer gave an unsatisfactory explanation of why, as Kings County District Attorney, he had dropped prosecution of Albert Anastasia, whom he called the "lord high executioner" of "Murder, Inc.," syndicate.

Ambassador O'Dwyer said that the key witness in the murder charge had died in a fall from a window while under police protection. It was difficult to visualize how the fall could have happened, but it had. O'Dwyer was among those New York officials most criticized in the Kefauver Committee report. The report declared that "Neither he [O'Dwyer] nor his appointees took any effective actions against the top echelons" of the gangster world.

Kefauver's report concluded: "His [O'Dwyer's] defense of public officials who were derelict in their duties, and his actions in investigations of corruption, and his failure to follow up concrete evidence of organized crime, particularly in the case of Murder, Inc., and the waterfront, have contributed to the growth of organized crime."

Having alienated the Democratic organization in Kansas City, Philadelphia, New York, Chicago, and Miami, Senator Kefauver won the hearts of the people but he lost power of the big-city political bosses and their allies in the Mafia and in the big labor unions. Senator Kefauver's only real concession was to try to avoid clashes with Big Labor, by simply telling his investigators that labor disputes were not within the jurisdiction of his Committee.

But as he dug into the organized crime picture in each city it was inevitable that Kefauver would get into the fringes of the big-labor union activities. The big unions had the power, the big tax-exempt money, and the political clout that were to cause such grave problems of corruption in the Teamsters Union a few years later.

In Detroit, Senator Kefauver's investigators turned the spotlight on the activities of Santo Perrone, a Mafia racket figure who had several convictions including one six-year sentence for violation of the Prohibition laws.

The Committee report related that when John A. Fry, President of the Detroit, Michigan, Stove Works, "whose social respectability in the City of Detroit is beyond question, entered into a relationship with one Santo Perrone, the obvious effect was to enlist the assistance of Perrone's gangster friends in Fry's labor problems."

"The second stage is that in which Fry's close friend, William Dean Robinson, likewise socially impeccable and a high official and now [1951] President of Briggs Manufacturing Company, concocted a legal fiction whereby Perrone's son-in-law, Carl Renda, obtained a contract [to haul away scrap metal]," the report said. In fact, Renda's duties were so slight that "a contract for doing nothing . . . has given him an income ranging from fifty to one hundred thousand dollars a year." The real purpose of the contract was "to have Perrone exert his and gangdom's influence in the Briggs Manufacturing Company's labor problems," the Kefauver report said.

"It is not the function of this Committee to inquire into labor disputes, but the Committee must point out the sinister relationship between the lucrative contracts granted to the gangster Perrones and the ability of the Detroit, Michigan, Stove Works to keep labor unions out of its plant."

"The most important fact uncovered in the Detroit hearings of this Committee was that some manufacturers have entered into and are today continuing intimate business relationships with racketeers for the purpose of affecting their labor relationships," Kefauver stated.

"The granting of the Renda scrap contract preceded the first of the notorious Briggs beatings by a little more than a week," the report said. "The Committee's record indicated that approximately six prominent labor officers of the Briggs Manufacturing Company were beaten in a most inhuman fashion by unknown persons in the year that followed the granting of the otherwise inexplicable Renda contract."

Senator Kefauver and his crime investigators barely scratched the surface of the manner in which the Detroit gangsters exploited the power of union labor as a tool for extortion from business. The Tennessee Democrat had clashed with organized crime just enough to demonstrate that it could result in political profit, and far enough to show the great political hazards in probing too deeply into the links between the big-city machines and the alliances with big labor and the Mafia.

It was left for Robert F. Kennedy and Senator John McClellan, an Arkansas Democrat with no presidential aspirations, to put the focus on the activities of another Detroit labor figure—Teamsters Boss, James R. Hoffa. Before the Kennedy tussle with Hoffa was concluded with two federal prison terms for Hoffa for jury tampering and pension fund frauds, the American public had learned the hundreds of ways that the Teamsters Union control over transportation can be made into rackets. Also, both Kennedy and McClellan learned the first lessons of how vital eavesdropping and wiretapping are to the effectiveness of law enforcement.

6

ROBERT KENNEDY—LESSONS FROM HOFFA TO VALACHI

"Former Attorney General Robert F. Kennedy appeared as a witness, describing the criminal organization as a private government of crime that handles billions of dollars in annual income that is derived from human suffering and moral corrosion. The Attorney General testified that federal investigative agencies now are certain, because of intelligence gathered from Joseph Valachi and other informants, that the national crime syndicate is operated by a commission of top-ranking criminals, varying in number from nine to twelve members, and that their identities are known. This Commission makes policy decisions for the combine, settles disputes among the various factions or 'families,' and allocates territories for each family's operations." *From Report No. 72 of the 89th Congress, 1st Session, by the Permanent Subcommittee on Investigations on Organized Crime and Illicit Traffic in Narcotics.*

SPECIAL agents for the Federal Bureau of Investigation arrested James R. Hoffa in Washington as he entered the Dupont Plaza Hotel elevator shortly after 11 P.M. on March 13, 1957. From that moment Robert F. Kennedy, then the counsel for the McClellan Labor Racket Committee, felt he had an airtight case against the tough little president of Teamsters.

Kennedy would not have to depend on some pimp or burglar for testimony that Hoffa had to bribe an employee of the Senate Committee to obtain information: he had a chief witness, John Cye Cheasty, who was a lawyer-investigator. Cheasty would testify that Hoffa had tried to bribe an employee of the Senate Committee to give him information. Cheasty had kept a careful log on his meetings with Hoffa in Washington and in Detroit.

FBI agents had monitored Cheasty's meetings with Hoffa and had even taken pictures of Hoffa slipping $2,000 in cash into Cheasty's hand. They had listened when Cheasty talked with Hoffa on the telephone. An FBI agent, Paul Morrison, had been driving the taxi that brought Cheasty to his meetings with Hoffa. Morrison had heard some of the conversation between Hoffa and Cheasty in the cab.

There was every reason for Kennedy to be a bit cocky. Within a few weeks after he had officially launched the labor racket investigation, he had discredited Teamsters President Dave Beck. Now Hoffa, who was the raw power in the 1,500,000-member union, seemed certain to be convicted.

"If Hoffa isn't convicted, I'll jump off the Capitol," Kennedy quipped in what was supposed to be an off-the-record press conference in his office in the Old Senate Office Building. The remark found its way into print in a Detroit newspaper and became the focal point of considerable attention because Hoffa's attorney, Edward Bennett Williams, tried to exploit it as prejudicial to his client.

Kennedy treated the subject of Hoffa as if the rowdy Detroit Teamster boss had already been pushed out of power. He said that the Hoffa arrest made him less uneasy about exposing Beck. He said he considered Hoffa "a worse influence than Dave Beck," and had been afraid that exposing Beck might simply be delivering the Teamsters organization to a ruthless pal of the underworld.

Four months later, on July 19, 1957, Robert Kennedy learned that the best-laid plans of mice and men can go astray. In the months between March and July, Kennedy had seen how truly resourceful Hoffa and his lawyers could be.

As the Hoffa trial was starting, Edward Bennett Williams contended that he had information from a Detroit man named Lawrence Burns that some of the evidence against Hoffa came from illegal wiretapping. Prosecutor Troxell declared that the government had used no wiretaps or other interception devices in any phase of the case against Hoffa.

During the trial, Joe Louis, the former heavyweight boxing champion, had come into the courtroom to shake hands with "my pal" Jimmy Hoffa in front of the jury that included eight Negroes.

Over the objections of United States District Judge Burnita Shelton Matthews, Williams had injected a race issue into the trial by asking a series of questions on Cheasty's role in a Florida bus boycott and in an investigation of the National Association for the Advancement of Colored People (NAACP).

First Williams asked Cheasty if he had taken any drugs during the period of time he was testifying. Cheasty answered he had taken nitroglycerine for a heart condition.

"Have you taken any form of narcotics?" the defense lawyer continued to press the theme, and Troxell said angrily:

"I object, Your Honor. This is an infraction which is disgraceful."

Williams followed this by asking if Cheasty had not used fictitious names when acting as an investigator. Cheasty said he had used fictitious names on some occasions, but could not say how many.

"When you were employed by the City of Tallahassee to investigate the National Association for the Advancement of Colored People, you used a fictitious identity, didn't you?" Williams fired the question quickly.

Reporters were startled by the suddenness with which Williams had rammed the race issue into the trial.

"I object to that," Troxell shouted, leaping from his seat too late to block Williams' question.

Cheasty remained calm. He retorted that he had not used a fictitious name in Florida, he had not investigated the NAACP, and added that he would be glad to tell Williams all about it.

Williams tried to stop Cheasty's answer. But Judge Matthews ruled that since Williams had opened the subject, Cheasty was entitled to explain. But before Cheasty's explanation could be placed in the record, Williams repeated his charge that Cheasty was investigating the NAACP "to break up the bus boycott."

"You are testifying, Mr. Williams," Cheasty complained.

When Williams was finally shut off, Cheasty testified: "In Tallahassee, I didn't use a fictitious identity. I went down there as John Cye Cheasty, a New York lawyer. I showed my credentials to the Chief of Police under that setup there."

And Cheasty testified in direct contradiction to the self-serving comments by Williams that Cheasty had gone there "to break up the bus boycott."

"I recommended that they cut the color line on the busses down there, and they let people come in and sit as they wanted on a first-come-first-served basis," Cheasty explained.

Williams blustered about the unfairness to Hoffa of having Cheasty's comments in the record, but Judge Matthews showed no sympathy toward Williams. She said that if the race issue had been improperly injected into the trial it was because Williams had done it.

"I was amazed that Mr. Williams went into that in the first place, but . . . it seemed to me, after he mentioned it . . . [it] should be allowed," Judge Matthews explained.

On July 6, 1957, *The Afro-American,* a newspaper, published a highly inflammatory pro-Hoffa issue that was circulated to Negro homes in Washington, D.C. It contained an attack on Judge Matthews, identified her as from Arkansas, and called her the tool of Big Business from the Old South. Hoffa and Edward Bennett Williams were praised as champions of civil rights and Negro equality.

Judge Matthews received reports that the newspaper had been delivered to the homes of jurors in the Hoffa case. Without public explanation of her reason, she ordered that the jury be isolated from the general public for the duration of the trial.

Williams told reporters he had no knowledge of the *Afro-American* newspaper incident until after the paper was circulated. He said he strongly disapproved of such prejudicial material, but couldn't be accountable for what was printed in every newspaper.

The Hoffa jury returned a "not guilty" verdict on July 19, 1957, and the announcement turned the courtroom into a carnival. "Jimmy is a real guy," declared Louis (Babe) Triscaro, the Cleveland Teamsters boss, who has a robbery conviction in his past. "Jimmy is a winner."

Robert (Barney) Baker, a twice-convicted thug from the New York waterfront, declared: "Jimmy's a real champ. Jimmy was right on this one, and I hope some of you newspaper boys will give him a break and write something nice about him."

At the front of the courtroom Hoffa was saying: "This proves once again that if you are honest and tell the truth, you have nothing to fear." He commended "all my attorneys," but particularly Williams, for a "masterful job of presenting facts, not fiction, in this case."

Edward Bennett Williams called attention to Bob Kennedy's comment that he would jump off the Capitol dome if Hoffa is acquitted. He quipped: "I'm going to send Bobby Kennedy a parachute."

Robert Kennedy was shocked by the acquittal, but lost no time brooding. He obtained some court-approved wiretaps from New York District Attorney Frank Hogan. He put together a devastating pattern of evidence, including proof of Hoffa's association with some of the worst Mafia-connected hoodlums in the New York and Detroit areas.

Some of Hoffa's conversations with John (Johnny Dio) Dioguardi had been tapped. These involved the manner in which Hoffa and Tony (Ducks) Corallo, a convicted narcotics-law violator, obtained charters in the UAW-AFL and used these to set up seven "paper" Teamsters locals in New York. These phantom locals, with only a few members and little legitimate function, were being used by Hoffa and his racketeering friends to grab control of New York Teamsters Joint Council 16.

To Johnny Dioguardi, trade unions were just another racket. He had operated a nonunion dress shop in Pennsylvania. When he sold it, he took an $11,000 bribe to make sure through his connections that it would stay nonunion.

Dioguardi and Corallo had brought into organized labor 40 men who had convictions for extortion, burglary, accessory to murder, robbery, bookmaking, possession of stolen mail, bootlegging, larceny, dope peddling, and bribery.

"Such racketeers as John Dioguardi and Anthony Corallo present a dangerous enough problem, but when they have the backing of top officers of the nation's largest union, particularly James Hoffa. . . the situation becomes one for national alarm," the McClellan Committee was to report later.

Hoffa was his usual fluent and cocky self when he appeared before the Senate Committee on August 20. But after one week, Bob Kennedy had him reeling. Repeatedly he forced Hoffa into corners with evidence, and then played recordings of the telephone taps that had been legally obtained by District Attorney Hogan.

The tough and agile Teamsters boss could explain almost any documents or circumstances, but he could not explain the conversations with Johnny Dioguardi. He had to fall back on claiming a lack of memory for things that obviously he could not have forgotten.

"To the best of my recollection, I cannot recall, and this [recording] does not refresh my memory as to this conversation," Hoffa testified, repeating the evasion time and again. He claimed he couldn't remember whether he had sent Teamsters Union business agents equipped with Minafones (electronic recording devices) to spy on a grand jury. He claimed he had no recollection of other matters that would have been equally difficult to forget. Senator Irving Ives of New York declared that Hoffa had "the best forgettery" he had ever seen.

Chairman McClellan and other Committee members concluded that Hoffa was finished, even though Robert Kennedy had barely scratched the surface of the wiretap information available. They had implicated Hoffa in a pattern of the most sordid misuse of Teamsters power, and in a 48-point summary McClellan outlined the worst examples. The national network of racketeering Teamsters was starting to emerge from Anthony (Tony Pro) Provenzano in New Jersey; through Babe Triscaro and William Presser in Cleveland; Joseph Glimco, a Chicago Teamster boss who was identified by the McClellan Committee as an associate of Capone mobsters in the Chicago area; Luigi (Lew Farrell) Fratto in Des Moines; and Gerald Connelly in Minneapolis.

Kennedy again was overoptimistic about the power of public opinion over the decisions within the International Brotherhood of Teamsters—"Hoffa's Hoodlum Empire." When Dave Beck, ousted from the Executive Council of the AFL-CIO, retired as General President of the Teamsters, Hoffa was elected by an overwhelming vote—1,208 to 453.

But Hoffa was not seated. The McClellan Subcommittee made evidence of union election frauds available to a group of rank-and-file dissidents who filed an action in the United States District Court.

On October 24, 1957, the AFL-CIO executive council suspended the Teamsters and said that the union would be expelled if Hoffa continued as an officer. The vote was 25 to four. Hoffa angrily strode out of the AFL-CIO headquarters. At that point, Hoffa had enough problems to break the nerve of the average man. His name was mentioned in scandals in Tennessee, in Philadelphia, in Los Angeles, and in Chicago.

But the thing that concerned him most was the federal perjury indictment hanging over him in New York, along with a charge of illegally arranging to have the telephones in his Detroit headquarters tapped.

Hoffa was unusually glum as he went into federal court for preliminary hearings in connection with the perjury and wiretap charges that were soon to go to trial. The government planned to use wiretapping evidence against Hoffa. The courts had held that although it was illegal for federal investigators themselves to use wiretaps to obtain evidence, it was permissible for them to make use of wiretaps which had been legally obtained by state law-enforcement officials.

Kennedy claimed that he had not used some of "the best ones" from the Hogan collection of wiretaps. Hoffa was obviously worried about it. He commented to reporters about the "unfairness" of the government's use of wiretaps of his conversations, saying the practice was a violation of his rights. He hoped there would be a United States Supreme Court ruling in the Salvator Benanti case that would prohibit federal bootlegging conviction based on evidence gained from wiretapping by state officials. The conviction had been upheld by the Second Circuit in line with prior Supreme Court decisions, but Jimmy Hoffa was hanging his hopes on that decision being upset.

United States Attorney Paul Williams believed he had two strong cases if the Benanti case was not upset. But he said that if the United States Supreme Court reversed the Benanti conviction because it depended on evidence obtained through wiretapping, the perjury case against Hoffa would be destroyed. If the conviction was sustained, the perjury case would be the better bet for Hoffa's conviction than the charge of tapping his union's phones.

On December 9, 1957, midway in the Hoffa trial in New York, the United States Supreme Court handed down a decision in the appeal of the Benanti bootlegging case. It was precisely what Jimmy Hoffa wanted. It prohibited the use of wiretaps in federal court cases. This meant that Paul Williams would not be able to use the most conclusive evidence he had against Hoffa, and Hoffa no longer had to be concerned about his own words being played back to him in court.

Paul Williams was disappointed at the decision, and a few weeks later, after a hung jury, was forced to abandon prosecution of Hoffa on the perjury charge as well as the wiretapping charge. "Without the wiretaps of Hoffa's conversations, the government just doesn't have much of a case," the prosecutor said.

At the time that President Kennedy named Robert F. Kennedy as Attorney General in 1961, the President quipped that "Bobby needed the experience." It always brought a laugh, because it was widely known that Bob Kennedy had never tried a case in his life and was notoriously bad as a law researcher.

But Bob Kennedy had strengths that far outweighed the lack of experience in research or trial work, and the most important of these were the hard lessons he learned in the pursuit of the elusive and imaginative James R. Hoffa. Hoffa could always find a reason for not taking aggressive action to clean up the union or to prohibit Teamsters Union members from associating with persons clearly identified with the Mafia. He managed it by surrounding himself with such men as Frank Fitzsimmons, the long-time Teamsters crony from Detroit who could be counted on to corroborate a Hoffa story or to take the Fifth Amendment.

Fitzsimmons was only one of a handful of men Hoffa used as a protective shield on matters that might involve violations of the law. These men vehemently denied that Hoffa knew what they were doing, or took the Fifth Amendment; in turn Hoffa would defend their right to refuse to testify. With only slight coaching from his lawyers, Hoffa would eloquently proclaim his duty to permit these men to claim their constitutional rights. He consistently promised to look into the questions raised by the McClellan Subcommittee, or the court monitors. But from his experience, Bob Kennedy knew that the only way to shake Jimmy Hoffa was to play his own words back to him—only in that way could he tangle such a glib liar.

Kennedy concluded that what was needed was federal legislation permitting the FBI and local law-enforcement officials to engage in electronic surveillance under court order. He favored an "immunity" statute to undermine the conspiracy of silence that protected Hoffa and other criminals.

There was also the problem of intimidation: dozens of witnesses before the McClellan Committee had been afraid to talk. It was necessary to guarantee protection for a witness and his family in order to obtain testimony.

By this time, Robert Kennedy had become a great admirer of the work done by Senator Estes Kefauver in his crime probe. If he still had doubts that there was an organized crime syndicate, these doubts were erased on November 14, 1957, when the New York Bureau of Criminal Investigation staged a raid on a mobster convention at the palatial home of Joseph Mario Barbara, Sr., near Appalachia, New York. Many of the top names in the Mafia, labor leaders, labor relations consultants, vending-machine operators, old-time bootleggers, and convicted robbers were among the 58 taken in the raid.

Among those arrested was Vito Genovese, one of the top gangsters in the country. He had been on the fringes of many labor rackets, and was identified as a key figure in an international narcotics ring.

The public and Congress were still not ready to accept wiretapping as essential in the war against organized crime. Then on June 22, 1962, Joseph Michael Valachi, a prisoner at the U.S. Penitentiary in Atlanta, Georgia, seized a two-foot length of pipe and beat another prisoner to a bloody dying mass. Valachi, who was serving time for selling heroin, later explained that he believed his victim was a member of the Cosa Nostra and had marked him for execution.

Months later, Attorney General Kennedy made arrangements for Joe Valachi to go before the McClellan Subcommittee on Organized Crime and Illicit Traffic in Narcotics to spell out the dramatic inside story of the Cosa Nostra. Before the Subcommittee, Joe Valachi revealed for the first time the inside story of life in the Mafia, which he called the "Cosa Nostra."

According to Valachi, the smooth-working and experienced combine had evolved from the gang wars of the 1930s in the New York and Chicago underworld. The national crime syndicate is operated by a "Commission" of from nine to twelve top-ranking criminals. Federal investigative agencies were then certain of their facts, because of the Valachi intelligence and the corroboration from other informants.

"This Commission makes policy decisions for the combine, settles disputes among factions or 'families,' and allocates territories for each family's operation," the McClellan Subcommittee reported.

It was noted that Kennedy had described the criminal organization of Cosa Nostra as "a private government of crime that handles billions of dollars in annual income . . . derived from human suffering and moral corrosion. . . . As a result of the Valachi testimony, federal investigative agencies are now pooling information on more than 1,100 major racketeers."

Robert Kennedy pointed out to the Subcommittee that as criminals become more adroit in insulating themselves from the law, the value of informants increases correspondingly but does not provide hard evidence. "Being able to identify a top racketeer is one thing," Kennedy said, "securing the evidence to convict him in a court of law is quite another."

He declared that one major purpose of using Valachi's testimony was to seek the help of Congress in obtaining additional legislation, including the authority to offer immunity to witnesses in racketeering investigations, and the reform and revision of the wiretapping law.

Robert Kennedy made the strongest request for new wiretapping authority. He said he believed that the present law was completely inadequate, that it did not protect individual privacy because the law required proof of both the tapping of the wire and the disclosure of the information, and he believed that either tapping or disclosing should be a violation of the law. He also proposed that legislation tighten the law on unauthorized wiretapping but permit tapping under court order by law-enforcement officials.

"Last January, the Department of Justice resubmitted to Congress a carefully worded bill, S. 1308, with strong procedural safeguards, which would afford a clear-cut basis for the legitimate and controlled use of wiretapping by law-enforcement officials," Kennedy told the Subcommittee. "At the same time, the bill would expressly forbid all other types of wiretapping." He noted that "this bill empowers the Attorney General, or his specially designated Assistant, to authorize application to a federal judge for a wiretap order."

"The judge can . . . issue an order permitting wiretapping in cases involving national security, murder, kidnapping, and racketeering," Kennedy said. And he summed up in these words: "We are dealing with a problem that is getting greater and greater in this country. Either we are going to get the tools to deal with it, or we are going to slip along as we are."

In *The Enemy Within,* his book on the labor racket inquiry, Kennedy concluded that the racketeers and corrupters of government represented a greater threat to the United States than any foreign subversive elements.

"To meet the challenge of our times . . . we must first defeat the enemy within," he wrote in 1959. At that time he had concluded that we could do this only if wiretapping and eavesdropping under court order were legal.

In the years as Attorney General, Robert Kennedy had an opportunity to view at firsthand how underworld figures tried to wield their influence through political channels. He fought with the Democratic machines of the big cities as much as with Republicans, and he learned to recognize the subtle efforts at "the fix" and the links the Cosa Nostra used in the Senate, in the House, and even in some of the highest offices in the Executive Branch.

In the end, the Cosa Nostra and the gambling mob from Las Vegas were able to stop what Kefauver had suggested in the early 1950s and what Kennedy proposed in the early 1960s as the vital tool in the war against crime—court-authorized eavesdropping and wiretapping for federal and state police.

During the time he was Attorney General and later as a U.S. Senator, Robert Kennedy was to have a ringside seat on one of the most amazing stories in Justice Department history: the case of Robert G. (Bobby) Baker, Fred B. Black, Jr., and Edward Levinson.

Baker was secretary to the Democratic Majority in the Senate. Fred Black was a highly-paid lobbyist for North American Aviation and other space industries. Edward Levinson was a Las Vegas gambling figure whose financial fortunes merged with those of Baker and Black in the period immediately following the award of the Apollo contract. All the cases involved wiretapping and eavesdropping and an unusual series of decisions by the Johnson Administration.

7

BUGGING BOBBY BAKER, BLACK, AND THE BOYS FROM LAS VEGAS

"The most sophisticated use of these electronic surveillance techniques for the purpose of gathering criminal intelligence has been made under Department of Justice authorization by the Federal Bureau of Investigation. The body of knowledge built up by the Bureau concerning the structure, membership, activities, and purposes of La Cosa Nostra was termed 'significant' by the President's Commission on Law Enforcement and Administration of Justice. Indeed, the Commission recognized that only the Bureau has been able 'to document fully the national scope of' the groups engaged in organized crime. Because this information was not gathered for the purpose of prosecution, however, it has not generally been made public." *American Bar Association Project on Minimum Standards for Criminal Justice, Standards Relating to Electronic Surveillance, page 53.*

UNTIL the Bobby Baker case broke into the open in the early fall of 1963, only a few people knew the power of Fred B. Black, Jr. The secret to Black's success was his contacts.

Top officials of North American Aviation Corporation (NAA) recognized the value of those contacts at the National Aeronautics and Space Administration (NASA). Despite the fact that Fred Black was under indictment on charges of federal income tax evasion, North American was paying the University of Missouri dropout more than $200,000 a year for his services in Washington.

Similarly, the fact that he was under indictment by a federal grand jury in Kansas City, Missouri, had not hurt his connections at the Defense Department, NASA, or in Congress. His friends included Robert G. (Bobby) Baker, then Secretary to the Democratic Majority in the Senate. When Lyndon Johnson had been Majority Leader, Baker was his "strong right arm." Later, as Vice-President, Johnson was chairman of the National Aeronautics and Space Council. James E. Webb was administrator of NASA. Senator Robert S. Kerr, wealthy Oklahoma Democrat, was chairman of the Senate Committee on Aeronautical and Space Sciences. Bobby Baker was close to all three.

Independently or through Baker, Fred Black had access to essentially any information he wanted about space contracting and space spending. Webb could rest assured that Kerr would not conduct unreasonable investigations of decisions which benefited the Senator and his associates. Black was one of Kerr's gin-rummy-playing friends.

He lived on a cul-de-sac around the corner from Vice-President Johnson who had purchased Les Ormes from Perle Mesta. A gate in a common back fence connected their gardens in those days before assassinations had frightened the nation into tighter security.

Baker and Black had worked diligently to obtain the Democratic nomination for Lyndon Johnson in 1960, but the Kennedy victory at the convention did little to damage their influence. The Kennedys had never understood the jockeying for control of contracts; consequently the trio of Johnson, Kerr, and Webb continued to be influential in the space field.

Their major worry initially was Attorney General Robert F. Kennedy's income tax prosecution of Black.

Attorney General Kennedy's suspicion of Fred Black and Bobby Baker increased as he learned of their association with Las Vegas gambling figures including Edward Levinson, Benjamin Siegelbaum, Edward Torres, and Cliff Jones, former Democratic Lieutenant Governor of Nevada who doubled as a hotel and casino operator. The Internal Revenue Service and FBI were cooperating in a major investigation of the "skimming" of millions of dollars off the top of the take in such Las Vegas hotels and casinos as the Flamingo, the Fremont, and the Stardust. The Justice Department authorized eavesdropping and wire-tapping to uncover information in these cases.

This surveillance convinced Kennedy that Fred Black and, perhaps, Bobby Baker deserved special attention from the organized crime unit. Consequently in February 1963, a bug was installed in Black's plush suite at the Carlton Hotel in Washington.

The bug remained operative until late April. Manned on a 24-hour-a-day basis, it furnished an intriguing insight into what organized crime could accomplish with a few highly placed political contacts. Both Baker and Black operated out of the Carlton, and their monitored conversations disclosed an arrangement between the late Senator Kerr and North American officials in the awarding of the Apollo contract.

The first phase of the multibillion-dollar contract was let to North American in the late fall of 1961 instead of to Martin Marietta which was at first judged the best qualified. At the same time, North American Aviation switched its vending-machine dealer. Baker's Serv-U Vending Corporation was substituted for a firm which had handled NAA's vending machine business for years. This change was made despite the fact that Serv-U had no employees, vending machines, or experience when the multimillion-dollar contract was awarded. The partners were Bobby Baker, Fred Black, Jr., Edward Levinson, and Benjamin Siegelbaum.

The financing of Serv-U Vending was arranged through the Kerr-controlled Fidelity National Bank in Oklahoma City, one of whose major stockholders was James E. Webb. This same bank was used by Baker, Black, and the two gamblers in buying into the District of Columbia National Bank during the same period.

The wiretap on Black raised questions about Senator Kerr's influence in the awarding of the Apollo contract to North American. Following his death, an inventory of Kerr's estate showed that he had owned an interest in lands which had benefited from North American's decisions to construct new plants in Oklahoma. Kerr held the land in the name of an Oklahoma City lawyer.

Kerr had died on January 1, 1963, a few weeks before installation of the bug. Black, in a conversation on February 11, 1963, with Dean McGee, the surviving half of Kerr-McGee Industries, deplored the fact that James Webb was less dependable now that the Senator was dead. He was apologetic about the adverse economic effects this might have on Oklahoma.

"First of all, since the old man died, this fellow Webb has gotten weaker and weaker where the state of Oklahoma is concerned," Black said. "We sent them [NASA] several things before the Senator died—

OK—when we got them back an OK on a third of what we wanted to put there. He's just not going to do anything for us. I'm getting concerned about a few things in Oklahoma City itself. NASA is not helping us. When the Senator was alive, he'd be helping."

Then Black assured McGee, "I want you to know, North American and Fred Black aren't backing up one inch."

Some of the tapes included comments about Lyndon Johnson, but for the most part these were vague. When it became apparent in 1965 that the tapes might be made public, Johnson was naturally anxious. He requested copies of transcripts from the FBI so he could personally review them. From the day he took office, Johnson was worried that Attorney General Kennedy had obtained recordings of conversations which might prove embarrassing to him.

He revealed his distrust of Kennedy to a number of Senators and Congressmen, who in turn repeated it to Sidney Zagri, Washington lawyer-lobbyist for the International Brotherhood of Teamsters. The Teamsters Union under James R. Hoffa had supported Johnson for the Democratic Presidential nomination in 1960, and Zagri shared with the Vice-President an intense dislike of Robert Kennedy.

At the 1964 Republican convention in San Francisco, Zagri sought support for Hoffa on the grounds that Kennedy had used illegal wiretap evidence to convict the Teamsters president. Although some Republicans bought this because of their dislike of Kennedy, the Party wanted no obvious alignment with Hoffa.

Hoffa and Zagri were successful, however, in selling the idea that there was too much eavesdropping and wiretapping by federal agencies to the Senate Judiciary Subcommittee on Administrative Procedures. Democratic Senator Ed Long of Missouri conducted the investigation. Long admitted collecting a $48,000 "referral fee" paid to his law firm by the Teamsters, but he denied it was in any way connected with his Subcommittee work.

At the same time, wiretapping was under attack from three other points: the Supreme Court, the Justice Department and, perhaps most significantly, the Executive Branch.

In response to a Presidential Crime Commission recommendation to legalize eavesdropping and wiretapping as essential tools in fighting organized crime, President Johnson launched an unusual tirade. (It was reported that, coincidentally or not, a lawyer from Texas on the Commission had threatened to write a dissenting report.) Nevertheless, the House and Senate passed legislation permitting eavesdropping and wiretapping by federal and state authorities on proper showing of due cause to the federal court and on application by the Attorney General or one of his assistants.

In signing that general crime bill into law on June 19, 1968, President Johnson declared:

"Congress, in my judgment, has taken an unwise and potentially dangerous step by sanctioning eavesdropping and wiretapping by federal, state, and local law officials in an almost unlimited variety of situations.

"If we are not very careful and cautious in our planning, these legislative provisions could result in producing a nation of snoopers bending through the keyholes of homes and offices in America, spying on our neighbors. No conversation in the sanctity of the bedroom or relayed over a copper telephone wire would be free of eavesdropping by those who say they want to ferret out crime."

President Johnson said he signed the law only because other provisions outweighed the evil; but he asked Congress to repeal the wiretapping provision. The President had developed a fixation on the subject not apparent when he was Majority Leader or Vice-President.

He announced that a 1967 Justice Department memorandum barring federal eavesdropping and wiretapping, except in national security cases, would remain in effect.

This policy became the subject of a bitter exchange between Senator McClellan and Ramsey Clark, during Justice Department appropriations hearings on June 27, 1968. The Attorney General argued that electronic eavesdropping was a "wasteful and unproductive" means of obtaining evidence. He said that out of a total of 38 federal electronic surveillance investigations under way, all dealt with national security cases; none with organized crime. Chairman McClellan, however, charged that Clark was flouting the law by refusing to use tools provided by Congress.

"This Administration has never and will never flout the law," Clark said, insisting that the law "authorized" but did not direct federal officials to use electronic surveillance.

"Then why did you fight the bill so hard?" McClellan asked with regard to those sections.

"It is undesirable and leads to invasion of privacy," was Clark's response.

Against the opinion of such seasoned experts as FBI Director J. Edgar Hoover, New York District Attorney Frank Hogan, and former Attorney General Robert F. Kennedy, Clark characterized wiretapping as having marginal value as a law enforcement tool.

Associate Supreme Court Justice and former Attorney General Tom C. Clark, who previously had rarely commented on the dangers of eavesdropping, now lined up with his son and President Johnson. In his majority opinion on Berger v. New York, Tom Clark stated: "Few threats to liberty exist which are greater than that posed by the use of eavesdropping devices."

In the Berger case, the Supreme Court reversed by a six-to-three vote the conviction of a Chicago public relations man for bribing the New York State Liquor Authority and various political figures for illegally issuing a liquor license to the Playboy Key Club.

Chairman McClellan and members of the President's own Crime Commission did not discount the possible misuse of eavesdropping, but noted that the legislation provided concrete safeguards against this. Requirements called for a court order, limited periods of tapping backed by affidavits, and a periodic report on how many telephones had been tapped. Experienced law-enforcement officials recognized the danger of uncontrolled tapping, but they pointed out that under present conditions the FBI and other law-enforcement agencies were really the only ones barred from eavesdropping. Lawless elements employed electronic listening devices for blackmail and other illicit practices and did not worry about evidence being admissible in court.

In general, experienced law-enforcement officials felt that Ramsey Clark was demonstrating his own inexperience when he characterized electronic eavesdropping as "wasteful and unproductive." The record was full of instances in which it had proved invaluable in gaining leads and evidence involving manipulative schemes, narcotic rings, gambling, and other crimes.

The stand of President Johnson and Ramsey Clark on wiretapping, however, had definite consequences for the prosecution of Fred Black.

In the early spring of 1966, Black told me he would not go to jail quietly but would "take some others along." He asked me to arrange a conference with Senator John J. Williams of Delaware. Senator Williams, at the time, was urging a vigorous investigation of Bobby Baker by a reluctant Senate Rules Committee. Black said he wished to "tell all" to Williams, and that what he had to say would involve some of the highest officials in the Johnson Administration. I informed the Justice Department prosecutors, who were handling the case, of Black's desires.

Then suddenly Fred Black changed his mind. Within a few weeks of our conversation, actions taken by the Johnson Administration and the Justice Department resulted in an unprecedented decision that saved Black from going to federal prison.

The chronology of the case is this:

Fred Black was indicted early in 1963 on federal income tax charges alleging he had failed to report income from a number of firms he represented in Washington, D.C. The indictment was returned in Kansas City before he had gained notoriety in the Baker case, and he quietly moved for a change of venue to Washington, where it might be lost in the maze of United States District Court cases in which only big names received much attention.

In May 1964, Black was found guilty and Judge John Sirica sentenced him to prison for 15 months to four years. Black was still confident, because the Circuit Court of Appeals for the District of Columbia was notorious for exploiting every technicality to upset convictions for well-known defendants. Black's friend, Lyndon Johnson, was President and appeared likely to be reelected despite the Baker scandal.

Even so, in 1965 Black lost his appeal. The Senate Rules Committee had issued a report on the "gross improprieties" of Bobby Baker. This report was also critical of the "conflicts of interests" inherent in the awarding of the North American Aviation contract to the Serv-U Vending Corporation.

In the meantime, two former Baker lawyers were nominated by President Johnson for key positions in the prosecution and appeals process. One was Abe Fortas, Johnson's personal lawyer and long-time crony. He was proposed as Associate Justice of the United States Supreme Court. At Johnson's request, Fortas had represented Baker from September 1963, until the week after President Kennedy's assassination. David Bress, who had represented Baker's vending-machine company, was nominated as United States District Attorney for Washington, D.C.

Senator Williams questioned the propriety of these nominations. Nicholas deB. Katzenbach, then serving as Attorney General, assured the Senate Judiciary Committee that Bress would not be in charge of the Baker investigation. Instead, Assistant Attorney General Herbert J. (Jack) Miller had obtained a court order under which the case would be handled by a team of special prosecutors that included William O. Bittman, Austin Mittler, Donald Moore, and Charles Shaffer.

In January 1966, Black was a grim man as he appealed his conviction. He complained he was broke, was getting only lip-service from friends in high places, and he threatened to talk if forced to go to prison. That same month Bobby Baker was indicted. This raised more doubts in Black's mind about the power of those who were urging him to be "patient" while they tried to arrange special treatment for him. Baker and Black knew the Bittman team meant business and would not soft pedal the case regardless of political pressure.

In February, President Johnson named Mitchell Rogovin as Assistant Attorney General in charge of the tax division. A protégé of Carolyn Agger, tax specialist and wife of Justice Fortas, Rogovin had been serving as Chief Counsel in the Internal Revenue Service.

Rogovin took seriously President Johnson's concern about wire-tapping. Digging into Justice Department files, he learned of the FBI bug on the Black suite. At the Internal Revenue Service, Rogovin had been a major block whenever the Senate Committee on Administrative Procedures had sought evidence of bugging taxpayers. At the Justice

Department, however, his attitude on electronic surveillance changed.

Now he insisted that the Justice Department had an obligation to go to the United States Supreme Court and reveal the bug on Black. Spokesmen for the criminal division and the FBI maintained it was an unprecedented step at this stage of a case. They informed Rogovin that the eavesdropping had taken place long after the obtaining of evidence which had resulted in the indictment of Black. Furthermore, even if those investigating Black's income tax picture had been aware of the eavesdropping, they would not have sought that kind of evidence, for theirs was a so-called "net-worth" case.

"The Department of Justice's investigation of this incident indicates that none of the evidence presented to the grand jury or used at petitioner's [Black's] trial was obtained, whether directly or indirectly, from any improper source," Rogovin was told. "Nor was anything learned by the government's trial counsel from the monitoring of petitioner's discussion with his attorney which had any effect upon the presentation of the government's case or the fairness of petitioner's trial."

It was stressed that the "prosecution's evidence . . . was founded solely upon material contained in reports of investigating agents of the Internal Revenue Service."

A routine audit examination in 1960 had initiated the Black case and, by October 1960, the case was classed as a "tax-fraud investigation." The investigation was completed in October 1962, months before the bug was placed in Black's suite.

"During the preparation and trial of petitioner's case, no attorney involved in its presentation [or, so far as appears, any other attorney for the Department of Justice] knew that a listening device had been installed in petitioner's suite," it was explained to Rogovin.

Nevertheless, the young lawyer insisted he felt so strongly about the abridgement of Black's rights that he would take the matter into his own hands. Accompanied by Solicitor General Thurgood Marshall, who argued the government's cases before the Supreme Court, he disclosed the eavesdropping to the Court. This ploy was successful. The Supreme Court upset the conviction and called for a hearing on whether the evidence in the tax-fraud conviction was "tainted" by illegal eavesdropping.

Judge Sirica conducted an extensive hearing and found no indication that any wiretap or bugging evidence had been used to obtain the indictment. But even though it was established that Black had received a fair trial, the conviction could not be reinstated and it was necessary to try him again.

Prosecutor Bittman suggested that instead of trying Black again on the same charge, a simpler approach be employed. A net-worth case is always difficult to prove; it can be quite complicated and requires a jury that will pay attention to details. Bittman reasoned that it would be more practical to indict Black for willfully failing to pay the taxes he owed the government. Proof could be established in a few hours through the introduction of his tax returns for several recent years in which he had reported in excess of $150,000 and $200,000, but had paid no taxes.

Rogovin rejected this suggestion for some "technical reasons" which were never made clear to Bittman and other veteran prosecutors. He proceeded to assign another lawyer to the case, and moved into the second trial with a good chance that Black would be acquitted. Meanwhile, Senator Williams couldn't help wondering why the Internal Revenue Service, usually so eager to grab the assets of every taxpayer, was permitting Black and his wife to continue living in luxury in their $150,000 home, despite the fact that it had piled up claims against them of nearly $500,000.

Before the second trial was completed, Justice Tom Clark resigned from the Supreme Court at President Johnson's request, so that Ramsey Clark could be named as Attorney General without incurring charges of impropriety by having a father on the high court while his son served as the nation's chief federal prosecutor. The vacancy on the Court was promptly filled by naming Solicitor General Thurgood Marshall.

Black was acquitted in his second trial, and resumed his work as a public relations man. At the same time, it was difficult to believe the Bobby Baker case would ever come to trial. Rogovin's stand in connection with Fred Black's conviction required the team of prosecutors headed by William Bittman to turn over all its wiretapping logs to Edward Bennett Williams, famed Washington mouthpiece who served such clients as Jimmy Hoffa, Frank Costello, and others identified with organized crime. As Baker's lawyer, Williams would make the most of the logs.

Bittman found it hard to keep his team working enthusiastically in the face of press reports that President Johnson was cool to the prosecution of his "strong right arm." Coincidentally, certain pressures contrived to split up the smoothly functioning unit.

Charles Shaffer was fed up working in a Justice Department where it was impossible to send reports "upstairs" without fearing how they would be handled. He resigned and set up a law practice in Rockville. Don Page Moore, also discouraged, joined a Chicago law firm. That left only Austin Mittler, a bright young law graduate employed at roughly $12,000 a year on what had once seemed an exciting project but now appeared to be a lost cause. He accepted a much higher salary to become law secretary to New York Supreme Court Judge James Crisona. Bittman argued he needed someone he could trust and who was familiar with the Baker case, but he could not in good conscience tell Mittler that the case was certain to go forward.

Over the Christmas holiday Bittman had to fight off a move in the Justice Department to eliminate two of the nine counts against Baker that he considered crucial. But the trial date was finally set. Persuaded to quit his new job, Mittler returned to Washington at a lower salary. He arrived the day before the trial started.

Throughout all, Bittman was the man who held the Baker prosecution together, even though he had been hard-pressed to move his large family to Washington and still manage on his salary. In the midst of his preparations for the trial he was offered promotions at a substantial increase in pay, either as Special Assistant to Attorney General Ramsey Clark or as United States Attorney in Chicago. There was only one condition: he would have to leave the Baker case.

He rejected the offers and continued with the case until January 29, 1967, when Baker was found guilty of income-tax evasion, theft, and conspiracy to defraud the United States government. The three-week trial revealed that Baker had received $100,000 in cash from West Coast savings and loan executives for "political contributions" to the Democratic Party.

Baker tried to convince the jury that he had delivered this money to Senator Robert Kerr, and had been "loaned" at least $50,000 of it—for Bittman had traced at least that much of the "contribution" to Baker's floundering Carousel Motel. Fred Black testified that the late Senator Kerr had "loved" Baker and regarded him "like a son." He said Kerr had told him of loaning the $50,000 to Baker.

However, Bittman contended this was not characteristic of Kerr. The late Senator's son, Robert, Jr., testified that his father kept notes on loans to his family "even as much as fifteen or eighteen dollars." There was no record of the $50,000 "loan," nor any to substantiate Baker's contention that in late December 1962, a few days before Kerr died, the Senator had changed the "loan" to a Christmas "gift."

Although Black made an impressive witness as he was led through his testimony by Edward Bennett Williams, he was not so impressive under cross-examination by Bittman. Black admitted not mentioning the alleged loan at the time he was questioned by Internal Revenue Service agents about Baker's initial claim that it was a $40,000 loan. He insisted he had given the agents a false story. Finally, under grilling, he lost his composure and declared he wouldn't tell IRS or the FBI anything.

Bobby Baker's conviction did not end Senator Williams' concern that the Johnson Administration might still get Baker off the hook. There were a thousand ways to throw a case into the Circuit Court of Appeals, where the Administration had made a lot of appointments. Williams learned that a young lawyer from the University of Texas had been assigned to work with Bittman and Mittler in connection with the appeal. On December 3, 1968, he wrote to Attorney General Clark:

"A situation has been called to my attention which may be all right, nevertheless it can cause possible embarrassment to the Justice Department.

"I am advised that Mr. Albert Alschuler has been appointed by the Department to assist in representing the government in its opposition to the appeal of Mr. Robert G. Baker while at the same time his wife, who is also a lawyer, is serving as a law clerk for Justice Fortas. Since this is a highly sensitive case I am sure you can recognize the delicacy of such an arrangement."

Fred M. Vinson, Jr., Assistant Attorney General in charge of the

Criminal Division, replied on December 13, 1968:

"Mr. Alschuler is a respected and competent attorney. I have the utmost confidence in his trustworthiness and loyalty to the Department.

"Quite apart from that, you should know that Mr. Alschuler's participation in this matter in connection with a hearing to be held in the District Court has been both minimal and ministerial. His work in this regard has been at the direction and under the supervision of two of the original government prosecutors who handled the trial and who have been specially retained for the forthcoming hearing in this case."

The letter from Senator Williams caused a tremor through the Criminal Division. It was just a gentle way of letting the Justice Department know that someone was watching.

Baker entered the Lewisburg federal penitentiary in 1970 to serve a one-to-three-year term, a light enough sentence in view of his conviction on seven out of nine counts involving nearly $100,000 in political payoff money. On entering prison, he piously said that he would "serve with honor."

As for the Las Vegas gamblers, some of whom were associates of Fred Black and Bobby Baker, they too were involved in cases which were undermined by Justice Department decisions.

In May 1967, a United States grand jury in Las Vegas returned indictments for federal income-tax evasion against Ed Levinson, former president of the Fremont Hotel; Edward Torres, former vice-president; P. Weyerman and Cornelius Hurley, former stockholders and employees. The Riviera Hotel also yielded defendants: Ross Miller, chairman of the board; Frank Atol, stockholder and employee; and Joseph Rosenberg, stockholder and casino manager.

The key to these cases consisted of FBI taps which had been made on Las Vegas casinos for the purpose of gathering information on the "skimming" of profits from the gaming places. Unfortunately, Nevada law, designed to provide a favorable atmosphere for the kind of people who run gambling casinos, made it illegal to wiretap for such information.

Nevada Democratic Governor Grant Sawyer condemned the electronic surveillance and challenged the FBI to "give us your evidence, or call off your dogs." Nevada Democratic Senator Howard Cannon went to the White House to complain to President Johnson about the taps. Subsequently United States District Judge Roger Foley, a Cannon appointee, sealed the records of the eavesdropping. It was a decision that would later stand in sharp contrast to a more vigorous effort by the government to fight organized crime.

In June 1967, all four former officials of the Fremont entered pleas of innocent. Judge Foley indicated that the trial would not take place for several months. There followed a frantic behind-the-scenes attempt to stop the trial and block publication of the FBI tapes; but the heart of the gamblers' "defense" seemed to be a $4.5 million suit which Edward Bennett Williams' law firm filed for Levinson against the four FBI agents who were responsible for the electronic surveillance of the Fremont Hotel, charging invasion of privacy.

In March 1968, Levinson and Rosenberg pleaded nolo contendere (no contest) to the "skimming" charges, admitting that they had "wilfully aided and assisted in the preparation of false corporate tax returns for the fiscal year ending in 1963."

Surprisingly, Judge Foley accepted the pleas over the government's pro forma objections, and fined Levinson $5,000 and Rosenberg $3,000. In light of the millions of dollars involved in the case, it was a slap on the wrist and considered as such by the FBI and by the Organized Crime and Racketeering Division of the Justice Department which had been bypassed on the arrangement by Assistant Attorney General Mitchell Rogovin.

This acceptance of the pleas was followed by a government motion to dismiss other charges against Levinson and Rosenberg, as well as the five others named in the two indictments. Thus, under Attorney General Ramsey Clark, the government swiftly brought to a close two cases which had required more than two years' preparation and the testimony of more than one hundred witnesses in the six months' investigation before a federal grand jury.

The Los Angeles *Times* reported that the organized crime fighters in Justice were "shocked and demoralized by the sudden end of a major tax-evasion case against Las Vegas casino operators." Henry E. Petersen, then Chief of the Department's Organized Crime and Racketeering Division, had not even been informed of the "arrangement" until it was all over. Two days after the government dropped its charges, Levinson's lawyers dropped his suit against the FBI agents. A related suit against the Central Telephone Company, which had assisted in setting up the electronic surveillance, was settled for an undisclosed amount.

Edwin L. Weisl, Jr., Assistant Attorney General in charge of the Civil Division, handled the dismissal of the suit against the agents and defended this disposition of the case as proper. Weisl was the son of Edwin L. Weisl, Sr., then the Democratic Committeeman from New York and a close friend of President Johnson.

Weisl contended the case "served notice that skimming will have to stop." But not all Justice Department officials were satisfied by this declaration. The case had cost more than $100,000 to develop and had required major cooperation by the FBI and Internal Revenue Service. The settlement also "served notice" that it was still possible to make a deal with the Justice Department if serious charges were filed against the FBI.

It also put Assistant Attorney General Rogovin in a difficult position on eavesdropping and wiretapping. Rogovin, so eager to disclose wiretaps when it was helpful to Fred Black, now opposed disclosure.

The cases of Fred Black, Bobby Baker, and the Las Vegas gamblers clearly showed how political corruption and organized crime both benefited from the same questionable policy under the Johnson Administration. The last chapter in the story was Johnson's unsuccessful attempt to appoint Abe Fortas, his old friend who had represented Baker during the first months of the scandal, as Chief Justice of the United States Supreme Court.

On October 2, 1968, the President withdrew the nomination after the Senate refused to invoke cloture to end a filibuster against the appointment. Then, in May 1969, a *Life* magazine article by William Lambert exposed an arrangement Fortas had made with the Louis Wolfson Foundation while on the Supreme Court to receive $20,000 a year as a consultant. Wolfson, in trouble with the Securities and Exchange Commission, had agreed to pay Fortas this sum for advice on the dispersal of funds from the family foundation. *Life* disclosed that Fortas had accepted and, 11 months later, returned a $20,000 payment. Serious ethical questions were raised by Senator Williams, Senator Robert Griffin (Rep., Mich.), and others, and Fortas was forced to resign on May 14. His was the first resignation under pressure of public criticism in the 178-year history of the Court—a man who had been proposed as Chief Justice only a few months earlier.

The new Administration now had two vacancies to fill on the Court and President Nixon named Warren Burger, a 61-year-old judge on the U.S. Court of Appeals for the District of Columbia, as Chief Justice. Judge Burger had a reputation for being tough on issues dealing with law enforcement and for having what Nixon considered a more realistic view on the importance of eavesdropping and wiretapping in the battle with organized criminals.

Bitter discussion will continue for years about the decision that resulted in springing Fred Black. Equally bitter controversy will rage about the settlement of the Levinson suit against the FBI.

However, there was little disagreement among law-enforcement men over the job Robert Blakey, former Notre Dame University professor of criminal law, did on the Ramsey Clark theory that electronic surveillance is of doubtful value as a law-enforcement tool. Blakey, as a "consultant" for the President's Crime Commission and later as counsel for Senator John McClellan's Senate Judiciary Subcommittee on Criminal Law Procedures, used the disclosures of the Patriarca logs from the tax-evasion trial of Louis (The Fox) Taglianetti to destroy Clark's contention that electronic eavesdropping is a "wasteful and unproductive" means of obtaining evidence.

8

PATRIARCA AND LOUIS THE FOX

"Like informant information, accomplice testimony, moreover, most often relates to past acts. It helps in solving, not preventing crime. For example, using the electronic device installed to cover the activities of Raymond Patriarca, the Cosa Nostra official . . . the Federal Bureau of Investigation was unable to prevent the murder of William Marfeo. The device was removed in July 1965 pursuant to the orders of Attorney General [Ramsey Clark]. Marfeo was killed, however, just about one year later on June 13, 1966. Only when another man was marked for death, was the Bureau able to solve the Marfeo killing by persuading that individual to testify against Patriarca. Would it not have been preferable to have brought a conspiracy rather than a murder indictment?" *American Bar Association Project on Minimum Standards for Criminal Justice, Standards Relating to Electronic Surveillance.*

THE Federal Bureau of Investigation bugged the office of New England's crime boss, Raymond Patriarca, from March 1962 until July 1965. Monitoring of conversations in the office of the National Cigarette Service, a vending-machine corporation in Providence, Rhode Island, was stopped on orders from President Lyndon Johnson who told the public he was against obtaining evidence in this way.

FBI Director J. Edgar Hoover had been using the electronic device to cover the activities of Patriarca, head of the New England "family" of La Cosa Nostra and a member of its national ruling board called the "Commission." From the activities of the Patriarca gangs, the FBI was able to corroborate some aspects of the story Joseph Valachi had told to them and to the McClellan Subcommittee.

As a young man, Patriarca had been convicted of armed robbery, arson, and violation of the White Slave Act. But like Valachi and others, he had succeeded in organized crime and enjoyed the immunity that often goes with this success.

Patriarca had not been successfully prosecuted in years. The recorded conversation could not be used in court, because the Benanti decision in 1957 had barred such use even when recording had been properly authorized by state court orders.

The Johnson Administration's decision to assure "fair play" for Fred Black, Jr., had repercussions throughout the country. Since by disclosing the complete bugging file on Black the Department of Justice had enabled him to avoid a federal prison term, it had to apply the same rule now in similar cases. Only in that way could President Johnson avoid being accused of giving special treatment to Bobby Baker's friends.

The decision threatened to overturn the conviction of Louis (The Fox) Taglianetti, who had been convicted of federal income-tax evasion in 1966. Ten of the "airtels"—summaries of the daily FBI logs on wiretapped conversations—from the Boston field office contained information on Taglianetti. Taglianetti himself had not been bugged, but the FBI may have uncovered leads against him while bugging Patriarca. Under the new "Black" rule, Taglianetti had to be given access to any government information that dealt even remotely with him while he was under investigation.

In May 1967, Justice Department lawyers delivered the airtels of the bug in the Patriarca office to Chief Judge Edward Day of the United States District Court in Providence. Judge Day reviewed them all, and concluded that only ten had to be made available to Taglianetti and his lawyers.

Those ten airtels appeared in the federal court record, and a tremor went through the East Coast Cosa Nostra and the entire political-criminal world of New England. The airtels revealed that Patriarca was engaged in extortion, fraud, bribery, perjury, loan sharking, gambling, kidnapping, and murder. Information from the airtels could not be used against Patriarca in court; but once it became public Patriarca could no longer pose as a reformed bad boy. The records also involved him with legal businesses in which he had denied a role—Nevada gambling, labor unions, race-track operations, and liquor distribution.

The airtels spelled out Patriarca's contacts with Vito Genovese, head of the New York Cosa Nostra and successor to Frank Costello and

Lucky Luciano; Anthony (Tony Ducks) Corallo, a *caporegima* in the Thomas (Three Finger Brown) Luchese family in New York; Carlo Gambino, who had succeeded Albert Anastasia as head of one of the New York families; and Joseph Bonanno, head of another New York family. Numerous other high Mafia figures were also included among those with whom Patriarca had direct or indirect dealings.

The ten airtels made public were only a small sample of the important information the FBI had gathered in more than three years of electronic surveillance. No wonder Raymond Patriarca was starting to question whether it had been a good idea for Taglianetti, one of his subordinates, to try to upset his income-tax conviction by raising questions about the bugging!

At Taglianetti's tax-evasion trial in the fall of 1966, Patriarca had appeared to identify Taglianetti as a "good will" man who had obtained many locations for his National Cigarette Service. This was no great risk for Patriarca, because questioning was held to the specific trial issue.

However, when defense lawyers John Varone and Bruce Selya tried to undercut the government claim that none of the FBI information was used against Taglianetti, the more they cross-examined government witnesses the worse things looked for Patriarca. Cross-examination by Selya detailed how the FBI handles electronic surveillance and elicited the information from government witnesses that the "subject" of the bug was in fact Patriarca rather than Taglianetti.

Before it was all over, Patriarca was forced to decide whether going to state prison was preferable to allowing the result of more than three years of electronic surveillance to be made public. (It is possible that some of the public officials with whom he did business in the New England area had a role in persuading him to forget about a defense based on disclosure and to take his medicine in prison.)

The ten airtels that had already been published were damaging enough to the New England crime boss. There was conversation by Patriarca of some illegal transaction involving a supply of whiskey, and a comment that in one area the gangs were competing with each other and that a man known only as "Pete" had "taken" a couple of banks alone. Patriarca commented that Pete was "all done and he is going to the [can]."

There was brief discussion of a controversy involving a woman who had past-posted a bookie, and there was mention of Johnny Barborian of Providence. "At the end of the conversation Patriarca told Eddie [otherwise unidentified] to pay the hit."

On April 17, 1963, Patriarca had a conversation with Rudolph Sciara, who had only recently been acquitted of murder in a state court. Patriarca warned Sciara not to let bail bondsmen know his identity because "all bondsmen are stool pigeons."

In that conversation Patriarca indicated his own suspicions of a dentist as a "stool pigeon for the FBI" and indicated he was contacting an unidentified (blanked out) individual in an effort to obtain the parole of Leo Santaniello and Lawrence Baiona, two lower-echelon figures in the Patriarca organization. He cautioned Sciara that the organized crime syndicate is fighting scientific crime detection and that there was a need for great care.

Although Patriarca, or his associates, frequently commented on the fact that their phones might be tapped they continued to use them but employed a code much of the time. Nevertheless, enough information came through so that law-enforcement officials knew very well what was being talked about.

On November 22, 1964, Raymond Patriarca discussed the difficulties in "trying to line up some man for a hit." He was extremely angry that all his witnesses in a libel case against the Boston *Herald Traveler* had been held in contempt for taking the Fifth Amendment. That same day he told of his own strategy in the event he was questioned about the Mafia or La Cosa Nostra. "He is going to reply that the only Mafia he ever heard of is the Irish Mafia that the Kennedys are in charge of," the airtel stated. "Patriarca will deny knowing of Cosa Nostra until Valachi mentioned it at recent hearings."

That airtel also revealed that "Taglianetti is considering feigning a heart attack in order to postpone his tax case."

On November 20, 1964, Patriarca told Joe Modica of Boston "to contact his friend who is allegedly extremely close to Attorney General Edward W. Brooke of Massachusetts, and have him arrange to release the one hundred thousand dollar-bond that is being held by the Massachusetts court. . . ."

Many of the conversations related to gangland murder victims: Samuel Lindenbaum and Steven Hughes in Middleton, Massachusetts; Joseph Francione, gunned down in Revere; and Henry Reddington, killed in his Weymouth home. Patriarca was told "Joe Barboza of East Boston" killed Francione. This corroborated leads indicating that Joe Barboza had later changed his name to Baron and moved to Swampscott. At the time of the conversation, Baron was confined and awaiting trial as a habitual criminal.

The Taglianetti airtels confirmed Patriarca's financial interests in various race tracks in New England, as well as his visits to New York in connection with problems in the Cosa Nostra "Commission" because of the troubles Joseph (Joe Bananas) Bonanno was having. Bonanno, one-time head of one of the New York City Mafia families, had been kidnapped because he failed to answer summonses to appear before the Commission.

The airtels gave a first-hand account of the turmoil within the Cosa Nostra over the Valachi testimony, and they showed how the mobsters viewed the testimony of government officials before Congressional Committees. When Col. Walter E. Stone, Superintendent of the Rhode Island State Police and a retired Providence Police Chief, appeared before a Senate Committee he testified that Patriarca "is as ruthless in the 1960s as he was in the 1930s." Patriarca said that Colonel Stone had been advised by an unidentified person not to testify about him but that Stone had "made a fool out of himself."

The Mafia chief contended that 90 percent of Stone's testimony was untrue. He particularly resented Stone's implying "Patriarca's dishonesty among his friends" and interpreted this as an effort to get Patriarca "knocked off."

"Raymond says Bobby Kennedy must have made him [Stone] do it," the airtel related. "Raymond says he [Stone] made a goat out of me—with the neighbors—the family—I have nieces and nephews—no one could go to work the next day."

"Raymond says if he didn't answer back he could never walk the street again. He [Stone] said I was a dishonest man with friends. I have always been an honorable man with friends," Patriarca was quoted as insisting.

One airtel quoted Patriarca as "worried about being questioned about his meetings with Jerry [Gennaro] Anguilo." Anguilo was identified in the Valachi hearings as a part of La Cosa Nostra.

The arrogance Raymond Patriarca developed during his long tenure as head of the New England Cosa Nostra was demonstrated when he threatened to talk to the leader of one of the underworld factions then warring in Boston, and warn him: "If the killings don't stop I'll declare martial law!"

Had there been reason for doubting the testimony of Joe Valachi, the few airtels on the conversations in Patriarca's office should have ended those doubts.

The so-called "Taglianetti logs" were made public by Judge Day on May 19, 1967. In the next few weeks they were devoured by the local newspapers from Providence, Rhode Island, to Portland, Maine.

Boston newspapers predicted that Patriarca was probably destroyed as leader of the New England Mafia, and Boston Superintendent of Police John T. Howland commented that the FBI tapes "won't help Raymond's image any."

"He was looked upon with awe as a smooth, sure and careful man," Howland was quoted as saying.

A Rhode Island police official commented: "I think Patriarca destroyed himself with this one. Prior to this, the only information about Cosa Nostra came from Joe Valachi."

On June 20, 1967, a federal grand jury indicted Patriarca on charges that he and two others had conspired to engineer the murder of William Marfeo over a competitive gambling enterprise Marfeo was running. Those indicted with him were Henry Tameleo, a subordinate in the Cosa Nostra, and Ronald Cassesso, a strong-arm man then serving nine-to-twelve years for armed robbery.

Named as a coconspirator, but not as a defendant, was the man they had tried to hire in 1965 as the "hit man" to kill Marfeo. Joseph (Barboza) Baron, named in the tapes by Tameleo as the man who had murdered Joseph Francione, had decided to cooperate with the Attorney General's office in April, immediately before the revelation that Patriarca's office had been bugged.

Although court rulings meant that the Patriarca wiretaps could not be used as evidence, or even as leads, the information gleaned from the airtels could still be of great help in documenting the involvement of Cosa Nostra leaders in crime. Publicity about Patriarca's operations was more devastating to him than the amount of usable material.

He could deny his role as a leader of the Cosa Nostra, but with his own mouth he had spelled out his connection with some of the best-known racketeers from Boston to Florida. Other related information would now be believed. The tapes gave federal and local investigators reason to join forces in developing the Joseph (Barboza) Baron testimony. So long as the case originated from Baron's discussion and not from the FBI eavesdropping it could be used to prosecute.

Baron voluntarily furnished a statement to agents of the FBI in April of 1967 concerning the offense in 1965.

At the trial of Patriarca, his counsel chose not to cross-examine Baron. But Baron was subjected to a rigorous cross-examination by other defense counsel relative to his dealings with federal and state authorities, and the record indicates that the defense was "afforded wide latitude to probe Baron's background, character, and ties to the authorities."

In November 1966, stories appeared indicating that the President's National Crime Commission had split with the Justice Department on the question of wiretapping and electronic eavesdropping by law-enforcement officials. The majority of the members of the President's National Crime Commission had taken the position that police eavesdropping is necessary in the fight against organized crime.

This was despite strong protests by Acting Attorney General Ramsey Clark, who had tried to get the Commission to avoid the subject. In a November 11, 1966 meeting, FBI officials disputed Clark's assertion that the "insignificance" of the information received (on the Fred Black bug) had convinced him that bugging and wiretapping were a waste of time.

Reports on the closed meeting indicated that Cartha DeLoach, Assistant to FBI Director Hoover, interrupted Attorney General Clark to state that the FBI would be seriously handicapped in the fight against organized crime unless eavesdropping and wiretapping were legalized.

Clark claimed that the eavesdropping issue could be a "red herring" to distract attention from important but less controversial recommendations; but only two members of the Commission voted with the Attorney General—Federal Judge Luther Youngdahl, and Mrs. Robert Stuart, President of the League of Women Voters.

Appearing before the House Judiciary Subcommittee, Clark maneuvered the Justice Department into a 180-degree turn from the opinion that wiretapping is essential in the fight against organized crime to the position that it was a waste of time. "I think it would be fair to say that over a period of six years the Department has come more and more to the view that wiretapping should be prohibited," Clark said.

"I think the last testimony . . . on this subject was by Attorney General Katzenbach," Clark testified. "He said, among other things . . . that if we could not seek some control and security, 'the best thing we could do was to prohibit wiretapping altogether.' I am sure he was excepting the national security area.

"We have looked at hundreds and hundreds of bugs and wiretap logs, and I think we have an experience on which to base a judgment now that we did not have as clearly earlier," Clark explained.

Representative Robert McClory (Rep., Ill.) said that the Johnson position, of opposition to wiretapping as an invasion of privacy coming on the heels of the Hoover-Kennedy controversy as to who had authorized certain wiretaps, "seemed to be a rather blunt rebuke to former Attorney General [Robert] Kennedy."

"That was not a factor at all," Clark replied. "I think I know from many years back that the President has been deeply opposed to wiretapping and electronic surveillance. . . . [In] my recollection of the chronology of the Hoover-Kennedy dispute . . . it took place primarily in November and December of 1966 and pretty well subsided then. When the President's State of the Union message came . . . I do recall that there was large applause at that part of the State of the Union message."

McClory: "Not by Senator Kennedy."

Clark: "I did not see Senator Kennedy at that particular time."
McClory: "I did."

Ramsey Clark was graduated from the University of Texas and the University of Chicago Law School. He practiced law in Dallas from 1951 to 1961. In that period of time he had essentially no experience in criminal law investigations. In 1961 he was named by Robert F. Kennedy as an Assistant Attorney General with the Land Division, largely because of his political background in Texas. He was recognized as the political person in the Justice Department, and moved up in rank, in 1967 becoming Attorney General. Tom Wicker, in a foreword to Clark's book, *Crime in America,* characterized him as "the most revolutionary public voice in America today. . . . Here he is, for instance, saying the kind of things most of us would never think to say, probably wouldn't say if we did think it, for fear of being ridiculed by 'practical' men."

McClory read just a few excerpts from the testimony of New York District Attorney Frank Hogan before the President's Crime Commission. Hogan had said that although wiretaps were installed in a very small percentage of cases, "they have produced, I think, remarkable results, especially in the toughest of all investigations to break—investigations involving organized crime and the corruption." He had called authorized wiretapping "the single . . . most valuable weapon in law enforcement against organized crime. . . ."

He credited this investigative tool with making possible the conviction of such top figures in the underworld as Charles (Lucky) Luciano, Jimmy Hines, Louis (Lepke) Buchalter, Jacob (Gurah) Shapiro, Joseph (Socks) Lanza, George Scalise, Frank Erickson, John (Dio) Dioguardi, Frank Carbo, and Joseph (Adonis) Doto.

Hogan noted that the late Senator Kefauver had written to him in 1951 endorsing a statement that wiretap information from the New York County District Attorney's Office "helped make the crime investigation a smashing success," and added: "Senator Robert Kennedy, then counsel to the [McClellan Labor Rackets] Committee, made constant use of our information and knows how valuable electronic surveillance is to the preservation of law and order."

Hogan declared that the position taken by Attorney General Ramsey Clark was "ridiculous."

"If you are going to make an out-and-out attack on organized crime and then say 'This isn't cricket, you mustn't do this,' then it is just asinine.

"I may say that within my experience, going back to 1935, this is the first time an Attorney General has reflected such thinking," Hogan said. "Every living former United States Attorney from the Southern District of New York," he testified, "has agreed that electronic eavesdropping was essential."

Hogan, however, dodged a personal criticism of Clark: "With respect to the Attorney General, a fine person and a fine lawyer, I don't think he has had any experience in this particular field."

Less than two months after the Patriarca logs had been made public in the Taglianetti case, G. Robert Blakey, a professor of criminal law at Notre Dame and a member of the President's Commission on Crime, appeared before the Judiciary Subcommittee to testify on the value of eavesdropping and wiretapping. He had read only the ten airtels made public, but he joined Hogan, Robert Kennedy, and all the former Attorneys General to point out the "sharp contrast" between the testimony of Ramsey Clark and nearly every other person with real experience in gathering evidence against organized crime.

"It is because I love privacy more, not less," Blakey said, explaining his position in relation to his membership in the American Civil Liberties Union, "that I support a system of court-ordered electronic surveillance. I agree with the judgment of the President's Crime Commission that if we can regulate this situation and bring it into some sort of court-order system, we will be able to curtail police abuse. . . . The primary victims of organized crime are the people in the urban areas, chiefly the poor, the people who, in so many other contexts, the American Civil Liberties Union stands up for. I believe if we are to ever do anything about getting organized crime off the backs of the urban poor, it will only be through the authorization of electronic surveillance techniques.

"So it is also because I share with many other members of the American Civil Liberties Union a deep concern for the urban poor that I think it is time we get organized crime off their backs. And I believe electronic surveillance is needed to do the job," Professor Blakey said.

Blakey inserted a *New York Times* story that quoted William Bittman, the man who won the convictions of Hoffa and Bobby Baker, commenting on Ramsey Clark's evaluation of wiretapping.

"We are losing the battle against organized crime. . . . Since we are not staying even, I don't think we should deny reputable law enforcement any legitimate tool."

Bob Blakey had been a Special Prosecutor in the Organized Crime and Racketeering Section of the Justice Department from August 1960, until June 1964. He declared that the Taglianetti airtels were far and above the best information that he had obtained. "[I read] . . . investigation reports that were the product of the use of normal investigative methods. There is just simply no comparison in the two kinds of reports. In light of this, I find it nothing short of incredible that Mr. Clark and others would seriously suggest that the use of electronic-surveillance techniques is 'neither effective nor highly productive.' "

Following an analysis of information obtained from the logs in the Taglianetti case in Providence, Blakey commented:

"If I had had those airtels, and they were legally admissible, and a couple of FBI agents to do a little legwork, I could have made murder cases hand over fist. I wouldn't even have bothered about the gambling cases. But to find now that the Attorney General suggests that this equipment is 'neither effective . . . or highly productive' in light of my own personal experience and my analysis of this information in the public record. . . . I find it just incredible. Mr. Clark must be taking advice from the wrong people."

Blakey stressed Ramsey Clark's lack of knowledge about organized crime in a moving statement in the record:

"The horse trainer who got word to Patriarca to help him get a license at the Rhode Island tracks knows something about our society today that Mr. Clark does not.

"The man who contacted Patriarca about his labor troubles at his construction sites in Maine, Connecticut, and Rhode Island knows something about our society today that Mr. Clark does not.

"Nick, the young man who got Patriarca to get him a membership in La Cosa Nostra, knows something about our society that Mr. Clark does not."

He quoted from the President's Commission on Law Enforcement and the Administration of Justice:

"In many ways organized crime is the most sinister kind of crime in America. The men who control it have become rich and powerful by encouraging the needy to gamble, by luring the troubled to destroy themselves with drugs, by extorting the profits of honest and hard-working businessmen, by collecting usury from those in financial plight, by maiming or murdering those who oppose them, by bribing those who are sworn to destroy them. . . .

"Organized crime is not merely a few preying upon a few. In a very real sense it is dedicated to subverting not only American institutions, but the very decency and integrity that are the most cherished attributes of a free society. As the leaders of Cosa Nostra and their racketeering allies pursue their conspiracy unmolested in open and continual defiance of the law, they preach a sermon that all too many Americans heed: the government is for sale; lawlessness is the road to wealth; honesty is a pitfall and morality a trap for suckers."

"This is what I wish Mr. Clark understood," Professor Blakey said.

Louis the Fox thought he was sly when he had his lawyers request the disclosure of all FBI eavesdropping records. He hoped that just one of those records had been involved in the evidence leading to his income-tax conviction. As it turned out, Louis Taglianetti and the whole New England Cosa Nostra would have fared better had The Fox just served his seven months for federal-tax evasion.

On March 4, 1968, a federal jury in Boston returned verdicts of guilty against Patriarca, Tameleo, and Cassesso for conspiracy to murder Willie Marfeo. All three received five-year federal prison terms, and all appealed.

Though the bugging of Patriarca's headquarters in Providence had taken place when the results were not admissible evidence in state or federal courts, the revelation of the ten airtels in connection with Taglianetti's income-tax case produced the example that Professor Blakey needed to demonstrate that Ramsey Clark didn't know what he was talking about.

9

THE ADDONIZIO STORY AND NEW JERSEY

"It is impossible to estimate the impact ... of the cost of these criminal acts to the decent citizens of Newark, and indeed, of this state, in terms of their frustration, despair and disillusionment. How can we calculate the cynicism engendered in our citizens, including our young people, by these men—how does one measure the erosion of confidence in our system of government, and the diminished respect for our laws, occasioned by these men. These very men, who as government officials, inveighed against crime in the streets while they pursued their own criminal activities in the corridors of city hall?" *Judge George H. Barlow, September 22, 1970, at the sentencing of Newark Mayor Hugh J. Addonizio and his codefendants in Trenton, New Jersey.*

HUGH J. ADDONIZIO had been an all-state quarterback at West Side School and at St. Benedict's Prep in Newark, and later had been a star quarterback at Fordham behind the famous "Seven Blocks of Granite." He had served 37 months in the Army overseas, took part in eight campaigns, and was discharged in 1946 as a captain. Two years later he was elected to Congress, and represented his New Jersey district in Washington until he ran for Mayor of Newark in 1962.

Some said that Hughie Addonizio wanted to be Mayor of Newark because it was a more lucrative position than that of Congressman. There were reports that he had unsavory connections with Anthony

(Tony Boy) Boiardo, who was recognized as an underworld figure even before Joe Valachi blew the whistle in 1963. Addonizio denied knowing Boiardo personally and that appeared to end it.

Addonizio's career flourished in the face of the Kefauver hearings, and continued through the McClellan labor racket investigations. It seemed secure even though much-publicized revelations of wiretaps and eavesdropping on various colorful figures raised the question of mob influence in New Jersey politics.

President Richard Nixon's stress on the evils of organized crime was of little concern to Addonizio; he had ridden out other crusades. But he wasn't prepared for Paul Rigo.

Paul Rigo was a frightened man. As a New Jersey engineering consultant, he had been involved in a series of under-the-table payoffs to public officials in connection with city contracts. They started in 1966. In late 1969, Rigo was subpoenaed to appear before a New Jersey state grand jury investigating corruption and organized crime.

Addonizio was not especially concerned. He had faith in the power of his political position in New Jersey and he knew the Cosa Nostra could protect those it dealt with.

The battle against organized crime requires many bits of information, laboriously gathered and assembled. Important pieces fall into place on those infrequent occasions when someone on the inside decides to talk, and when the right men listen. One of the right men to listen was James Featherstone, a Special Attorney from the Justice Department who headed the Strike Force investigating corruption in New Jersey.

The Strike Force, a specially trained group, combines experts from Justice, the Internal Revenue Service, the Narcotics Bureau, the Alcohol and Cigaret Tax Division, and the Immigration and Naturalization Service. A Strike Force is given a stiff orientation program, which includes lectures on the federal statutes applicable to each government agency represented. In this way every member of the team recognizes evidence of possible violations of the laws in any of these areas. Working side by side in the same offices and "on the spot," members are able to check with each other immediately when their suspicions are aroused.

Until the institution of the Strike Force concept, agents working on their own who happened to be sufficiently familiar with the law in other areas to spot potential evidence had to forward the information they uncovered to their headquarters in Washington. There (if all went well) it would be referred to the proper agency. Speaking off the record, law-enforcement officials and departmental lawyers will admit that the old system was at best haphazard and at worst hampered by interagency rivalries.

Featherstone's Strike Force was coordinating its work with the United States Attorney Frederick Lacey and those New Jersey state officials who could be trusted.

In Washington, the Criminal Division was under the direction of Will A. Wilson, an Assistant Attorney General. Wilson did not have the look of physical strength that television has led Americans to associate with the typical crime buster. As Texas Attorney General, however, he was tough enough to be the man who first pursued Billy Sol Estes.

On December 1, 1969, in his booklined inner office at the Justice Department, Will Wilson was talking with a man who had called him from Acapulco the previous week claiming to have firsthand information about organized crime in New Jersey. The caller was Paul Rigo, an obviously successful professional man in his mid-40s, attractive, well-groomed, and suntanned from his stay in Mexico. But the tan did not hide his genuine fright.

Paul Rigo told Wilson he had been subpoenaed by the state grand jury investigating corruption and organized crime in his home state of New Jersey. Not only that, but the Internal Revenue Service was preparing an indictment against a member of his consulting engineering firm, and possibly against him. He wanted to avoid being picked up in connection with either investigation, and had insisted on seeing Wilson because he felt he didn't dare talk to subordinates.

A discreet attempt to contact the Strike Force in New Jersey had brought prompt and emphatic threats that he would be silenced for good. This immediate response from members of the mob had terrified Rigo. Obviously they had sources close to federal officials. He could not risk being trapped between those who insisted that he answer their questions, and those who had threatened him and his family if he did.

Fear had sent him to Mexico; discretion had prompted him to pay cash for his plane tickets, hoping no one could trace him. But before leaving he did confide in one friend, and that friend arranged for him to talk with Wilson.

After Wilson determined that Rigo had potentially useful information, he got in touch with the Organized Crime Division of the Bureau. Rigo was brought together with Thomas Kennelly, Deputy Chief of the Division. It is the policy of the Justice Department that officers not talk alone with informers, so Gerald Shur, head of the Intelligence and Special Service Unit, joined them.

Later, Kennelly recalled that Paul Rigo was nervous and even resentful at what he felt was pressure being applied by Joseph Lordi, Essex County Prosecutor, in the investigation. Rigo wanted to get off the hook, but he had not as yet committed himself to the dangerous move of telling all he knew. He offered the Justice Department officials enough information to convince them he was on the level, but had stopped short of committing himself as a full-scale informer.

He told them how, shortly after receiving his first contract as an engineering consultant for the City of Newark, he was contacted by a "Joey B." and his sidekick "Ralph." These men demanded 10 percent of the value of the contract as a kickback to "Tony Boy." At first Rigo ignored the demand, but in a short time Joey B. and Ralph reappeared on the scene. They picked him up for a little ride out to an Essex Falls estate to meet Tony Boy.

Anthony (Tony Boy) Boiardo made his demands bluntly: Everyone with city contracts paid 10 percent to Tony Boy because he was a friend of "the Pope," as he called Mayor Addonizio. That, together with Boiardo's threats to break his (Rigo's) legs and harm his children, convinced Rigo he should pay.

When Paul Rigo left Kennelly and Shur that day, with an appointment for the following morning, the men met with Kennelly's chief, Bill Lynch, to review the information. Lynch shared their feeling that Rigo was holding back, and they thought that they had learned enough from him to notify U. S. Attorney Frederick Lacey in New Jersey that Rigo had come in voluntarily and was talking.

Kennelly and Shur decided, with Lynch's concurrence, to try the "hard sell" the following day. They informed the still-nervous engineer that he had provided them with very little new information. If he did not want to tell his whole story, he was free to face the New Jersey grand jury on his own.

According to Kennelly, "Rigo began mopping his brow and saying he needed a 'drink' while he thought it over. First he told the law officers that doing as they demanded would mean 'hurting a lot of friends.' " But he was going to need protection from either the law or his mob "partners." Paul Rigo decided to give the Justice Department all the information he had.

It was not an easy decision. Rigo knew from his past attempts to reach federal officers in New Jersey that the men about whom he would be talking would be aware of his every move as soon as he made it. He also was sure they would attempt to carry out their threats against his family. But he opened up, and the pieces began to fit together.

After Rigo's second day with Kennelly and Shur, Frederick Lacey arrived in Washington to direct the legal action that was to follow this information. Lacey took the threats against Rigo and his family seriously and arranged for them to have protection.

A scant two weeks later the City of Newark, the State of New Jersey, and the country were astounded when a 66-count indictment for conspiracy, extortion, and tax violation was returned against Newark Mayor Hugh Addonizio. Also indicted were three City Councilmen and former Council members, other city officials, city contractors, and Anthony (Tony Boy) Boiardo, the son of one of the Mafia's most dreaded members. Even his Cosa Nostra colleagues were in awe of the senior Boiardo, Ruggiero (Richie the Boot) for, among other reasons, the efficiency with which he disposed of embarrassing bodies at his Essex County estate.

The indictments against Addonizio and the others were not based solely on the information provided to the Justice Department by Paul Rigo. Before Rigo talked, both state and federal grand juries and a federal Strike Force had been following leads to a situation of pervasive corruption throughout the state and turned up ·by a study of the Newark riots.

Before the riots in 1962, the FBI had received information linking Hugh Addonizio to members of La Cosa Nostra. There were charges that he had received their support for his campaign for Mayor. Irvin Berlin, Tony Boy Boiardo, Antonio (Tony Bananas) Caponigo, Angelo (the Gyp) DeCarlo, and Anthony (Ham) Dolasco were said to have contributed up to $5,000 each in return for gambling rights in Newark after the election. Another source of information suggested that Addonizio's Police Director Dominick Spinza was taking payoffs from Newark bookies and that the Mayor had attended clandestine meetings in New York with Spinza and several of his reputed Mafia backers.

Again, in 1968, law officers had questioned Mayor Addonizio about $14,000 to remodel his summer home which had allegedly been paid by Paul Rigo. The Mayor explained this as a "loan," and went to court in an effort to keep his bank and broker's records out of the hands of the investigators.

The court upheld Addonizio's contention that his own personal records were protected by the Fifth Amendment, but ordered his banker and broker to make their records available to the special grand jury. Addonizio claimed he had to borrow the money from Rigo because he needed his own available funds (which were far in excess of $14,000) for "anticipated expenses."

The New Jersey probe had received brief national attention when Frank Sinatra was subpoenaed to testify; Sinatra was still fighting the order when the Addonizio indictments hit the newspapers.

At the same time (in 1969) that Paul Rigo was closeted with Kennelly and Shur at the Justice Department, Union County District Court Judge Ralph De Vita was suspended from the bench and bar in New Jersey pending his appearance before the grand jury. Somerset County Prosecutor Michael R. Imbriani charged that De Vita had offered him a bribe to influence the outcome of a case pending against members of organized crime—an offer which Imbriani claimed to have tape-recorded.

Two reputedly high-ranking Cosa Nostra figures, Angelo De Carlo and Simone Rizzo (Sam the Plumber) DeCavalcante, had been called before the grand jury and were indicted for loan-sharking and gambling.

Not even employees of the federal government in New Jersey were free of the taint of corruption. Earlier in the year, two IRS employees had been indicted for tax-law violations and another removed from his post for his close links with Mafia Boss Gerardo (Jerry) Catena.

The Newark papers were full of stories of corruption and allegations of graft. But then, New Jersey has had a long-time reputation as the playground of the Cosa Nostra—with the government safely under the thumb of the mob. This was not the first time there had been a flurry of investigations; wide-ranging charges against important people; a rash of indictments against a few small-fry to give the impression of reform and good government; some minor convictions; and then—"business as usual."

But this time things were different. The investigations were handled by a Strike Force determined to prove to a skeptical American people that opposition to organized crime was more than campaign rhetoric, or that the Mafia was invented by TV script writers. They wanted to show that it is possible for dedicated law enforcement to obtain indictments that bring convictions; that the "mob" is not beyond the reach of the law. In this they had the full support of Attorney General John Mitchell. Rigo's decision to talk was the break that made it possible for the Strike Force to put together the scattered information they had gathered and take their case to the courts.

On Addonizio's first appearance before the grand jury he "took the Fifth." The Mayor also hid behind the Sixth Amendment, which deals with the rights of a defendant in a trial, and the Fourteenth, which says that the rights of citizenship shall not be abridged without "due process of law." On his second appearance he did admit knowing Tony Boy Boiardo but refused to answer further questions.

On Sunday, December 14, Addonizio broke his silence and announced that corporation counsel Philip Gordon, also summoned before the grand jury, had admitted receiving kickbacks from a city contractor. Addonizio said he had accepted Gordon's resignation, and was asking the City Council not to pay the bills of any of the implicated contractors until a thorough investigation could be held.

This was the forthright action that citizens of any city should be able to expect from their officials. But two days after the Mayor's civic-minded pronouncements hit the papers, he stood indicted on charges of conspiracy, extortion, and tax evasion. In this case, testimony at Addonizio's trial showed that he himself was on the receiving end of the kickbacks. Rigo's bills had not been paid because his payoffs were not up-to-date.

Fourteen others were indicted with Hugh Addonizio, ten of the present or past city officials: Gordon; Lee Bernstein, a former Councilman; Judge Anthony Guiliano; Water Authority Director Anthony La Morte; City Councilmen Calvin West and Frank Addonizio (a distant relative of the Mayor's); Irvin Turner; Water Authority Secretary James Callaghan; Public Works Director Ben Krusch; former corporation counsel Norman Schiff. Also indicted were contractor Mario Gallo, whose construction firms had major city contracts, and three employees of the Valentine Electric Company—Joseph (Joey B.) Biancone, the general manager; Ralph Vicaro (referred to by Rigo as "Joey B.'s sidekick"); and Anthony (Tony Boy) Boiardo, the Mafia man listed as a "salesman." Schiff, Krusch, and Gallo were not included in the income-tax indictments but charged only with extortion and conspiracy.

Before Hugh Addonizio went to trial on June 2, 1970, he tried every delaying move. By April of that year it had become apparent that Addonizio was going to be forced to a runoff in his bid for reelection. The runoff was scheduled for mid-June, when his trial would probably still be in progress. His attorney went to the Supreme Court in a futile effort to have the trial postponed until after the election. Attempts were also made to have Addonizio's trial "severed" from those of his codefendants to lessen the full impact of the Mafia-connected conspiracy. In fact several of the defendants did receive severance from Addonizio for various reasons; but his own trial proceeded as originally scheduled.

By the time the Addonizio conspiracy extortion trial began, the original list of 15 defendants had been cut to eight. Five had received severances; two were dead. Judge Guiliano died in his sleep on February 4, 1970, at the age of 72. Six days later, contractor Mario Gallo was killed when his car ran into a road abutment only three hours after he met with U. S. Attorney Lacey and agreed to cooperate with the prosecution.

There was still another death associated with the case. Bank official Paul Anderson, on his way to court to corroborate the testimony of a witness, also perished in an auto crash not more than two miles from where Gallo had had his fatal accident. There had been no evidence to indicate that anything more than coincidence connected these fatalities.

When the jury was selected, the defense used challenges to excuse eight Negroes from hearing the trial; the jurors and alternates were all white. The Newark riots had not been forgotten; in addition Addonizio was facing a runoff election against Negro Assemblyman Kenneth Gibson after a campaign which had exploited racial fears and antagonisms on both sides.

Next to Paul Rigo, billed as the government's "star" witness, the most dramatic testimony came from Irvin Kantor. Lateral sclerosis (the disease which killed baseball's Lou Gehrig) had left the 49-year-old Kantor bedfast and under constant medical attention. His body was wasted, he breathed laboriously, and his voice was no more than a painful whisper.

Kantor's doctors informed the court that to move him from the East Orange Veteran's Hospital where he was confined could prove fatal. Even the effort of answering questions in the hospital could drastically shorten his life. If he began, he might not live to finish his testimony. Despite all this, Irvin Kantor agreed to testify about his role in extorting funds from companies doing business with Mayor Addonizio's Newark.

Judge Barlow moved the court to the hospital, leaving the jury behind in Newark, to determine whether Kantor could appear as a witness. Defense attorneys insisted that their own doctors be permitted to examine Kantor. They also objected to Judge Barlow's allowing Mrs. Kantor to stay by his side and repeat his nearly inaudible answers. But after assurances from Kantor that he was willing to appear, and that he was aware of the danger to his life, Judge Barlow ordered the jury brought to the hospital to hear his testimony.

The "courtroom" provided by the hospital was a makeshift affair;

but what it lacked in the dignity of an orthodox courthouse was supplied by the atmosphere of courage that surrounded the dying man, summoning the strength to disclose his corrupt past even at the cost of his own life. Kantor's hospital bed, with the head cranked up, was placed directly in front of the judge and facing the jury. Behind the bed stood two doctors, watching for danger signs in their patient and enforcing the rest periods to which Judge Barlow had agreed.

Kantor's slim blond wife, Jane, sat holding his hand, calmly repeating the answers which revealed her husband's alliance with the Mafia and the officials they had corrupted. They were two slight figures against what Valachi had called "the invisible government"; one man and the woman who loved him, trusting in the law and the legitimate government to protect their family.

Kantor had set up a dummy corporation, the Kantor Supply Company, with its address a vacant lot his father had owned. Payoffs which came by check were deposited in the company's account. Invoices for "supplies" covering the amount of the checks were sent to the victims to mislead nosey accountants and IRS auditors. (The idea for the invoices, Kantor admitted, had been his.) Kantor would then, in turn, draw checks for cash on the account of the Kantor Supply Company, and deliver the money to Joey B. or to his brother-in-law "Tony Gee" Gagliano at the Valentine Electric Company. The operation flourished from 1963 to 1967. Kantor's share was 5 percent of the take. In the two days of tortuous testimony, Kantor identified nearly $1 million in Kantor Supply Company checks as money passed to Biancone and Gagliano for distribution to the other conspirators.

Jane Kantor, under oath, repeated her husband's almost inaudible story about hearing Joey B. tell a contractor that the kickback money was needed for Mayor Addonizio's successful 1966 campaign for reelection.

Kantor, like Paul Rigo, told the jury that he feared for the safety of his family. His fear was brought home to the jury by telephoned bomb threats to the VA hospital on both of the days he testified. Each day the jury was evacuated from the temporary courtroom while authorities searched for explosives. None, however, was found.

Bomb threats in East Orange were not the only threats of violence associated with the Addonizio trial. The special grand jury, continuing to hear witnesses, received information that Paul Rigo's barber had been approached and offered $15,000 for any information which would lead the mob to the government witness. It was worth $100,000 to Tony Boiardo, according to the reports passed on to the FBI, to have Paul Rigo killed.

The problem facing the government was how to investigate these threats without further endangering Rigo. The normal procedure in cases such as this would be to inform Judge Barlow of the investigation. But then he would be compelled to tell the defense that a further investigation was in progress, related to the trial, against Boiardo. Lacey feared that this would make Boiardo intensify his efforts to have Rigo killed.

The FBI further advised the Justice Department that Assistant U. S. Attorney Goldstein would start no investigation until the Department had decided whether the investigation should be conducted without informing Judge Barlow and getting his consent.

Meanwhile, the grand jury was turning up more unsavory material. Not every firm had agreed, as Rigo had, to make "contributions" to the Mayor and his cronies in and out of City Hall. Joseph Foley, a vice-president of Elson Killam Associates, a construction firm, had reported to Killam himself and to Peter Homack, a top executive of the firm, that a Joey B., whom he could not identify further, had been introduced to him at lunch by defendant Sonny LaMorte, the Newark Water Department Director. This Joey B. had solicited a payoff from Foley on a city contract that Killam Associates had recently received.

Joey B. described himself as "a businessman" whose business was to collect "political contributions or what-have-you" for the City Administration. He told Foley the money was needed "to keep the war-chest campaign fund full." Joey B. also told Foley that the Killam company had been awarded the contract by mistake, that "it slipped through" before arrangements for a kickback had been completed. When Foley protested, Joey B. wanted to know, "How we could be so naive . . . anybody who did work for the City of Newark had to give some percentage of their [sic] fee."

A few days later, Homack, one of the operating executives, and Elson

Killam (who had since died) had been called to City Hall by Sonny La Morte. They went willingly, Homack told the grand jury, because Killam wanted to check out Foley's story. It wasn't that he didn't believe Foley; he was sure his employee had simply been mistaken about what he thought Biancone had said.

La Morte introduced Killam and Homack to Biancone and the group proceeded to the Mayor's office. Killam was introduced to Addonizio as the man who had the new city contract. The meeting was brief. Homack said they believed it had been set up simply to prove to Killam that Joey B. was indeed authorized to speak for City Hall. Back in the corridor outside the Mayor's office Biancone got right to the point: pay for the contract. Killam refused.

The "regular" payoff was 10 percent of the value of the contract. Killam had only been asked to come up with 5 percent, possibly because the city had mistakenly granted it without arranging the kickback in advance. When Killam refused to pay, he was offered a special rate of 4 percent; then 3 percent. Finally he was asked to name his own figure!

Killam still refused, and made a counter offer. His firm would give up the contract, and would also withdraw from two other city projects on which they were working. Two days later, Homack continued, La Morte telephoned and "intimated our offer . . . had been accepted." He wanted a letter from Killam explaining the withdrawal to cover any questions by city officials who weren't included in the deal and might get suspicious.

Homack drafted the letter and obtained La Morte's approval at lunch that same day. Over Killam's signature, the letter claimed that the company had too much business at that time to continue or accept any new work for the city. However, Homack admitted "it was not true . . . we wanted an excuse to break all ties with the City of Newark."

While Killam Associates had refused to pay the price of doing business with the city, the firm's officers did not report the solicitation to the proper authorities. In Newark this would have been difficult. There was no sure way of knowing on which side any of the authorities were.

Ralph Cestone of the Verona Construction Company did pay for his city contracts, at least $170,000 during 1965 and 1966. When at first he seemed reluctant to fulfill the usual prerequisite for doing business with the City of Newark, Paul Rigo was instructed to explain to him how it was done and to pick up Cestone's "contributions." By this time Rigo had been appointed "bagman" by Tony Boy, a dubious honor not easily declined.

It was Rigo who had to handle the more complicated details of converting Cestone's large checks into cash. The mob operated in an efficient, businesslike manner. Since unnecessary violence gives the Mafia a bad name and draws unwanted publicity, a simple system was devised to ensure prompt payoffs. The City simply wouldn't pay a contractor's bill until his graft payments were up-to-date.

In October 1965, when Ralph Cestone called Rigo seeking his help in getting his money from the city for the work he was doing, Rigo promptly dispatched one Charles Robinson in his company's helicopter to fetch Cestone's payoff check. As soon as the last installment of Cestone's $90,000 quota for that month was airlifted to Rigo, a City car arrived at the Verona Construction Company and a messenger paid Cestone $657,907 of his bill to the City. A second check from the City, for over $1 million arrived more conventionally the following month.

Cestone's company completed its work for the City of Newark in early November of 1965. By February of the following year, nearly half a million dollars was still not paid. Cestone called Rigo again, and Robinson got another helicopter ride to pick up the final payoff checks from Cestone. But the Mayor and his friends were in no hurry to close out the account. Finally nearly a year after the job was completed, Ralph Cestone received the final payment.

The trial of Angelo (Gyp) De Carlo rocked New York and New Jersey with one revelation after another. DeCarlo, Daniel (Red) Cecere, Joseph (Indian Joe) Polverino, and Peter (Pete the Bull) Landusco were charged with extortion and conspiracy to extort funds through loan-sharking.

The most sensational testimony came from Gerald Zelmanowitz, a securities analyst whom Louis Saperstein had introduced to DeCarlo and his group. Saperstein was a former Newark insurance man and labor racketeer. In 1967, when the Internal Revenue Service agents seized his brokerage records, DeCarlo demanded that Saperstein return the $100,000 DeCarlo had put into the venture.

Zelmanowitz gave an eyewitness account of DeCarlo's methods. He testified he was present when Saperstein was beaten until "his face was purple, his tongue bulged, and he was pleading for mercy." DeCarlo "threatened him [Saperstein] with death unless he paid them all he owed by December 13,"—two months from the date of the beating. Zelmanowitz said DeCarlo told Saperstein that $5,000 would be due every Thursday until it was all repaid.

The terror-stricken Saperstein was beaten at The Barn, the DeCarlo hangout, and when released he fled to a New York hotel where he hid out. He died on November 26, 1968, from what were originally believed to be "natural causes." But Saperstein had sent a letter to the FBI on the day before he died, and because of what it said his body was exhumed and an autopsy performed. The autopsy found that Saperstein's body contained "enough arsenic to kill a mule."

Part of this letter to the FBI was introduced into the trial record. There was no means to establish who had been responsible for Saperstein's death, but the letter was sufficient to establish the attempted extortion.

Two of the defendants, Polverino and Landusco, were granted a severance because of illness before the case went to the jury and were to be tried later.

DeCarlo's record included a conviction for breaking and entering, a counterfeiting conviction, and one for highway robbery. On March 4, 1970, Judge Shaw sentenced him and Cecere to 12-year prison terms. The two other defendants were tried later.

The DeCarlo and the DeCavalcante logs gave the greatest insight into the mob's operation in New Jersey, and some idea of the price the public paid because of corruption in government contracts and law enforcement. There were other illustrations. On the same day that Judge Shaw sentenced DeCarlo and Cecere, a federal grand jury brought back a nine-count indictment charging that Zelmanowitz and eight other defendants had conspired in the theft and transportation of securities valued at well over $1 million. On that same day, in Manhattan, John (Gentleman John) Masiello and his 27-year-old son,

John, Jr., both members of the Genovese Mafia family, were sentenced for bribing Post Office officials.

The trial of Newark Mayor Hugh Addonizio began on June 6, 1970. "In the Addonizio administration, everything had a price on it," U. S. Attorney Frederick Lacey told the jury. "The extortion went on right in City Hall."

The Mayor and two Mafia figures—Joseph Biancone and Ralph Vicaro—were found guilty of conspiracy to extort on a wide range of public building contracts in Newark. They were sentenced to ten-year prison terms, and fined $25,000. They had shared the proceeds of extorted kickbacks totaling $1.5 million from contractors and work on city water and sewer lines.

The success of the Addonizio trial gave a boost to the belief that honest government could triumph over the evil of the Mafia. Convictions followed. Two days later, Sam (the Plumber) DeCavalcante and two of his Mafia friends were found guilty of crossing state lines into Pennsylvania to extort money. Less than two months after that, John V. Kenny, the 78-year-old Democratic boss of Hudson County, and Jersey City Mayor Thomas J. Whelan were indicted with ten others on 34 counts of conspiracy, extortion, and tax evasion.

The federal grand-jury indictment charged that the 12 defendants had extorted $181,682 from three companies between 1965 and 1970.

In addition to Kenny and Whelan, those indicted included Bernard Murphy, the Jersey City Purchasing Agent; James Corrado, the Superintendent of Polk Hospital in Jersey City; Thomas Flaherty, President of the Jersey City Council; Fred Krokpe, Hudson County Police Chief; John J. Kenny (no relation to John V. Kenny), a public official; William Sternkopf, Jr., a Commissioner of the Port of New York Authority; Frank Manning, Hudson County Engineer; Joseph Stapleton, Hudson County Treasurer; and Philip Kunz, Business Administrator for the City of Jersey City. Four members of Boss Kenny's family were named as coconspirators but not indicted.

After the successful prosecution of Addonizio, the Kenny probe picked up momentum. Witnesses talked more freely. By the time the Kenny case went to trial in May 1971, the New Jersey Strike Force from the Justice Department had more than 70 indictments of organized crime figures in the northern New Jersey area. The top figures in La Cosa Nostra and their political allies had been convicted of federal or state crimes and were on the way to prison or already in prison.

A New Jersey state investigation had resulted in the indictment of Joe Zicarelli, one of the major organized crime figures in New Jersey, and John Theuer, the Hudson County Republican Chairman. The indictment charged that the two men conspired to get a county prosecutor appointed who would be easy on the gambling rackets.

The New Jersey State Investigating Commission was going at its work with a drive reminiscent of the days when Thomas E. Dewey was cleaning up New York in the late 1930s. The New Jersey legislature had passed new laws to provide for eavesdropping and wiretapping, to grant immunity to witnesses, and to provide for protection of witnesses.

As the trial of John V. Kenny moved forward, it revealed the same pattern of corruption that had taken place in Newark. There had been even more arrogance in the way that the 78-year-old Jersey City Boss had handled kickbacks.

Hugh Platt, Jr., president of Hay Palmer and Associates, when granted immunity from prosecution, told how City Purchasing Agent Murphy, had dunned him for 10 percent of a contract. He said that he had delivered exactly $2,884.04 in cash to the official.

In another vignette James Crawford told how he had been sent to Jersey City at Murphy's request. The purchasing agent had suggested that he come to discuss a bid on a $42 million water and power project. Crawford met Murphy in a 20-passenger plane belonging to Crawford's company. Crawford said Murphy asked for $3 million, and that he rejected it. He did not go to the FBI because he did not want "to be involved," Crawford said.

The Strike Force in northern New Jersey, under John Bartels, was by far the most productive. It had been helped a great deal by a decision made by Judge Robert Shaw in the trial of Gyp DeCarlo.

He had ruled that the 2,100 pages of FBI recordings made available to DeCarlo and the other defendants should be made public. New Jersey Governor Richard Hughes denounced the court for publishing the logs, for they reflected unfavorably on many high officials in his administration. The American Civil Liberties Union (ACLU) also denounced Judge Shaw's decision. The revelations had dramatized the real need for reform, and the New Jersey legislature had provided the laws for court-authorized eavesdropping and wiretapping.

But nowhere in the country was there a clearer example of the value of eavesdropping to break up a Mafia gambling combine than in Kansas City. There, electronic surveillance obtained the evidence for major narcotics law prosecution. At the same time it provided the leads to stop a murder and to solve a bank robbery. It was unfortunate that Ramsey Clark had never had an experience like the one David Martin had in his first year of coordinating the eavesdropping and wiretapping in Kansas City.

10

THE CIVELLA GANG AND KANSAS CITY

"Today this country is painfully realizing that evidence of crime is difficult for governments to secure. Criminals are shrewd and constantly seek, too often successfully, to conceal their tracks and their outlawry from law officers. But, in carrying out their nefarious practices, professional criminals usually talk considerably. . . . The eavesdrop evidence here shows this petitioner [Berger] to be a briber, a corrupter of trusted public officials, a poisoner of the honest administration of government, upon which good people must depend to obtain the blessing of a decent orderly society.

"No man's privacy, property, liberty or life is secure if organized or even unorganized criminals can go their way unmolested, ever and ever further on their unabandoned lawlessness. However obnoxious eavesdroppers may be, they are assuredly not engaged in a more 'ignoble' or 'dirty business' than are the bribers, thieves, burglars, robbers, rapists, kidnappers, and murderers, not to speak of others. And it cannot be denied that to deal with some specimens of our society, eavesdroppers are not merely useful, they are frequently a necessity." *Justice Hugo Black's dissent in the Ralph Berger case, October 1966. Justice Tom Clark wrote the majority opinion freeing Ralph Berger.*

DAVID MARTIN graduated from George Washington Law School in June 1967, at the time when President Johnson was vigorously refusing to support wiretapping legislation. After passing the bar examination in Maryland, Martin went to work for the Justice Department. He understood the apprehension of those who feared that wiretapping might be abused. What he could not understand was the Johnson Administration's opposition to any wiretapping in the organized crime area. And, above all, he failed to see how Attorney General Ramsey Clark and the President could take the position that wiretapping was effective against subversives but "neither effective nor highly productive" in connection with gambling, narcotics, union racketeering, or similar crimes.

David Martin and other young lawyers in the Organized Crime Section obeyed the Attorney General's order barring use of the 1968 law authorizing court-approved wiretaps; but it made little sense to them, especially considering the safeguards required by the law. Consequently there was no opportunity to test the effectiveness of wiretapping against organized crime until February 1969, a month after the Nixon Administration came into office. The new Attorney General, John Mitchell, rescinded Ramsey Clark's order. Immediately, lawyers in the Organized Crime Section went to work to show how effective wiretapping was against the Cosa Nostra.

Within two years, two court-authorized wiretaps enabled David Martin to solve a bank robbery, break up a major gambling ring, and two narcotics rings in Kansas City. One of the narcotics rings was linked to a Cosa Nostra murder inside the federal penitentiary at Leavenworth, Kansas. Another narcotics wiretap made it possible to prevent a murder by a heroin wholesaler. Unfortunately one Mafia-directed murder of a key witness in an interstate gambling case could not be prevented; but Martin used the new crime legislation to preserve the testimony of a key witness in the case.

By the summer of 1971, the young attorney was convinced that Senators Estes Kefauver, John McClellan, and Robert F. Kennedy had been right to urge wiretapping as essential in fighting organized crime in America.

Martin's baptism of fire began when he was named "area attorney" to coordinate efforts of the FBI, the IRS, the Bureau of Narcotics and Dangerous Drugs, and other federal agencies in Kansas City and St. Louis. What he accomplished paved the way for the establishment of Strike Forces in Missouri. In developing the case against the narcotics rings in Leavenworth, Martin was fortunate to be teamed with Abraham Poretz, one of the late Thomas E. Dewey's crime fighters. In dealing with the Kansas City underworld, he was helped by FBI agents William N. Ouseley and Leoni J. Flos, both of Italo-American extraction. Ouseley and Flos spoke Italian, and were knowledgeable about the history of Kansas City mobsters in politics. From his superiors in the Criminal Division, Deputy Assistant Attorney General Henry Peterson, William Lynch, Ed Joyce, and Thomas Kennelly, Martin learned how to button-up a case while at the same time scrupulously adhering to the requirements of the wiretap law.

At the time of the Kefauver hearings in 1951, Buster Wortman was one of the leading bookmakers in the St. Louis area and he continued as such until his death in August 1969. Many were ready to take his place, and David Martin was eager to move in on them. But for a number of reasons, including the strict rules in implementing electronic surveillance and the wariness of the St. Louis gambling fraternity, he was never able to obtain Justice Department authorization to wiretap in St. Louis. Within a few months, however, he hit the jackpot in Kansas City.

Kefauver Committee reports had only briefly identified Nick Civella as a figure to watch in organized crime in Kansas City. At that time, Civella's gang was just beginning to muscle in; later it joined forces with labor racketeers to move the Gargotta mob off center stage. Civella had ties with Carlos Marcello in New Orleans, and other Mafia figures in Las Vegas and Chicago. He controlled gambling in eastern Kansas and western Missouri in the same way Charles Binnagio had during the 1950s, and left the racket activities in St. Louis to John J. Vitale, Tony Giardano, and other successors to Buster Wortman.

In the fall of 1969, Martin, a tall lanky Virginian, arrived in Kansas City with only a sketchy knowledge of Missouri politics. In short order, Ouseley and Flos acquainted him with the problems of operating against the Mafia in that area.

Martin relayed to them his instructions from the Justice Department to avoid all possible unlawful invasions of the rights of privacy. He had been advised to err on the side of restraint rather than disregard the rights of a citizen—even a hoodlum. Martin's superiors emphasized the necessity of obtaining federal court orders to engage in wiretapping, and of showing "good cause" in requesting such orders. The law required annual reports on wiretap authorizations, for these authorizations might have to be justified later in open court.

From mid-October until late December, surveillance of the Nick Civella gang by Martin and the FBI agents convinced them that a telephone at the Northview Social Club was being used by Tony Civella and Frank Tousa to conduct an interstate gambling operation. Long-distance telephone records established that calls were being placed from Las Vegas by a Martin Chess, the man who apparently was supplying the betting line for the day.

While in Washington for Christmas, David Martin demonstrated to the Justice Department that he had "good reason" for tapping the telephone at the Northview Social Club. He returned to Kansas City with a request for approval of a wiretap signed by Assistant Attorney General Will Wilson, and obtained the signature of United States District Judge William R. Collinson. He then turned it over to the FBI to execute.

From January 7, 1970, until January 17, 1970, the FBI overheard conversations indicating that Nick Civella, Tony Civella, and Frank Tousa were engaged in a conspiracy to violate the gambling laws. On January 17, the FBI, armed with search warrants, moved to search the residences, automobiles, and persons of those three men. Money, books, and records were seized from Frank Tousa at the Northview Social Club. There was also evidence involving Tony Civella; but not a scrap of documentary proof tied Nick Civella to the operation even though he was recognized as the boss.

By diligently listening to the recorded conversations over the Northview Social Club telephone, Martin and his team were able to identify the voices of Sol Landie and Alvin Hurst—two of the biggest gamblers in the area. The tapes clearly identified Nick and Tony Civella as part of the gambling conspiracy.

The next move was to subpoena Landie and Hurst before a federal grand jury, but that step was delayed until the decision was made to grant them immunity from prosecution under the recently passed crime package. The Justice Department asked United States District Judge Elmo B. Hunter to grant the immunity in secret proceedings on the grounds that an open hearing would reveal that the testimony of Landie and Hurst was crucial to the case. Judge Hunter balked at this request. As a result, although the actual testimony was given in a closed session, it was obvious that the two nervous men had testified against the Civella gang.

A few days later, partly to mislead the Civellas, gambling conspiracy indictments were returned against 12 individuals, none in the Civella gang. It was assumed by many that Landie and Hurst had been granted immunity to testify against those named in the indictment, but it is doubtful that the maneuver fooled the hardened criminals of the Kansas City syndicate for very long. On October 22, indictments were returned against Nick and Tony Civella, Frank Tousa, and the Las Vegas gambler Martin Chess.

Exactly one month later, Sol Landie was murdered in his home by four young Negro men. The men had first asked if there was any money in the house, then put a pillow over Landie's head and shot him through the pillow while his wife watched. One had then shoved the gun in Mrs. Landie's vagina and threatened to "blow your insides out" if she resisted their rape attempts. When police arrived, Mrs. Landie was in a state of shock but was able to give them a description of the men. Initially it was assumed to be just another rape and robbery. But identification came from neighbors who had seen the men in the vicinity and from fingerprints carelessly left around the house. A neighborhood service-station operator identified the men's car. Several days later, when three of the men were arrested, it became clear it was a "contract" killing for the Mafia. Questioned separately, all three gave essentially the same story and the same basic reason for doing it—money.

Tommy Lee, an associate of some members of the Civella mob, was identified as the man who had arranged the "contract." Each man received $500 and Lee told them that the reason for the job had to do with testimony Landie had given in a gambling case. The men had been hired by Lee and others to carry out earlier acts of violence—arson, bombing, robbery; but this was their first murder. Carl Civella, another brother, was implicated in the transaction as was John Frankoviglia, a small-time member of the gang. Lee was found guilty of murder. John Frankoviglia and three of the killers are awaiting trial, while the fourth faced charges in juvenile court.

Immediately after the murder of Sol Landie, David Martin returned to Kansas City to take a deposition from Alvin Hurst, for his testimony was now paramount. Legislation providing for such depositions to preserve evidence had been signed into law only a few months earlier by President Nixon. It was not an insurance policy for Hurst, but it did represent some assurance that merely wiping out a witness would not destroy the evidence.

While Martin was waiting to make his moves in the Civella case during the spring and summer of 1970, he had not been loafing. He supervised the surveillance of Eugene James Richardson, who had become a major narcotics wholesaler in Kansas City.

Initially there was a problem in establishing sufficient evidence to prove the need for a wiretap, but finally it was obtained. On April 30, approval was authorized for a tap to be installed on a telephone used by Richardson and his employees.

The tap was productive almost immediately—and for more than simply tracing the activities of Richardson and the dozen or so people who worked for him. On May 8, narcotics agents listened as Michael Piggie and others planned to rob the Southgate State Bank in Kansas City on the following day. Leads from the tapes enabled narcotics agents and local police to arrest Piggie, Eddie David Cox, Maurice Lanear, and Cleveland D. Ford shortly after the robbery occurred. The best evidence at the trial of the four men was the voice of Piggie on the telephone outlining their plans.

Only a few days later, narcotics agents heard Richardson and a James Dearborn planning to murder a Negro narcotics pusher who owed Richardson more than $2,000. The pusher, Roy Dean Jordan, was not selling the stuff sent him but instead was using it himself.

David Martin and a team that included narcotics agents and local police converged on Jordan's home. There was also a helicopter hovering overhead as Richardson and Dearborn approached the front door. Agents in the plane signaled others on the ground when to surround the house. Following Richardson's and Dearborn's arrest on charges of assault to murder, a grateful Jordan agreed to help develop the case.

On May 20, federal and local officials made a surprise raid at 8 A.M. on more than a dozen narcotics centers in Kansas and Missouri. Richardson, out on bail, was arrested at his home. The required knock on the door preliminary to entering gave him the time necessary to flush the heroin down the toilet.

Richardson opened fire with a .38 caliber gun, but when shots were returned he threw out his gun and emerged with hands in the air. He was one of 17 arrested in the roundup and charged with violation of the Harrison narcotics laws through possession and sale of heroin. Because of the eavesdropping evidence against them, 14 of the 17 defendants either entered pleas of guilty or were found guilty in a jury trial. One woman died of an overdose of heroin which, it was suspected, had been given to her intentionally because she was a key witness. One person was acquitted, and the judge directed a verdict of not guilty for another defendant.

The death of Willard Hardaway in Leavenworth penitentiary on September 22, 1968, called attention to a regular organization for smuggling narcotics into the federal prison. The "horse" for bringing the narcotics into the prison was one of the guards, Charles Lee Wray; but the long supply line stretched to New York and New Jersey and included a bookkeeping operation in Rockford, Illinois, operated by Herbert Hoover Franks, a lawyer.

The East Coast supply source was identified as Anthony Pisciotta, who had served a prison term for narcotics violations. The sale of the heroin inside the prison was handled by Frank Cappola. Wray pleaded guilty and was sentenced to five years. Cappola and Pisciotta did the same and received ten years. They were among nine defendants who served time after realizing it would be futile to fight the overwhelming evidence the government could muster against them.

During the Kefauver hearings it had been learned that a mobster contributor to the Missouri gubernatorial campaign of Forrest Smith had attempted to obtain appointment for his friend to the board of police commissioners. The friend was Morris Shenker, attorney for many of the St. Louis witnesses who appeared before the Committee.

When the Justice Department established its official Strike Force in St. Louis in May 1970, it had to contend with problems which arose from Mayor A. J. Cervantes' appointment of Attorney Morris Shenker to head a newly formed Commission on Crime and Law Enforcement for the city. Lawyer Shenker could not be criticized for his lack of knowledge in the crime field. He had a 30-year record of representing persons connected with the Mafia, labor racketeering, and organized crime in general.

Shenker had been attorney for Jimmy Hoffa over an extended period of time. He represented gamblers Buster Wortman, John Vitale, Anthony Giardano, and convicted labor racketeer Lawrence Callanan of the St. Louis Steamfitters Local 563. Mayor Cervantes proudly declared there was no organized crime in St. Louis, and with Shenker's help he expected to prove it.

The traditional association between politics and organized crime in St. Louis and southern Illinois made it difficult for the St. Louis Strike Force to accomplish very much in its first year. But in February 1971, Anthony Giardano was indicted on a charge of concealed ownership of the Frontier Hotel gambling casino in Las Vegas, Nevada.* In the

*The indictment charged that the defendants, including Anthony Joseph Zerilli, age forty-two, of Grosse Pointe, Michigan, had engaged in a conspiracy to violate federal laws by engaging in interstate activity for the purpose of acquiring and concealing ownership of the Frontier Hotel in 1966 and 1967 in violation of Nevada state law. The Nevada law requires all persons holding financial interest in a Las Vegas casino to be licensed by the state.

Zerilli, president of the Hazel Park Racing Association of Detroit, had been identified by the McClellan Subcommittee on Organized Crime as a *capodecina* in the Detroit crime hearings on the crime syndicate in 1969.

Also indicted were Michael Santi Polizzi, 46, of Grosse Pointe Shores, president of Valley Die Cast Association. He had also been identified as a *capodecina* in the McClellan hearings on organized crime. Also indicted was Arthur James Rooks, 67, identified as former Municipal Court Judge in Hamtramck, Michigan, and owner of a Michigan construction company and ski resort.

indictment Giardano was identified as a member of the board of directors of Banana Distributing Company—since the Justice Department had ceased referring to racket figures as members of the Mafia or La Cosa Nostra.

The indictment charged that on September 14, 1967, Giardano and Anthony Sansone, Jr., a campaign manager for Mayor Cervantes and son-in-law of Jimmy Michaels, notorious gang leader of Syrian extraction, traveled from St. Louis to Las Vegas, to deliver $150,000 to Jack S. Shapiro in carrying out a conspiracy to acquire hidden ownership. Shapiro was formerly a partner in the Silver Slipper Casino and managing director of the Frontier Hotel in Las Vegas.

That was the only top Mafia figure indicted in St. Louis, but the Strike Force there was just getting under way in the summer of 1971. Thanks to the work of Dave Martin and the use of wiretapping evidence, the Kansas City Strike Force under Mike Defeo was winding up an important phase of its work against the Civella mob.

11

LONG'S LOUISIANA AND CARLOS MARCELLO

"We have been in repeated public conflicts with Orleans District Attorney Jim Garrison, who denies the existence in our city of provable organized crime. He and his staff have blocked our efforts to have grand juries probe the influence of the Cosa Nostra and other syndicate operations. Prosecutive trickery and public deception have successfully prevented grand jury action in the pinball gambling racket, suspected liquor license irregularities, bookie operations, and numerous others." *Aaron M. Kohn, Managing Director, Metropolitan Crime Commission, New Orleans, Louisiana, before the House Government Operations Subcommittee on August 13, 1970.*

CARLOS MARCELLO was known as the "Little Big Man" of Louisiana. When Senator Estes Kefauver took his crime hearings into the Mafia-infested Bayou State in 1950, Carlos and his brother, Anthony, declined to answer questions from the Committee on grounds of self-incrimination. In his book, *Crime in America,* the Tennessee Democrat predicted that unless drastic action was taken, Marcello would build "a criminal dynasty that one day may rival Al Capone's."

Calogero Minacori was born in Tunis in 1910, while his Sicilian parents were enroute to the United States. The family took the name of Marcello when they settled in New Orleans. The records of the Metropolitan Crime Commission in New Orleans show that young Carlos had been in trouble from boyhood, and that as a youth he had served a four-year prison term for assaulting and robbing a Chinese grocer. In 1935, at the age of 25, Marcello received a full pardon from Louisiana Governor O. K. Allen, who was a puppet of the then Senator Huey P. Long.

Marcello was arrested in 1938 on charges of peddling marijuana in association with one of the largest narcotics rings in the history of New Orleans. He pleaded guilty and served a one-year term in the federal penitentiary in Atlanta. It was the last time he was to enter a plea of guilty and take a jail term.

The Kefauver Committee found that Marcello was a small operator on the fringe of the big-name national syndicate that included Frank Costello, Joe Adonis, Jake and Meyer Lansky, and Phil Kastel. When Costello had been chased out of New York, he and his slot machines found the climate in New Orleans pleasantly hospitable.

"They created a monopolistic arrangement whereby only the machines of their syndicate were permitted," the Kefauver Committee reported in 1951. "They built up a business with a profit in millions. Costello and Kastel were tried in 1939 on charges of trying to evade payment of $500,000 in federal income from slot machines." They were acquitted.

New Orleans Mayor DeLesseps Morrison was one of the organizers of a drive against organized crime. Before the Kefauver Committee, he spelled out the problems which arise when the national syndicate moves into an area. He told the Committee that Huey Long's welcome to

Costello led to the alignment of interstate and local operators in slot machines, gambling houses, bookmaking, and other racketeering activities.

"From 1936 to 1946, the successive companies of New Yorkers Phil Kastel, Frank Costello, and Jake Lansky, in cooperation with local gentry such as the narcotics vendor Carlos Marcello, operated slot machines illegally and openly throughout New Orleans," the Kefauver Committee stated.

When, in 1947, police raided the warehouses of the Louisiana Mint Company, they confiscated 1,000 machines. They smashed nearly 400 before Costello and Kastel filed suit for damages and enjoined the city from destroying any more. But the courts sustained the city's contention that, although the machines dispensed mints, they were still slot machines and illegal.

Kefauver reported that the Kastel and Costello combine opened an elaborate nightclub outside of the jurisdiction of New Orleans. This Beverly Club provided a retreat for the mob's operations when the heat was on inside New Orleans. Marcello had a small piece of the Beverly Club, Kastel told the Kefauver Committee.

In every line of inquiry, the Committee found his trail. Several witnesses testified that he had an interest in another luxurious club, the Old Southport, which he was rumored to have bought outright for $160,000. Marcello owned interests in racing wire services, horse parlors, and bookie joints such as the Bank Club and the Billionaire Club. He had an interest in Kastel and Costello's Louisiana Mint Company, in the L. & B. Amusement Company with his brother-in-law, and in half a dozen other slot-machine companies operating in and around New Orleans.

"King" Clancy, Sheriff of Jefferson Parish, told the Kefauver Committee that Marcello advanced money to people who were building business establishments of one kind or another, and put his slot machines in these locations.

"Whether or not he and his brother Anthony had boats running narcotics into New Orleans, it is a fact that Marcello had served time for dope peddling among other things and had asked and been refused a Presidential pardon," Kefauver reported. "Toll calls connected Marcello with Harry Brooks, close associate of Mickey Cohen [in Los Angeles]; Joe Civello, narcotics violator [Texas]; and Sam Yarras, brother of Chicago hoodlum Dave Yarras, a prominent figure in the fight between the 'mob' wire service and Continental Press."

Kefauver noted that Marcello was in touch with Charles Gordon, identified as a main cog in a national football-betting syndicate. "Carlos talked over the phone to one Vincent Vallone just before the latter was murdered in Houston, Texas, in a Mafia-type killing."

"He [Marcello] has never become a citizen," the Kefauver report said. "In view of this fact, and in view of his record which the chairman stated made him one of the leading criminals in the United States today, the question was raised as to why he had not been deported."

Nearly 20 years later, *Life* magazine, in its April 10, 1970, issue, wrote an "investigative report" under the title: "Louisiana Still Jumps to Mobster Marcello—The 'Little Man' is 'Bigger than Ever.'" The *Life* article contended that Louisiana Governor John McKeithen was either negligent or was involved in a long-time arrangement which favored Carlos Marcello. Governor McKeithen retorted that he did not know Marcello, and that the series of articles appearing on Marcello and Louisiana politics was a deliberate effort to hamper his wide campaign against the extent of school desegregation required of the Southern states.

Life charged that Marcello was friendly with several members of the McKeithen Administration, including the Director of the State Public Works Department, the Director of the State Highway Commission, and Tom Ashy, State Racing Commissioner identified by *Life* as "a bookie."

The *Life* author, David Chandler, wrote that the Louisiana Revenue Department failed to collect state taxes from Marcello and his friends. He further contended that Marcello persuaded officials of Jefferson Parish to drain a swamp that he owns at a cost of millions of tax dollars. The cost, said Chandler, would be $5 million; Marcello's land would increase in value from $1 million to $60 million!

The state held legislative hearings on the *Life* charges. They were conducted before a committee headed by state Senator Adrian

Duplantier of New Orleans, reportedly friendly to the McKeithen Administration. The Governor and local law-enforcement figures claimed they knew of no Louisiana officials who knowingly permitted organized crime to flourish in the state.

The Legislative Committee found that the treatment of Carlos Marcello and his associates by the state Revenue Department "was so noticeable and substantially improper as to create a suspicion of corrupt influence." The Committee also noted that this special treatment might be due to "systematic exploitation of the laxity and inefficiency" in the department operations rather than to collusion.

A Federal Strike Force in Louisiana was established in June 1970, under John Wall, a top Justice Department investigator-lawyer, to pull together federal enforcement functions and local and state officials in an effort to break Carlos Marcello's power in Louisiana and the Mississippi Gulf Coast region.

Marcello had continually solidified his position and became more powerful. More than 20 years before, he had succeeded Silvestro (Silver Sam) Carollo as head of the Cosa Nostra family in New Orleans.

The simple chronology of events since May 1951, when Senator Kefauver had urged that Marcello be deported as an undesirable alien, was a tragicomedy. The depressing picture of fumbling and ineffectiveness would have been funny if it had not indicated either incompetence or deep-seated corruption on the part of the government personnel involved. The federal court had entered a deportation order in the Marcello case in February 1953. Marcello had attached that order in a dozen ways in the intervening years. In every instance, when the issue got to the Supreme Court, the validity of the deportation order was upheld.

The Eisenhower Administration under Attorneys General Herbert Brownell and William Rogers had failed to deport Marcello. Robert Kennedy, who became Attorney General in 1961, pledged to get the job done. He was particularly critical of Rogers, whom he regarded as too much of a "playball politician" to risk a fight with the Long machine in Louisiana.

In April 1961, Kennedy had Marcello arrested, handcuffed, whisked to the New Orleans airport, and placed on an Immigration Service plane to Guatemala.

Why Guatemala? The Justice Department had learned that Marcello had obtained a Guatemalan birth certificate, and that periodically his friends and associates had been in that Central American country since 1956 with a farsighted view of establishing a base closer to New Orleans than Italy.

When Marcello landed there the Guatemalan press immediately challenged the authenticity of the birth certificate, which indicated that Marcello was born in the Guatemalan village of San Jose Pinula. The birth certificate (since admitted to be false) became a hot local issue. There were allegations that high Guatemalan officials had been bribed. Marcello was deported from Guatemala and, it was reported, dumped over the border into neighboring El Salvador.

Marcello made his way back to the U. S., reentered illegally, and sent his lawyers into federal court to challenge his deportation order. But the false Guatemalan birth certificate had complicated his problems. Marcello was indicted on three new charges: defrauding the U.S. by obtaining a fraudulent birth certificate; perjury in connection with its acquisition and use; and illegal reentry into the United States while a valid order of deportation was outstanding.

Government prosecutors believed they had a good case. They had a key witness, Carl Irving Noll, who had gone to Guatemala several times in connection with obtaining Marcello's fraudulent birth certificate. During the trial on the charges of defrauding the government, Noll reported threats on his life. Obviously Marcello and his group knew they were involved in a tough struggle against Attorney General Kennedy.

Marcello did not take the stand in his own defense. On November 22, 1963, a federal jury found Carlos Marcello not guilty on the charge of defrauding the United States with the Guatemalan birth certificate. It was on this day that President John F. Kennedy was assassinated. The effective power of Robert Kennedy was to end shortly.

Still pending for Marcello were criminal charges of perjury and illegal reentry. Then Marcello and an associate were indicted on a charge of conspiring to murder the key witness (Noll) in the false document trial. Finally Marcello was charged with tampering with the jurors who had acquitted him in his fraud trial. One juror, Rudolph Heifler, had told the grand jury he had accepted $1,000 to vote not guilty.

Marcello's lawyers managed to delay trial on any of the cases until August 1965. At that time United States District Attorney Louis LaCour dismissed the illegal reentry charge. He explained that there were other criminal charges pending which dealt with the same deportation.

In August, Marcello was brought to trial on the jury-tampering charge. Although Heifler repeated at the trial that he had accepted $1,000 to vote not guilty, the New Orleans jury acquitted Marcello of the charge. The government concluded that it would be impossible to win a verdict of guilty against Marcello in New Orleans. The Johnson Administration dropped all the remaining charges against him. Carlos Marcello was home free.

In September 1966, Marcello went to New York City to meet with the Cosa Nostra bosses of Florida, New York, and other centers. The group was arrested at a restaurant and taken before a New York grand jury. This meeting of Mafia figures, getting together to iron out jurisdictional problems, has been described as a "Little Appalachia."

Marcello took the Fifth Amendment, and avoided trouble. But back in New Orleans that night he took a swing at FBI Agent Patric Collins, saying, "I am the boss here," and bought himself a charge of assaulting a federal officer. He was tried first in Laredo, Texas; the trial ended in a hung jury.

The second trial on this charge was in Houston, after the Nixon Administration took office. It resulted in a verdict of guilty. Judge John Singleton sentenced Marcello to a two-year federal prison term. Marcello's lawyers contended that the New Orleans mobster's health was poor, and that the two-year prison term was "excessive in the light of the 'technical' nature of the charge of assaulting a federal officer."

Those arguments touched a responsive chord in the heart of Justice Hugo Black, who had jurisdiction in the Fifth Circuit Court of Appeals. His law clerk called the Justice Department's Criminal Division to make unusual inquiries about the FBI's activities and the whole problem of "excessive" punishment on a "technical" crime of assault.

A few days after Justice Black granted Marcello's plea for a review by the Supreme Court, Judge Singleton reduced the sentence from two years to six months. On October 13, 1970, the Supreme Court, in a seven-to-two decision, upheld the conviction. Black was able to persuade only one colleague, William O. Douglas, to join him in deploring the FBI's conduct in the Marcello case. On that same day Chief Judge John R. Brown of the Fifth Circuit denied any further stay of execution, and Marcello was ordered committed. Marcello served his light six-month's sentence in the federal prison hospital at Springfield, Missouri. He was back in business immediately after his release in March 1971.

Against that background Attorney General John Mitchell gave the go-ahead for the moves that were to strike at the Marcello political base in Louisiana politics.

When John Wall launched the Strike Force in the summer of 1970, he had great hopes of achieving Marcello's deportation. The Supreme Court had unequivocally stated that Marcello was a deportable alien. Wall felt that the efforts had been unsuccessful up until that time "due, for the most part, to Marcello's financial wealth and astute legal counsel." He might have added that Marcello's political connections in Governor McKeithen's administration hadn't hurt his "financial wealth."

However, the Nixon Administration's effort to deport Marcello hit a snag in a few months. When they tried to reinstate the charge of reentering as a deported alien, United States District Judge Lansing Mitchell dismissed the indictment. He ruled that the charge dismissed under the Johnson Administration could not be reinstated because the statute of limitations had expired.

Judge Mitchell declared that the statute of limitations had started running at the time that Marcello made his reentry in June 1961, because this was when the government "found" him. So the 1965 decision to dismiss the initial charge had cleared the deck for Marcello to remain in the United States indefinitely. The Johnson Administration had, in effect, given him immunity from prosecution by bringing the charge, dropping it, and permitting the statute of limitations to run.

Nevertheless, there is a bright side to the whole sordid story. In the 1950s the history of police corruption in New Orleans began to change. It was then that the Metropolitan Crime Commission, organized as a nonprofit civic group, began to have some impact. Aaron M. Kohn, its Managing Director, told a House Government Operations Subcommittee investigating the role of private efforts against organized crime: "Organized crime has grown to proportions which have caused it to be called America's biggest industry, mainly because the private sector has both stimulated and tolerated it." He charged that "commercial alliances. . .give wealth and false respectability to racketeers. . . . It is impossible to conceive that our adult tolerance of organized crime has not been a substantial cause of what is now being bitterly denounced as permissive misconduct of the young."

"When State Superintendent Francis Grevemberg resigned in 1955, we were confronted with the absence of a single public official in the entire state who was doing anything about organized crime, except those who protected and profited by it," Kohn said.

The turning point came in 1955, when Major Joseph De Paoli, Police Superintendent in New Orleans, was forced to retire. What undid him was an 88-page report documenting his corrupt collusion with important vice and gambling operators and his activities as the controlling "bagman."

This change, brought about by the action of the New Orleans Crime Commission, can best be described by saying that previously "it had been dangerous to be an honest cop. Thereafter, it became increasingly hazardous to be a dishonest one."

The Police Administrator for Jefferson Parish, near New Orleans, is an elected Sheriff. Until 1964, the office was notoriously corrupt, protecting the headquarters operations of La Cosa Nostra organization and its diverse criminal operations. Three successive sheriffs were ousted—Frank "King" Clancy in 1956, after 28 years; William S. Coci in 1960; and John Fitzgerald in 1964.

Kohn's report stated: "Since Sheriff Alwynn Cronvich took office in 1964, we have consistently supported his aggressive policies. An organized crime intelligence unit has worked effectively. . .and Sheriff Cronvich's activities are statewide in their impact and influence.

"One of the earlier sheriffs, John Fitzgerald, was indicted, but we were never able to get the prosecutor to bring him to trial."

The men in power went after Kohn for this report. He was indicted three times, and served a ten-day prison term for refusing to disclose the name of the police sergeant who had given him information.

"Beginning in 1966," said Kohn, "we have been in repeated public conflict with New Orleans District Attorney Jim Garrison, who denies the existence in our city of provable organized crime. He and his staff have blocked our efforts to have grand juries probe the influence of the Cosa Nostra and other syndicate operations. Prosecutive trickery and public deception have successfully prevented grand jury action on the pinball gambling racket [estimated $20 million annually], suspected liquor license irregularities, bookie operations, and numerous others."

The New Orleans Crime Commission Director accused Jefferson Parish District Attorney Frank Langridge of collusion and "nonfeasance." He said that Langridge's chief investigator, Joseph (Zip) Chimento, had been convicted twice for bribery and was a suspected enforcer for the Cosa Nostra, and complained that on the rare occasions when it had been possible to pressure Langridge to act there was never any meaningful result.

On the state level, Kohn gave an equally depressing picture: "Louisiana's Attorney General, Jack P. F. Gremillion, consistently refused or evades use of his discretionary powers to act against misconduct of the sheriffs, district attorneys, and judges. He takes no initiative against organized crime." Gremillion was then under Federal indictment for fraud and conspiracy. He won acquittal by a jury on the fraud and conspiracy charges.

Later, in September 1971, Gremillion was convicted by a federal jury on five counts of perjury arising out of his denial before a federal grand jury that he owned stock in the Louisiana Loan and Thrift Corporation. Gremillion was charged with lying under oath in an appearance before the federal grand jury that was investigating to determine the circumstances under which he gave rulings favorable to the now-defunct firm.

A secretary for the firm, Janyce Coman Degan, had testified that Gremillion was a stockholder in the firm and called her to ask her about his dividend checks. Edward Barnes, attorney for the Justice Department, told the jury that abundant evidence had been produced to corroborate her testimony. The Attorney General of Louisiana had lied to the federal grand jury in denying any economic interest and any stock interest.

The Metropolitan Crime Commission backed a merit plan for various positions rather than competitive elections. The group sparked the Louisiana Judicial Commission to investigate and recommend discipline against a number of judges, including the removal of one. It claims credit for the successful tax prosecution of a state Supreme Court judge and his resignation, and the discipline of several other Louisiana judicial figures.

Kohn claimed that although the "increasingly powerful Marcello Cosa Nostra family" had taken a virtual monopoly in New Orleans, the Metropolitan Crime Commission was able to prevent Governor McKeithen from appointing a Marcello man to the bench.

"Although obstruction and threats to destroy our crime commission have not ceased, it is no longer a lonely battle. We work cooperatively with a new Justice Department Strike Force, with a vigorous new U. S. Attorney, and with federal agents of the FBI, the Narcotics Bureau, Internal Revenue, and others," Kohn said in 1970.

The Strike Force wasted no time deploring Judge Mitchell's decision in the Marcello deportation case, or in going back to examine how the mistakes were made under Louis LaCour's term as United States District Attorney. They concentrated on chasing down all the illegal rackets in liquor counterfeiting, narcotics, prostitution, and the widest variety of gambling enterprises which stretched from Jefferson Parish through New Orleans and all along the Gulf Coast.

The Strike Force had moved against the Western Union Sports Ticker, had assigned 35 agents to raid bars in Bossier City, Louisiana, and had arrested a local rackets lord named John Henry Vice. In connection with the same raids, Michael Maroun, attorney for Marcello, and 13 others were charged with violation of the federal liquor laws. Maroun was identified as the owner of the Town and Country Motor Hotel.

"I feel I am being harassed and persecuted because I have acted as attorney for Mr. Carlos Marcello," Maroun complained at the time of his arrest.

United States Attorney Donald Walter declared this was "nonsense." "He was indicted because the grand jury felt he had broken the law," Walters said. It was charged that Maroun and Joseph Michael Faour, general manager of the hotel, had kept improper records on liquor sold so they could reuse the bottles.

United States Attorney Gerald Gallinghouse, backed by the federal Strike Force, has taken an aggressive position. One of the three members of the State Tax Commission, Leo J. Theriot, resigned after it was disclosed that he never went to the Commission's office while collecting a salary of $16,000 a year.

On November 24 and 25, 1970, the Strike Force in New Orleans directed more than 300 federal agents in raids on more than 1,300 narcotics and gambling places in Louisiana and Mississippi. John Wall limited the sweep to Louisiana and Mississippi, because in those states the slot machines were legal and the federal registration law did not pose the same Fifth Amendment problems on self-incrimination that it did in states where the machines were illegal.

Wall in the Strike Force headquarters in New Orleans, with Rick Giselson to help him, and Michael Carnes in the United States District Attorney's office in Biloxi, along the Mississippi Gulf Coast, were an effective team. More than 3,000 Balley type slot machines and 1,000 one-armed bandit types were seized. Just the physical job of taking possession of 4,000 slot machines and storing them in warehouses pending final court decisions on their destruction was a major undertaking.

The Strike Force soon learned that it was in for months of legal struggle against a tough and knowledgeable adversary with good political connections. Louis LaCour, former United States Attorney, was engaged by many of the major pinball operators in their challenge to the constitutionality of the seizures. LaCour had been appointed by President Kennedy and retained by President Lyndon B. Johnson.

In February 1971, the New Orleans Strike Force moved against a multimillion-dollar counterfeiting operation at the Stiglets Printing

Company in Baton Rouge, Louisiana. They caught John Stiglets and an employee in the process of printing $200,000 in $20 notes. It was estimated that more than $1 million of the total counterfeit currency that was passed in Mississippi, Louisiana, Dallas, and Los Angeles came from the Stiglets plant. Some even showed up in Iowa and Florida.

Stiglets and his employee, John Sims, Jr., were charged with possession of $500,000 in counterfeit bills. Other arrests were made in Newport, Kentucky, and Cincinnati, Ohio. At least 15 were arrested in what was described as the "largest single seizure of counterfeit bills made in Louisiana."

A few days later, the swiftly moving Strike Force took part in "Operation Flanker" against a huge narcotics ring. Among the more than a dozen indicted in New Orleans was Antonio Flores, identified by the Strike Force as "one of the largest importers of heroin in the country, with direct sources of supply in France and Spain." Nathaniel Brooks, also indicted, was then serving a 20-year sentence for violation of the narcotics laws.

"Operation Flanker" also resulted in the March 3, 1971, indictment of five members of a wholesale narcotics distribution organization which had been headed by Whitney A. Barconey, Jr., before he was shot to death in October 1970. Barconey, the Strike Force pointed out, had been a "well known and respected member of the community, his narcotics involvement being unknown to all except the narcotics community and law enforcement."

Barconey was described at his death as a civic leader and humanitarian. The Strike Force revealed that he was a major dealer who "received his narcotics from national sources of supply."

But all these strikes at specific violations of liquor, narcotics, and gambling laws, were only preliminaries. The major strike was to be at the heart of the political corruption that was the source of power for Marcello and dozens of others who preyed on Louisiana and her neighboring states. A political community that had worked with the Mafia, confident that it had things under control, was to find itself shaken out of its complacency.

Big Jim Garrison was arrested on June 30, 1971, on federal charges of taking payoffs from pinball-machine owners to protect illegal gambling in New Orleans. Claiming he was framed, Garrison said he guessed that being arrested was "better than being shot"—which was what he had been expecting since he started his controversial investigation of the assassination of President Kennedy.

Police Captain Fred Soule, assigned to Garrison's staff, and Police Sergeant Robert Frey, who headed the New Orleans vice squad, were also among the ten charged with taking part in the conspiracy and bribery plot.

Pershing Gervais, the key witness against Jim Garrison and formerly on Garrison's staff as an investigator, had been cooperating with the Internal Revenue Service and New Orleans Strike Force for nearly two years. Gervais had carried a recording device for several months, and the affidavit filed by the Internal Revenue Service contained material he had taped which left no doubt about what had taken place.

Gervais, so-called "bagman," said that for several years he had been collecting as much as $1,500 a month in payoffs for Garrison, but that FBI raids on the pinball operators had nearly eliminated these payoffs. Gervais had been "wired for sound" when he talked with the pinball operators, and also when he delivered the money to Captain Frederick Soule. Soule was given $1,000 every two months which, the indictment charged, he split with Sergeant Robert Frey, head of the vice squad.

Gervais said he had been the conduit from John Callery, a lobbyist for the pinball-machine industry, for payoffs from the industry to Garrison, and had delivered to him between $2,000 and $3,000 every two months. Gervais made recordings of Garrison's comments as (Garrison) received the payoff money, and of the District Attorney's description of how he intended to deal with Governor John McKeithen on the pinball issue.

The Strike Force action in New Orleans and excerpts from the recordings supported the contention of the Metropolitan Crime Commission that Garrison was not the "Fighting D.A. of New Orleans" his campaign literature portrayed him to be. The evidence backed up Crime Commission Director Kohn's charge of the "prosecutive trickery and public deception" that had killed grand jury actions in the pinball racket.

The taped recordings substantiated Gervais' charge that Garrison deceived the public of New Orleans and muted the voice of the Crime Commission. Perhaps the most devastating bit of corroboration was the fact that when Garrison was arrested at his home, he still had the last $1,000 in marked bills locked in a drawer, where Gervais had said it would be. Traces of the luminous powder used to mark the bills were found on Garrison's hands.

The recordings also corroborated the payoffs to Fred Soule. Soule told Gervais that he kept the money in a safe deposit box in Irving, Texas. Tax agents found $75,000 there, which Soule had never mentioned on his income tax returns.

Within a matter of a few months, the Strike Force in Louisiana hit deep into the heart of the state's corrupted politics. There was more to come. John Wall and Thomas Kennelly were satisfied that recording the voices of the culprits represented the only effective means of fighting political demagogues or the underworld figures they dealt with—and excused for a price.

12

CHICAGO—A CAPONE LEGACY IN POLITICS

"Organized crime would be a principal beneficiary of President Johnson's bill to abolish all use of wiretap and eavesdrop devices except in national security cases. In his 1967 State of the Union Message, the President proposed legislation to ban all use of wiretapping and eavesdropping by anybody except in national security cases under his direction. The bill would place the President under no scrutiny in his use of eavesdropping devices in national security cases—a questionable feature from a civil liberties perspective. But it would prohibit all use of eavesdropping equipment to fight organized crime." *Representative Joseph M. McDade (Rep., Penn.) on the House Floor on August 29, 1967, on a "Study of Organized Crime and the Urban Poor."*

> "The purpose of organized crime is not competition with visible legal government but nullification of it. When organized crime places an official in public office, it nullifies the political process. When it bribes a police official, it nullifies law enforcement." *The President's Crime Commission Report in 1967.*

THE Kefauver hearings were a setback for the Mafia in Chicago, but only temporarily. Learning from that experience—as they had learned from Al Capone's tax conviction—they slowed down their activities somewhat, changed their method of operation, and by 1969 were nearly as strongly allied with the Chicago Democratic Party as they had ever been.

The Strike Force established by the Justice Department in the last days of the Johnson Administration operated under restrictions, imposed by Ramsey Clark, that prohibited eavesdropping or wiretapping unless subversive activities were involved. In the war on crime, this was pitting slingshots against cannons. Government investigators were denied the one weapon the mob feared most.

The syndicate had become sophisticated since the days of Al Capone's conviction. Members now filed income tax reports even though they had to list huge sums under "miscellaneous income" to conceal their origins. Accountants and tax lawyers had become as important as triggermen, and transactions were made in cash to keep nosey IRS agents from finding damaging evidence in one's financial affairs.

When Anthony Accardo appeared before the Kefauver Committee, it developed that he was using "miscellaneous income" as a gimmick to hide hundreds of thousands of dollars. His tax lawyers had advised him that this was the way to account for income that could not be explained to federal tax investigators. Local political control was no longer enough. Now the IRS could claim jurisdiction over everyone, and had the facilities to document a "net worth case" to prove you were living beyond the income to which you admitted.

From 1924, when the Torrio-Capone gang manned the polls during the mayoralty election in Cicero, Illinois, the importance of political clout has been recognized. Now the mob has refined and enlarged its influence to control courts and national political figures as well as those on a local or state level. The Kefauver Committee identified Roland Libonati, a Democratic State Senator, and Representative James Adducci, a Republican in the state legislature, as part of the "bipartisan coalition against reform" that had openly opposed legislation proposed by the Chicago Crime Commission. Both Libonati and Adducci were later elected to Congress. Libonati became a member of the House Judiciary Committee, where he unsuccessfully tried to stop the FBI surveillance of Salvatore (Momo) Giancana. He also supported Hoffa's lawyers in trying, again unsuccessfully, to get a House investigation of Robert Kennedy.

Frank Nitti, Capone's successor, and Louis Campagna exerted enough pressure in the Illinois Legislature to prevent passage of wiretapping bills in the 1930s and early 1940s. However, wiretapping was responsible for jailing five of Chicago's top hoods in a shakedown of the movie industry in 1941. Wiretapping and eavesdropping, legal in New York, produced evidence of a coast-to-coast extortion racket which came to be known as the Browne-Bioff scandal. Frank Nitti, Louis Campagna, Paul (the Waiter) Ricci, Charles (Cherry Nose) Gioe, Phil d'Andrea, Nick Circella, and John Rosselli were indicted when New York officials, armed with wiretap evidence, got George Browne and Willie Bioff to turn state's evidence. Frank Nitti committed suicide; the others were convicted and imprisoned in 1943.

The Mafia network sprang to their aid. Tony Accardo assumed the name of a lawyer he knew and went to Leavenworth with Eugene Bernstein, mouthpiece and tax lawyer for the mob, to visit Ricca, Gioe, and Campagna. His use of an assumed name was discovered and both he and Bernstein were indicted, but were acquitted.

The three convicts applied for parole through Paul Dillon, a prominent member of the Missouri bar and President Truman's St. Louis campaign manager in 1934. Against the recommendations of the prosecuting attorney and the presiding judge, parole was granted in 1947, during the Truman Administration. The Kefauver Committee termed this early release from imprisonment of "three dangerous mobsters . . . a shocking abuse of parole powers."

The Kefauver Committee also criticized Eugene Bernstein for

springing the three from prison, and for the way he settled income tax problems for his clients. Bernstein notified Campagna's wife and Accardo that $190,000 would have to be raised. The cash was brought to his office. The Committee report charged: "He [Bernstein] had the almost inconceivable effrontery, as a member of the bar, to assert to the committee under oath, that although he saw some of the persons who delivered the money he never asked their names and that his office had no record whatsoever to indicate their identities."

The Democratic machine in Cook County was aligned against the "reform" packages sent to the Illinois legislature by Virgil Peterson, long-time Director of the Chicago Crime Commission, and his successor, Harvey Johnson.

The mob influence in the Illinois legislature had resulted in law prohibiting "electronic eavesdropping" in any form. It prohibited not only wiretapping, but the use of concealed recording devices which Peterson had characterized as "of tremendous importance to law enforcement officers—particularly in undercover work."

Proposed legislation, supported by the Chicago Crime Commission in 1969, provided that wiretapping could be used if authorized by the court after an application by appropriate law enforcement officials. This legislation would have allowed wiretapping to be used only in connection with murder, kidnapping, aggravated kidnapping, soliciting for a prostitute, narcotics, gambling, and conspiracy.

"Under the present law, racketeers and gangsters are given complete immunity against interception of their oral and telephonic communications," the Crime Commission report for 1969 said. "Hence they may communicate freely without fear of detection or prosecution by law-enforcement officers. By hiring small-fry to perform the routine jobs—pushing narcotics, operating a call-girl service, selling policy tickets—the higherups can reap the enormous profits of large-scale criminal enterprises without committing any of the overt acts which would implicate them. They merely direct the operations by telephone or word of mouth with complete immunity from prosecution. It is a sad commentary on the adequacy of our laws that these higherups are rarely prosecuted for their true crimes, and only occasionally are enmeshed in income-tax violations.

" . . . . While recognizing that citizens should be protected in their constitutional right against unlawful invasion of privacy, the Crime Commission is concerned that too broad interpretations of this privilege has resulted in an unwarranted protection for criminals."

The Crime Commission in Chicago suggested that whenever a judge "rules on a motion to suppress evidence on grounds that it was illegally seized, he shall file written findings of fact and conclusions of law in support of his order. . . . This legislation will force the judge to place on the record the reasons for the ruling and provide prosecutor, the observers, and the Appellate Court the opportunity to measure the judge's ruling against existing law to see if he has erred by going too far in favor of either prosecution or defense."

In this restrained understatement the Chicago Crime Commission placed in focus corruption in the federal as well as the state courts.

Union money and manpower in politics have influenced the decisions of an unfortunate number of United States district judges and some circuit court judges, but labor racketeers and syndicate hoodlums have never gained dominant control of the federal courts. Not, however, because they haven't tried.

One of the weapons in the warfare against public officials has been the oldest of all—sex blackmail.

Many corrupt and political figures were sleepless and nervous on the night of June 2, 1957. Dan Carmell, a smooth little union lawyer, was to go on trial the next morning. He was scheduled to appear in federal court on a charge of violating the White Slave Act by transporting an 18-year-old Davenport, Iowa, girl into Illinois for purposes of prostitution. Had the charge been filed in a state court, it might have been killed or at least limited to the narrowest possible technical grounds. Some federal judges in the Chicago area could have been counted on to give Dan—or his political friends who were involved—a break.

This was no ordinary White Slave Act case, for Carmell was no ordinary procurer. The tough, free-spending Chicago lawyer was counsel for the Illinois Federation of Labor, counsel for the Chicago Federation of Labor, and attorney for several local unions. With high good humor and back-slapping geniality, he had picked up the dinner and drink tabs of key city and state officials at The Chez Paree, The Swiss Chalet, and The Pump Room. Carmell's $100-tips or the $150 he gave an orchestra leader to play a favorite tune came out of the dues paid by union members.

When the more conventional entertainment had been concluded for the evening, Dan would whisk his friends off to private parties, complete with Oriental films, with women, and a huge man who performed interesting acrobatics. Young girls were available for those who were more interested in participatory than spectator sports. The girls were not assigned, but were under instructions to let the politicians do their own selecting. They were ordered not to accept money from Dan's guests. "I'll pay the bills," Dan told one of the girls, reprimanding her for accepting money. He wanted to play down the commercial aspects of his hospitality so his guests could be flattered by believing they had made personal conquests.

Those who accepted Carmell's hospitality were forever in his debt. Dan Carmell didn't guess at what went on behind the bedroom doors; he watched, strolling from bedroom to bedroom. A politician with even one such night behind him would find it difficult to say no to Carmell or to the labor groups he represented.

Carmell's downfall began in October 1955, at the Illinois Federation of Labor Convention on Rock Island. He was giving a party for some of the men attending the convention, and he invited an attractive 18-year-old Iowa girl to come along. Later some other girls joined them. It was understood that each girl would receive $100 for merely sitting at the table with the union men and their political friends. By the end of the fourth day, more intimate "friendships" had developed.

To Dan Carmell, it was just another convention fling. Nevertheless, with an eye always open for new faces and figures to bait his Chicago sex-trap, he told the girls that if they ever decided to move to the big city, he would pay their expenses and set them up in a high-class prostitution racket. When by February the Iowa girls were having trouble making ends meet and one called Carmell to see if his offer was still open, he lived up to his promise to set them up.

It was exciting for the girls to meet political big shots. One gray-haired man was introduced as "the Senator," but the girls weren't sure what his name was or whether he was a state Senator or a United States Senator. The pace, however, was too much. These girls had been around a little, but they found the extent of debauchery in their Chicago "jobs" sickening. They had never even heard of most of the things to which they submitted at the Carmell parties. In less than three weeks they packed and went home.

In Davenport, the boyfriend of one of the girls became suspicious and told the Federal Bureau of Investigation what he thought Carmell's operation had been. They investigated, and by early September the United States District Attorney in southern Iowa had enough evidence to take the case to a federal grand jury.

In Illinois, Carmell had the connections to fix legal problems like these. But in southern Iowa he had no such facilities. His only chance was to frighten all his political friends into coming to his aid. His closest associates passed the word that they were all in this together.

"If Dan goes down, we may all go down with him," was the message.

To Democrats and Republicans alike it meant that they would either have to pull political strings, or risk personal disgrace and smashed careers.

For ten months Carmell's political friends trembled. No one knew who would be implicated. Every effort was made to save Carmell. They tried to get the indictment quashed or, failing that, to get the trial moved to Chicago where a judge might be found who would give Carmell a break. Certainly federal Judge Henry Graven, stern and impartial, who was to preside over the case in Iowa, was completely unconcerned about the political upheaval the Carmell trial might create in Illinois.

The corrupt Chicago labor-political machine wanted no part of a trial in Iowa. They didn't want to tangle with District Attorney Stephenson, who was a tough prosecutor, a brilliant trial lawyer, and had a reputation for being incorruptible.

Judge Graven rejected the motion for a change of venue and set the case for trial in Iowa. Carmell's lawyers appealed the decisions, but the appeal ran head on into a published ruling by the Court of Appeals which stated:

" . . . in the interest of an expeditious, efficient and orderly administration of justice, controversies about venue [the site of the trial] should be finally settled and determined at the district court level." In other words, the circuit court believed it was good policy to avoid shifting trials from one federal court district to another.

Carmell pleaded that many prominent people, including six Illinois state court judges, had said they wanted to give testimony to his good character. Letters from the six judges were included in the petition, along with their assertions that they did not feel they could leave their courts in Chicago to appear for Carmell in person.

The bill of particulars filed by the federal District Attorney made it clear why Carmell and his friends were panicky. It charged that Carmell had transported one of the girls to Chicago with the understanding that " ... [she] would engage in excessive sex indulgence with the defendant and other men, would engage in unnatural sex acts, acts of sex perversion with the defendant and other persons, male and female, all for the entertainment of the defendant and his friends."

It was likely that some strait-laced Iowa farm women would be among the jurors—hardly the audience in which Carmell could expect any leniency on a charge involving such debauchery.

On February 25, 1957, the Eighth Circuit Court of Appeals reversed its policy and gave Carmell what he wanted. The case was ordered sent to Chicago. The trial would be in the area where Carmell was most at home in the political jungle.

Stephenson, disappointed at losing his trial, turned the files over to Robert Tieken, the United States District Attorney in the Chicago area. Tieken had been cooperating with Stephenson for months. The appeal had given him time to run down even more leads on some girls Carmell had imported from California. In Carmell's view, Tieken was no improvement over Stephenson as a prosecutor; but Carmell hoped a politically friendly federal judge would be assigned to his case. The indictment might yet be quashed. At least a major part of the evidence that had been amassed against him might be suppressed.

Hope turned to despair when the trial was assigned to federal Judge Julius Hoffman, a firm and impartial man who could not be approached by Carmell's henchmen. Despite all the legal maneuvers, Carmell was scheduled to go to trial before a judge who had a reputation for unflinching integrity.

The day before the trial Carmell was despondent. He told his wife, Mildred, that he dreaded the ordeal of going to trial before Judge Hoffman. In the late evening, Carmell went into the bathroom of their fifteenth-floor apartment. When he failed to return, Mrs. Carmell opened the door—and then rushed to the window. Below, on the newly sodded lawn, lay the crushed body of her husband. Carmell was dead when the police arrived, and so was the criminal trial which could have shaken the Chicago political world.

McClellan Committee Investigator Alphonse Calabrese had talked with Carmell a few weeks before the Chicago attorney jumped to his death. Smooth and genial, Carmell went out of his way to be helpful. Calabrese had been on the case for some time before he learned that the union attorney was under indictment on a white-slave charge. In addition to his own trial, Carmell had been scheduled to appear before the McClellan Committee that same week as attorney for officials of the Bakery and Confectionary Workers Union.

Carmell's activity is a vivid example of how a few union attorneys have used the money and position available to them to destroy the integrity of local government officials.

In 1960, Tony Accardo was finally convicted on a charge of income-tax evasion. It was a victory against organized crime. The immunity Accardo had enjoyed for years was broken. Judge Julius Hoffman sentenced him to six years and $15,000 in fines.

Though Judge Hoffman could not be bought off, it didn't mean Accardo could not appeal. On January 5, 1962, the United States Court of Appeals for the Seventh Circuit reversed the conviction on grounds of "prejudicial error."

Newspaper stories during the trial, the court said, were prejudicial, and Judge Hoffman's instructions to the jury on this subject "were inadequate protection." Judge Elmer Schnackenberg in a dissent, said there was no prejudicial error and the conviction should have been sustained.

The second trial for Tony Accardo ended with an acquittal on October 3, 1962. This was just the kind of immunity from conviction that the Mafia leaders were so good at obtaining for themselves. It was par for the course before the new tools were available. These tools are:

Court-approved eavesdropping and wiretapping; the immunity statute to force a witness to testify; and the new statute that assures preservation of evidence, making it less likely that witnesses will be killed to keep them from testifying at a trial.

The way the Capone mob took over the government of Burnham, Illinois, was to control politics in the Chicago suburbs. In 1924, the Torrio-Capone gang manned the polls during the mayoralty election in Cicero, Illinois, and following the election, Cicero became the head-quarters for gang operations and gang influence. It still is today.

When Tony Accardo was having his tax troubles, the overall leadership of the Chicago mob was assumed by Sam (Momo) Giancana, whose romance with Phyllis McGuire, of the McGuire sisters, gave him publicity very unwelcome to the Chicago syndicate. It was the couple's presence in the Cal Neva Lodge in Nevada that caused the Nevada State Gambling Control Board to move against Frank Sinatra, one of the owners of the lodge.

Giancana went to jail in 1965. He was convicted of contempt of court for refusing to talk after having been granted immunity. Giancana lost control of the Chicago crime syndicate. Later he was "exiled" by them to Mexico.

The top leadership of the Chicago mob was in doubt after Giancana was deposed. Joey Aiuppa was "Mr. Big" in Cicero, and "Jack the Lackey" Cerone also had a major role there.

But Sam (Teetz) Battaglia was the big man in the various suburbs of Chicago. In January 1968, Battaglia, his lieutenant Joseph Amabile, alias Joe Shine, and Dave Evans were convicted in a long federal court trial.

The mob had discovered that the construction business could be a lucrative shakedown, and now the defendants were accused of having conspired to extort money from builder William Riley and of obstructing the movement of materials to the construction site of Riley's King Arthur Apartments in Lansing, Illinois. The conviction was upheld by the United States Court of Appeals.

However, underworld connections reach into prison to smooth the way for the mob's beautiful people.

For five months before transfer to Leavenworth, Battaglia was housed in Tier E-1 of the Cook County jail. "Barn Boss" Martin Tajara, a convicted murderer awaiting execution, controlled Tier E-1 at that time. Battaglia used his wealth and prestige to curry favor with Tajara. Without the knowledge of the prison authorities, a refrigerator was brought into his cell. Gourmet food and liquor was stored in it, which Battaglia shared with Tajara. When Battaglia was transferred to Leavenworth, he left Tajara the refrigerator as a token of esteem. A few weeks later, Cook County Sheriff Joseph Woods conducted a surprise raid on Tier E-1 and confiscated the refrigerator.

Another case involving "Joe Shine" Amabile and extortion against the same contractor also resulted in the conviction of Henry Neri, the former mayor of Northlake, Illinois. Neri had demanded $70,000—$100 for each apartment under construction. Judge Hoffman, who also presided over this trial, called Neri a "sickening spectacle" as he sentenced him to 12 years in prison and a fine of $7,500. Amabile, Nick Palermo, Alderman Leo Shababy, and former alderman Joseph Drozd, were also convicted.

The conviction of Neri, Palermo, and Shababy, however, was set aside by the United States Circuit Court in an opinion written by Judge Otto Kerner, former Illinois Governor and United States Attorney. Joining with Judge Kerner in that opinion were Judge Walter Cummings and Judge Elmer Schnackenberg. They reversed Judge Hoffman on grounds that he had refused to permit questioning of jurors "about newspaper articles prejudicial to the defendant" that had appeared before the trial. They had also based the reversal on Hoffman's refusal to provide the defense lawyers with the addresses of government witnesses.

The Appeals Court freed Amabile on grounds of double jeopardy since the extortion involved the same contractor.

Before a second trial Neri, Palermo, and Shababy entered pleas of guilty in a deal for reduced sentences.

The head of the Strike Force in Chicago considered the Neri case an important demonstration of the Mafia's continued control of government contracts in some of the Chicago suburbs.

By that time it was apparent that the Chicago Strike Force meant business. James Featherstone, who had headed it for a year, was moved to Washington as a Deputy Director of the Organized Crime Division in the Justice Department. At his recommendation, Sheldon Davidson, then only 32, was appointed his successor. Davidson was already recognized as one of the real experts in the Justice Department on the "SCAM" racket—a racket where organized crime would move into a large company, use the firm's credit to run up hundreds of thousands of dollars in debts, then sell the inventory for cash and let the firm go under.

This was the modern gangster's version of nonviolent thievery. Of course, the Cosa Nostra could fortify its persuasiveness with a bit of violence from time to time, if the occasion demanded.

The Strike Force in Chicago, through the use of court-approved wiretaps, made dozens of mass moves in the field of syndicate gambling, prostitution, and narcotics. Strike Force boss Davidson was beginning to feel like a reincarnation of Elliott Ness, with a real live Chicago gangster scenario taking place around him every week.

But it was the political corruption that Davidson and his crew were seeking as they moved across the hottest Democratic political city in America. Justice had long recognized the impossibility of having the major thrust of criminal law enforcement under the Democratic-Republican combine of local political people in what was largely a bipartisan corruption. Mayor Richard Daley was apparently clean, but the same could not be said of many of those who were in some way involved with the politics of Cook County.

In *Captive City,* author Ovid Demaris had said that Chicago "is owned and operated by an invisible government." He tied together the compromises of the business community and the political deals, and maintained that the Chicago Crime Commission, under Virgil Peterson, represented one of the few forces that exposed wrongdoing and pushed for reform.

Many of the local courts were corrupt. Only the brave judges would stand up to the mob. One of those was Judge Julius Hoffman, and he was constantly being reversed by a Circuit Court that seemed to be over-influenced by major Mafia figures.

The Strike Force seemed to be making tremendous strides in

bringing Chicago under control, and President Nixon had a very practical reason for wanting to stop the political corruption by election time in 1972. He remembered what had happened in 1960, and he did not want to be counted out again by the invisible Mafia government.

The Justice Department Strike Force was just moving into high gear in the summer of 1971. In July and August, it was first revealed that the financial affairs of United States Circuit Judge Otto Kerner were under study by a federal grand jury. The investigation involved a possible "conflict of interest" in the period when Kerner had served as Governor of Illinois and had the responsibility for appointing the Illinois Harness Racing Commission.

That Commission had the responsibility for ruling on the assignment of racing days and had made a number of decisions that were highly favorable to the financial interests of Mrs. Marjorie Everett, known as the "Queen of Illinois Racing."

Kerner was one of a number of political figures who had been permitted to secretly purchase stock in various racetrack enterprises that had resulted in "windfall" profits that ran into hundreds of thousands of dollars. During that same period of time, the favorable decisions of the Kerner-controlled Illinois Harness Racing Commission had caused a phenomenal growth in Mrs. Everett's complex of racing interests.

On September 23, 1971, Representative H. R. Gross (Rep., Ia.) asked that the House Judiciary Committee initiate an investigation of Judge Kerner and of William J. Lynch, former law partner of Mayor Richard Daley, who had also owned some of the stock.

The Iowa Republican told the House that "on the basis of what is printed in the Chicago newspapers as having been admitted by Judge Kerner and Judge Lynch and other participants, it would seem to me that there should be impeachment started.

"If we are going to let this conduct pass unnoticed or without criticism then we will share in the responsibility if others later arrive at the conclusion that they can get by with it," Gross told the House.

He noted that the Chicago Strike Force appeared to be involved in an investigation aimed at the violation of federal laws, but that "the

Congress also has responsibility involving the ethical standards as to who are seated on our courts.

"I would suggest that the House Judiciary Committee immediately assign investigators to the job of seeking the facts," Gross said. "Regardless of whether the federal laws are violated, there is a vital responsibility to keep the Federal bench free from any and every hint of scandal.

"As Governor of Illinois, Otto Kerner had the control of the Illinois Harness Racing Commission and an authority that entailed a responsibility to keep himself out of such (financial) transaction," Gross said.

"If this had been unearthed before he went on the bench, it is extremely doubtful he would have been confirmed. The fact that he is presently sitting in the Appeals Court . . . does not make this spectacle any less sordid as far as I am concerned."*

Compromise of the courts had long been a goal of the organized crime figures in Illinois.

---

*From the remarks of Representative H. R. Gross in the Congressional Record of September 23, 1971, page H-8715.

13

MIAMI—MOVES AGAINST THE LANSKY MOB

"Some have seized upon two words from the dissenting opinion of Justice Holmes in the Olmstead case in 1928—the famous phrase, 'dirty business.' But they have not bothered to read the rest of the opinion. What they overlook is that Justice Holmes expressly disavowed the position that wiretapping was a violation of our Federal Bill of Rights, and, when he used the term 'dirty business' he was not describing legal wiretapping so much as he was characterizing the conduct of the federal officer who, in gathering evidence, committed a crime by tapping wires illegally in defiance of the laws of the State of Washington. . . .

"And, let us not forget that it was the same Justice Holmes who said on another occasion: 'At the present time, in this country, there is more danger that criminals will escape justice than that they will be subjected to tyranny." *New York District Attorney Frank Hogan, on July 12, 1967, before the Senate Judiciary Subcommittee on Criminal Procedures.*

GAMBLER Martin Sklaroff and two of his associates won a battle when the Fifth Circuit Court of Appeals upset their gambling conviction on the grounds that the evidence was obtained by an illegal wiretap in 1967. Justice Department lawyer William Earle, however, felt a bit more secure about using wiretaps in making a different gambling case against Sklaroff and his father, Jesse. This was in June 1969, a year after Congress had approved court-authorized wiretaps. Strike Force Director Dougald McMillan and Earle had requested the United States District Court's permission to tap four airport pay phones.

The Sklaroffs had ingeniously set up shop in the heart of bustling Miami International Airport. They had annexed these four public telephones as their office, hanging "out-of-order" signs on them to keep intruders away.

Armed with the court's authorization, FBI agents tapped the telephones for six days. In that short time the FBI had enough evidence to bring indictments against the Sklaroffs and eight of their contacts.

The FBI planted agents in the airport to keep the Sklaroffs under surveillance. One, in a Northwest Orient Airlines uniform, watched from behind the counter. Agent Tom Stickney squeezed his six-foot, two-inch frame into a refrigerator packing case so he could photograph the gamblers' activities. When a porter started to move the huge packing crate out of the main lobby, he was astounded to hear a growl from within: "Keep your cotton-pickin' hands off my box!"

An Airlines official whisked the startled employee around the corner for a scanty explanation.

By a system of signals, the agents were able to listen and record calls only when the Sklaroffs were using a phone; other calls were not listened to or recorded.

"I'm really relaxed these days," Martin Sklaroff told one of his callers. "The FBI doesn't even know where I am." That conversation was one of more than 200 which provided the substance for 23 indictments.

On July 3, 1969, the FBI conducted a nationwide bookmaking raid—the first time the new law had been used to combat organized crime. Armed with search warrants, FBI agents frisked Martin and Jesse Sklaroff in the airport on the basis of information gathered by wiretapping the previous week. They found an odd assortment of pay telephone keys, hatpins, and an electric drill. Agents believed that the drill had been used to make small holes in the airport phones, and the hatpins inserted to scramble normal operations and permit free long-distance dialing.

During the raid, Strike Force agents broke down a metal door in Philadelphia to enter an apartment where one of Sklaroff's contacts was operating. In Detroit the Strike Force discovered a previously unknown bookie joint in full operation in a quiet residential neighborhood.

Special Agent Edwin Sharp heard Martin and Jesse Sklaroff "make over two hundred calls and receive and furnish line information, discuss baseball activities about major league pitching, make and accept baseball wagers . . . layoff bets over the telephones with persons in ten major cities located outside the state of Florida."

Although the Sklaroffs' lawyers challenged the legality of the court-approved wiretaps, Judge Mehrtens ruled that the Miami Strike Force had complied with the law.

The trial of the Sklaroffs had been delayed for months while their lawyers appealed Judge Mehrtens' ruling on grounds that it was "overextending the tap" under a law that is specific in the length of time a tap can be kept on a telephone. The court did not agree.

At the trial, the prosecution had a "lay-down hand." The defense, faced with testimony of FBI agents, tapes of three hours of conversations, and pictures, could only admit that they had engaged in the acts, but didn't realize they were unlawful. McMillan, Strike Force head, said, "I feel this case has shown the real value and importance of wiretaps. The criminal element knows this is a critical area in which we hope to move against them."

The best endorsement for the court-approved wiretapping was the complaint of Marty Sklaroff. Just before the jury returned a verdict of guilty, he told Jim Savage of the *Miami Herald:* "You can't work without a telephone . . . I'm gonna have to find another business. The federal wiretaps are going to put us all out of business."

For 17 years Sklaroff had been shuffling around in the bookie business, getting a little bigger each year until he had taken over much of the operation headed by Gil Beckley, "King of the layoff bettors." He had never spent a night in jail in his life—he had successfully challenged every conviction. Now, with the legalized wiretapping, Sklaroff accepted jail as inevitable. "I wouldn't mind going to jail so much if they would let me have a couple of telephones in my cell," he told Savage. "You know, so I'd have something to do."

It was in Miami that the Justice Department demonstrated the value of court-approved wiretapping against the big narcotics wholesaling rings.

In June 1970, the Justice Department made coordinated raids in ten different cities on one Saturday night; by Monday morning they were able to announce the arrest of 139 persons. The simultaneous raids, which climaxed a six-months' investigation, resulted in the seizure of about 100 pounds of cocaine and heroin, $21,446 in cash, and automobiles and firearms.

Telephones were tapped in Miami, Chicago, and New York, and the Director of the Bureau of Narcotics and Dangerous Drugs, John Ingersoll, said that it was this technique that enabled the agents to trace the distribution of narcotics to identifiable individuals. The Bureau felt that conventional means of investigation would involve the agents in danger. The defendants, highly conscious of being under surveillance, could be caught only by the interception of their phone conversations.

Meyer Lansky and the intricate pattern of his financial maneuvering were of special interest to Will Wilson, head of the Criminal Division of the Department of Justice. Wilson was fascinated by Lansky's evolution from a brutal gun-toting mobster of the New York "Bug and Meyer mob" to the man Hank Messick described as "chairman of the national board of the crime syndicate."

To the *Wall Street Journal* and *Life* magazine, Lansky was the financial genius of the underworld. To his neighbors in Miami Beach, he was "a perfect gentlemen," an unobtrusive man whose main pleasure was walking his dog along the beach front. He was not, however, without protection. For more than ten years FBI agents had been tailing him and he had accepted them as bodyguards. He had been known to slow down when driving to allow the FBI car to catch up.

The Miami Strike Force had primary jurisdiction over Lansky because his home was in Florida. Any action would have to be initiated by a federal grand jury in Miami, but it was no secret that the Lansky group controlled four major casinos in Las Vegas, Nevada. His contacts—Carlos Marcello in New Orleans, and New Jersey's Gerardo Catena—shared "skimming" profits from the Las Vegas ventures. Two of the Lansky groups participated in Bobby Baker's activities in the Serv-U Vending Corporation.

In the spring and summer of 1971, Senator McClellan's Permanent Investigating Subcommittee started to zero in on some of Lansky's associates in the fencing of stolen securities. Strike Forces in New York, New Jersey, New Orleans, and Los Angeles were also running down information on Lansky's far-flung operations.

In addition, two indictments were returned against Lansky in mid-March of 1971. One was a contempt of court charge because he failed to return from Israel to appear before a federal grand jury in Miami, although a subpoena had been served through the U.S. Embassy in Israel.

Another indictment officially charged Lansky, four other persons, and the Nevada Corporation with conspiring "to engage in illegal gambling activity and to conceal and distribute proceeds from the Flamingo Hotel" in Las Vegas. It further charged that Lansky conspired "to use interstate and foreign commerce to carry on illegal gambling activity and to conceal and distribute the unlawful proceeds of that activity."

It was the first time that Lansky had been officially charged with participating in the income from the Flamingo, or having any role in the distribution of the "skim" from any of the Las Vegas casinos.

Samuel Cohen and Morris Lansburgh and others applied for Nevada gambling licenses and concealed the interest of Lansky and some of his associates in the hotel. It was alleged that all were involved in a great conspiracy to hide the real income from Nevada and U.S. Treasury officials, and to skim about $200,000 annually.

The Justice Department contended that Lansky was a key figure in the skim, and that his associates traveled between Florida, Nevada, Switzerland, and other points to distribute the so-called skim money and carry out various unlawful activities.

The indictment charged that Lansky had created the conspiracy to "cause payments totalling $200,000 to be made from the proceeds of the Flamingo operation . . . to Meyer Lansky."

Jerry Gordon, a corporate executive of Flamingo, was charged with having filed false tax returns for 1966 and 1967. Large amounts of cash from the Flamingo were taken to the New York office where they were turned over to certain unnamed persons. More large amounts of skim were channeled through the account of a Swiss bank in Miami, according to the indictment.

Some of the FBI wiretaps on this case brought out the unexpected information that Ed Levinson and others at the Fremont casino in Las Vegas had access to some top-level FBI reports. Just how this was managed was never made clear, but a number of political and legal channels were suspect. It had to be accepted as a fact of life that even the FBI might have its traitors near the top, and some of them might even rationalize that they were getting back as much as they gave in terms of Mafia intelligence information.

It was easy to believe that the Lansky group could have infiltrated the top level of the FBI, for there had been no doubt that Teamsters boss James Hoffa had access to many reports through a complex system of counterintelligence. These legal and political "leaks" from the FBI to the Teamsters was one reason for establishing the so-called "Hoffa unit" in the Organized Crime section in 1961. It was certainly the reason that only a few in the FBI were informed of the identity of Baton Rouge Teamster boss Edward Grady Partin, key witness against Hoffa in the jury-tampering trial, before he walked into the courtroom to testify. Those who did know Partin's identity turned down a number of inquiries from within the FBI which tried to uncover more than Partin's code name, "Andy."

The political contributions that the wealthy Las Vegas casino operators and their allies dispensed made it obvious that any complaints they had would fall on sympathetic ears. Then Governor Grant Sawyer of Nevada accused the FBI and the Internal Revenue Service of "Gestapo-like tactics" in the wiretapping network at several Las Vegas casinos. In Nevada, gambling was legal, and Governor Sawyer believed that the gambling community had a right to privacy in their business. He failed to understand that the government had an obligation to see that *all* of the casinos' income—legal, as well as illegal—was reported on federal tax returns even if the Governor wasn't concerned about his state getting its fair share.

Wiretaps picked up a conversation at the Fremont in which Ed Levinson discussed the amounts that should be contributed to Nevada public figures. A *Reader's Digest* article listed the Levinson contributions from $1,000 to Senator Alan Bible and $500 to Representative Walter Baring, down to the $200- and $300-figures allocated to a County Commissioner and a candidate for Justice of the Peace.

Writer William Schulz, in preparing the *Reader's Digest* story, asked Howard Cannon, Democratic Senator from Nevada, if he had received any political contributions from the casinos. Cannon said he could not remember any specific contribution from Levinson, that his records had been destroyed, and that his campaign manager was dead. However, he volunteered that he would have been disappointed if he had not received some political funds from the Fremont group.

Did Cannon recall doing anything for any of the casino operators in return for contributions? Cannon said he could not remember a thing—"unless you would count going to see the President about the Gestapo tactics being used by the FBI and Internal Revenue agents." Cannon said that he had talked to President Johnson because of his deep concern about such police-state tactics being used against the Las Vegas casinos. Only a short time after that, President Johnson issued orders to stop all wiretapping in organized crime cases and to limit the FBI's eavesdropping and wiretapping only to cases involving the national security of the United States.

Levinson's complaint had caused the President to take steps which assured that eavesdropping and wiretapping would no longer be used to catch the legal gamblers in Las Vegas—or illegal gamblers such as Meyer Lansky in Florida, with his complicated schemes for taking about $12 million a year in "skim" from Las Vegas.

President Johnson very strongly believed in the right of public officials to acquire additional income from side businesses. He had never criticized Bobby Baker or any House or Senate colleagues for engaging in business that more sensitive people might have found to be "conflicts of interest."

In early 1971, the Strike Force in Miami, Florida, was following up the many leads the Kefauver Committee had exposed 20 years earlier. In October of 1950, Lansky had gone before the Kefauver Committee to explain his financial dealings with Frank Costello, Lucky Luciano, Joe Adonis, Frank Erickson, Jimmy (Blue Eyes) Alo, Charles and Rocco Fischetti, Tony Accardo, Jack Dragna, John Roselli, Phil Kastel, Tony Gizzo, Jimmy King, Michael (Trigger Mike) Coppola, Bugsy Siegel, Longie Zwillman, James Lynch, Joseph Stacher, Gerardo (Jerry) Catena, and Willie and Salvatore Moretti—all big names in the underworld.

Dan Sullivan, Director of the Miami Crime Commission, and Virgil Peterson, Operating Director of the Chicago Crime Commission, had identified Lansky as having dealings with all of those syndicate figures.

The McClellan Permanent Investigating Subcommittee found Lansky's tracks all around the Mafia effort to clean up "dirty money" by routing it through Swiss bank accounts and back to the United States for investment in some of the major conglomerates.

Lansky was instrumental in working out a number of complicated maneuvers which involved posting stolen stocks as security for bank loans—more than $100 million worth, according to the Subcommittee, were stolen from the mails. Syndicate members, using tactics developed by Lansky, would manage to get these stocks into the investment portfolios of large insurance companies where it would be unlikely they would be noticed for some time.

Meyer Lansky's financial relationship with the Flamingo Hotel and Ed Levinson's activities at the Fremont had proved such an embarrassment to Supreme Court Justice William O. Douglas that he resigned in

1970 as president of the tax-exempt Parvin Foundation. He had drawn more than $100,000 at the rate of $12,000 a year and had been criticized in Congress for accepting income from the Flamingo, with its violence-torn history and its racket-laden present, and the Fremont, involved in the skim of millions.

But the skim of millions from the earnings of the Flamingo and the Fremont had been established to the satisfaction of the FBI agents, who listened in on Levinson's telephone, and to the satisfaction of the Internal Revenue agents who had put the case together.

The management of those casinos stood accused of cheating the government of millions of dollars in taxes. It was not good public policy for Justice Douglas to be using money from a gambling joint, even if it were legal earnings, to finance his favorite charities and social theories in the education of foreign students.

Justice Douglas defended his role as president of the Parvin Foundation on these grounds:

It was an outside interest not prohibited by law.

No one had proved that the actual money was tainted by illegal activities at the Flamingo and Fremont.

No one had proved that Albert Parvin was other than an interior decorator and businessman who had made a great deal of money and wanted to benefit mankind.

No one had proved that Parvin was involved in the operation of the Fremont with Edward Levinson and Edward Torres.

Minority Leader Gerald Ford, Representatives Joseph Waggoner, Louis Wyman and H. R. Gross, sought impeachment of Justice Douglas on grounds that his conduct reflected on the United States Supreme Court. Even if his conduct was legal, they felt that the ethics were questionable and his actions did not present a proper example to the young people of America.

Although Ford and others were confident they could get an impeachment of Justice Douglas through the House, they first had to get around the Judiciary Committee, whose chairman, Emanuel Celler, was a long-time personal friend of Douglas. They tried to establish a special committee to investigate the Douglas matter, but Celler fought it.

Impeachment is the only means by which a Supreme Court Justice can be removed. Justice Douglas had it made so long as Manny Celler headed the House Judiciary Committee, the only unit empowered to initiate impeachment proceedings.

The Justice Department was powerless to tackle this problem head on. No tough investigations could be expected because of Celler's own lax attitude on Congressional as well as Judicial ethics.

After 40 years in Washington, Celler still continued to draw income from his New York law firm by maintaining his widely known "two-door policy." Celler's name appeared on only one of the firm's two doors, and clients with business before federal agencies were supposed to enter by the other door to avoid any conflict of interest or suggestion that they might be trying to buy his prestige as Chairman of the House Judiciary Committee.

Celler has continued his law partnership with Milton Weisman, identified in the trial of Circuit Court Judge Martin Manton as the man who received large amounts of cash to get favorable opinions from Judge Manton. Weisman was never called as a witness in the trial or in any House or Senate hearing.

Against that background it is easy to understand how Chairman Celler would pass off as "guilt by association" the assumption that Parvin was a front man for Lansky, Levinson, and other mobsters. Of course, it was also necessary to disregard evidence that Parvin did not deal an arm's length away from the gambling casinos. Two of his employees, Levinson and Torres, gave him nightly reports on the operations of the casinos and hotels. *Life* magazine identified Levinson as one of several who delivered cash from Las Vegas to Meyer Lansky in Florida for transmission to Swiss bank accounts.

Albert Parvin, good friend of Justice Douglas, still under oath before the Securities and Exchange Commission, admitted he did not remove Torres, under income-tax indictment, from the management of the Fremont even though he had fired Levinson when he was indicted on the same charges. Torres, he explained, was a very efficient manager.

That testimony cast doubt on the Celler thesis that Parvin was "just another businessman," and that the Douglas-Parvin relationship was quite innocent.

The tolerant attitude toward Justice Douglas and other federal judges could be expected so long as Chairman Emanuel Celler remained as Chairman of the House Judiciary Committee, or until the House was willing to establish a special committee to conduct an investigation of Justice Douglas.

On March 1, 1969, the Miami Strike Force and other federal and state agencies had a welcoming committee at Miami International Airport to greet a group of Kansas City mobsters who were arriving in the city. The lawmen greeted their "guests" with subpoenas to go before the federal grand jury in Miami.

Although that airport confrontation was not the most productive from the standpoint of evidence, it did serve notice that mobsters could no longer consider Miami "free territory," as they had in earlier years. It was a most significant turning point in Florida history—perhaps the first time since Al Capone started wintering in Florida in the 1920s that there had been such a direct show of hostility to the Mafia and the mob money. If they wanted to enjoy the Florida sunshine, those mobsters would have to be prepared to go before the federal grand jury and let a little light shine in on what had been transpiring in the underworld.

In an earlier era, the mobsters could have relied on just taking the Fifth Amendment and walking out free. Under the new federal legislation, the Justice Department was able to grant the mobster immunity from prosecution if he would talk about his colleagues in crime. If he refused, they could cite him for contempt of court.

Doug McMillan pointed with pride to the conviction of Joseph Fischetti, brother of Rocco Fischetti and a friend of singer Frank Sinatra, on a charge of violating the Taft-Hartley labor law. Fischetti had arranged with the secretary-treasurer of a Teamsters local to cancel a labor-management contract between the owner of a construction company and a local union building trades group. Evidence indicated that Fischetti and the union official were paid more than $15,000 to have the contract stolen from the building trades group and destroyed.

There were many who felt, however, that their sentence left

something to be desired. The men received a $4,000 fine, six months in jail, and a year's probation. In a caustic editorial, the *Miami Herald* commented:

"As we see it, when a federal task force goes after what it considers a case of organized crime, the punishment should fit it when a conviction is gained. The federal agents who spent six months on this case must feel cheated. The taxpayers certainly should feel that way."

The Strike Force used electronic surveillance in connection with the arrest and jailing in Miami of Gary Bowdach, a loan shark from the New York area. Bowdach had served a sentence for manslaughter in New York in connection with the shooting of a 17-year-old girl. When he moved into Florida, he was working at his specialty—the loan-shark racket; but it was the guns which the arresting officers found in his car and his housetrailer that finally put him in prison.

Hershie Laff, an old-time bookmaker, had been operating with a low profile until the Miami Strike Force used court-approved wiretapping to turn the spotlight on his activities. Others turned up off the same wiretap were Nick Nardonne, identified with a La Cosa Nostra family in New Jersey, and Fred Romash and Murray Yunes, both Miami gambling figures. The use of court-approved wiretaps resulted in the indictment of one of the biggest gambling-line figures in the Los Angeles area.

Carl Fiorito was an important man in the Chicago narcotics traffic until the Miami Strike Force moved against him. He was charged with making a "false statement" to a government agency in connection with a government loan in Florida. It was believed that Fiorito was responsible for the deaths of two undercover agents in the Chicago area. Therefore, the minute that the "false statement" charge was filed, he was arrested at his home. Arresting officers found and seized an arsenal of 23 guns in Fiorito's apartment. With such a large stock of guns, the best charge to press was illegal possession of firearms.

On June 21, 1971, Alfred Felice, a member of the Bruno family from Philadelphia, was charged with failure to file federal tax returns. Among the crowd of witnesses called (120 of them) were celebrities Sammy Davis, Jr., and Dean Martin. However, at the last minute Felice entered a plea of guilty and was sentenced to two years in federal prison.

In that same week the Strike Force also hit it big with the conviction on stolen securities cases of five Cosa Nostra figures from other areas. They included David Iacovetti, a member of the Carlo Gambino family operating out of Connecticut, New York, and Miami; Anthony DeRose, who had been identified as a "button man" (gangland killer) in the Chicago area; William Dentamaro, of the Chicago Cosa Nostra; Ilario Zannino, an underboss in the Patriarca family who was also known as Larry Baione; and Philip Waggengeim, a close associate of Zannino and the Patriarca family of Boston.

Another stolen-securities ring was broken up with the arrests of a number of Cosa Nostra figures from New York City and New England.

Two mobsters indicted through the work of the Miami Strike Force skipped the country. Everisto Garcia Vidal, a gambling man in the Miami area, jumped $100,000 bail and reportedly left for Nicaragua and Costa Rica. Al Mones, known in Miami and elsewhere as "king of the handicappers," was indicted on gambling charges arising out of an earlier Internal Revenue Service investigation. He took off for Israel.

14

CALIFORNIA AND LAS VEGAS

"Our state has become the favorite investment area of the veiled finance committee of organized crime ... I can tell you that I am worried [about] hidden interests on state licenses; ... the intrusion of criminal cartelists into our sensitive world of finance; ... the layoff of huge sports bets into the Los Angeles area; ... loan-sharking and the reported moves of remnants of the old Mickey Cohen mob to control it, together with some new tough boys ... the conspiracy of silence that so often meets enforcement agencies, grand juries, and our courts when investigations are undertaken." *California Attorney General Thomas C. Lynch, on announcing the formation of a special organized crime unit within the California Department of Justice.*

MOB money and Teamsters money are behind so much of both the economic and political structures of Las Vegas that it is difficult to know if even the federal courts can be trusted. More than $50 million from the Teamsters pension funds financed everything from Caesar's Palace to the towering Landmark Hotel.

In California, more Teamsters millions funded new building projects, including the $11 million Beverly Ridge development which involved highly suspicious financial arrangements. This was only one of dozens of projects backed by Teamsters funds, investments which by the summer of 1971 were approaching the billion-dollar mark.

But the resources behind some other Las Vegas hotels and gambling casinos were more secretive. There was a well-founded suspicion that the money invested in these enterprises was "skim" money which had been "cleansed" by running it through a Swiss bank and a couple of corporations. The truth could not definitely be known until the Justice Department was able to have access to the names of those who held numbered and anonymous Swiss bank accounts. In the summer of 1971, the first tentative agreements were reached and it seemed that the whole filthy business might break open and reveal that the investments were a device for hiding the real owners and for cheating the United States Treasury.

The Los Angeles Strike Force under Alfred King had done much work on the Lansky indictments returned in March 1971, but it was finally decided (partly for the convenience of the witnesses) to return the indictments in Florida. According to the indictment, Albert Parvin, Justice Douglas' friend and benefactor, was believed by the Internal Revenue Service, the FBI, and Strike Force lawyers Mike DeFeo and Robert Thaller to be a front for the Lansky group. It was alleged that Lansky had arranged to be given $200,000 as a "finder's fee," although actually the indictment said that the payment was part of the Hotel Flamingo conspiracy involving the Albert Parvin Foundation.

Over the period of time during which Lansky arranged to receive installments on the $200,000 fee, Justice Douglas was the president of the Parvin Foundation. In those eight years he received more than $100,000 in salary. Conservative Republicans, who disliked the permissiveness in Douglas' Supreme Court opinions dealing with law enforcement, cried "Impeach him!" The arrangement looked too much like an indirect payoff to the High Court Justice as a reward for opinions that coincided with the mob's best interests.

Even before the indictments against Lansky in March 1971, Strike Force personnel had concluded that a special study should be made of the whole operation of the Parvin Foundation, the Parvin-Dohrmann investments in the Fremont, the Aladdin, and the Stardust, and the channeling of money through Swiss banks. They were intrigued by the mystery that surrounded so much of the Parvin-Dohrmann operation, and the manner in which multimillion-dollar moves were being made with new cash from international sources.

A special group was formed to operate in Florida, California, New York, and Washington, with an emphasis on breaking through all these complex financial matters. Called the "financial group," or "Strike Force 18," it had Robert Campbell, a 32-year-old tax-law specialist, as its head.

Campbell, a 1964 Harvard Law School graduate, had spent two years in the Army as legal advisor to a financial officer. Two years in the Tax Division of the Justice Department, followed by two years of trial work on the investigation of big-number operators, not only qualified him, but whetted his appetite for the task of untangling Meyer Lansky's whole complex financial network.

This was not, however, a "Lansky squad" in the sense of Robert Kennedy's "Hoffa squad." The international combination of Swiss bank accounts and U.S. investments had to involve a broader area than any one man covered. Lansky was just one of the many successful international money manipulators.

Papers from dozens of government agencies on Lansky alone filled four filing cabinets. They would be enough to occupy Campbell, his team of four attorneys, and as many FBI agents as they asked for. Los Angeles Strike Force boss Alfred King willingly gave up the major part of the Lansky probe and much of the Las Vegas "skimming" investigation to Strike Force 18.

House Speaker John W. McCormack's top aide, Martin Sweig, had already been indicted and convicted as an intervenor in a Parvin-Dohrmann stock case at the Securities and Exchange Commission.

Sweig was involved in the efforts of Nathan Voloshen, a friend of Speaker McCormack, to lift a trading ban on Parvin-Dohrmann stock. The ban was imposed on May 6 because of highly unusual trading patterns. Voloshen arranged a meeting with SEC Chairman Hamer Budge "through Sweig." Voloshen had been retained by Parvin-Dohrmann for $50,000. Although Voloshen pleaded guilty and Sweig was convicted by a jury, very little actual information came out.

Voloshen and Sweig were being investigated for other influence-peddling. They had intervened with the Labor Department on behalf of Jack McCarthy, a New York labor official and racketeer convicted in 1969 of filing false financial reports with the Department of Labor. This was only one of many investigations under way at that time on the activities of the two men.

Jack Dragna, a top Mafia figure in the days of the Kefauver hearings, died in 1957, but a whole new crop of underworld leaders was active. Louis Dragna, a nephew of Jack Dragna, was seeking to take the place of his much-feared uncle in lower California.

John Roselli, former Illinois labor-racket figure of the Brown-Bioff case, had been convicted in a card-cheating case at the Friar's Club. He had been introduced into the club in 1963. In short order, he took part in the scheme where one operator watched players' cards through a peephole and then used electronic devices to signal accomplices who were in the game. Roselli was now in prison, and the Los Angeles Strike Force was pressing deportation action to send him back to his native Italy.

One of the most significant cases taken over by the San Francisco Strike Force was the indictment of James Fratianno in August 1970. A decade earlier, Fratianno had been identified as one of the top ten individuals in organized crime on the West Coast. He had not limited his activities since. The indictment contended that Fratianno had engaged in "the express and implicit use of threats of violence and other criminal means" against Carl Held, former Sacramento bar owner, in an attempt to collect repayment of a $15,000 loan.

The Strike Force in San Francisco, originally operating as a unit of the Los Angeles Strike Force and now headed by James E. Ritchie, got its first major indictment only about four months after it was formally organized. And it was a big one.

On March 20, 1971, the federal grand jury indicted San Francisco Mayor Joseph Alioto, who was at that very moment in the White House attending a Mayor's Conference. President Nixon was aware of the investigation, but it was not certain whether he knew that Mayor Alioto might be indicted right then. Indicted with Alioto were John O'Connell, the former Attorney General of the State of Washington; George Faler, who served as a Special Assistant Attorney General for about six years, and former Assistant Attorney General John McCutcheon.

The nine-count indictment charged conspiracy, interstate travel to promote bribery, and two counts of mail fraud in connection with the settlement of a case involving price-fixing by electric equipment manufacturers. It was charged that Alioto had entered into a secret agreement to act as lawyer for the Washington State Group of electric utilities. He was to represent them in actions against the manufacturers of electrical and utilities equipment. His fee would be 15 percent of the sums recovered "but not exceeding one million dollars" and he would share the money with Attorney General O'Connell and with Faler.

Under this secret agreement, Alioto paid $50,000 to Faler and over $100,000 to O'Connell. It was alleged that under the agreement Alioto had an obligation to complete the Washington State Group's antitrust cases without payment of additional fees. However, as part of the conspiracy, Alioto, O'Connell, and Faler agreed that O'Connell "would unlawfully remove the fee ceiling" of $1 million.

The ceiling was removed by O'Connell in mid-1965, at about the time the antitrust cases against Westinghouse and General Electric were settled, and in a secret arrangement unknown to the State and the Group, Alioto then agreed to share 50 percent of his fees with O'Connell and Faler. Eventually he paid them $751,810, the indictment charged.

According to the charge, Alioto's fees totaled $2.3 million despite the fact that in a memo, Faler wrote "every expenditure or commitment for more than $100 should be made only upon the majority consent of the steering committee." It was alleged that Alioto paid O'Connell

$429,000 and Faler $222,000 in the 1965 to 1967 period, and that O'Connell passed on $39,000 of his money to John McCutcheon, County Prosecutor in O'Connell's home area of Tacoma, Washington.

Alioto answered the charges with the cry of "politics," saying that the Republican Administration wanted to knock him out of contention for the California governorship.

In February 1971, Strike Force boss Ritchie demonstrated how two court-approved wiretaps could yield a $2 million haul of heroin. Fourteen arrests were made as a result of those two taps, which provided the Strike Force and the Bureau of Narcotics and Dangerous Drugs with the information needed to trace the activities of the narcotics ring in the United States and in Mexico.

One of the taps intercepted a telephone call placed by Vernon Baca to the residence of Umberto Jose Chavez, in Fremont, California. The other was a follow tap a few days later, when Chavez placed a return call to Mexico. Federal charges of conspiracy to import and distribute heroin were filed several days later against Chavez, Baca, and eleven others in connection with the seizure of $2 million in heroin.

On November 5, 1970, fourteen people were indicted by a federal grand jury in Los Angeles in a massive Strike Force assault on the importation and distribution of pornographic materials. United States Attorney Robert L. Meyer said the indictment embraced an annual distribution of more than six million pieces of hard-core pornographic material, and was the result of a coordinated investigation lasting more than six months. The investigation was continuing, and more indictments could be expected.

Among the indictments were counts of mailing unsolicited obscene advertising, including to juveniles; mailing obscene literature to juveniles; and of transporting obscene films from Los Angeles to St. Paul. One man and a corporation were charged with contempt for disregarding a court order forbidding them to mail advertising circulars of an erotically arousing and sexually provocative nature. Two were charged with importing more than 100 cases of obscene magazines from Europe, in violation of U.S. laws.

Electronic surveillance with court approval set the stage for a

26-city, 11-state sweep, the focal point of which was Caesar's Palace in Las Vegas, a gambling venture financed with an $11 million loan from the pension funds of the Teamsters Union. Also seized was $1,792,000 along with an additional $200,000 in IOU's taken in the New York office of Caesar's Palace and a check for $133,000 written by a New York brokerage house to an individual. Buffalo raids yielded $10,000 in IOU's and about $117,500 worth of Las Vegas stocks and bonds.

But Attorney General John Mitchell declared that the large amount of cash seized in the raid should not minimize the great importance of the records the government found. "This information will enable us to trace further the illegal gambling activity which drains millions of dollars out of the economy every year.

"Conviction of the people who were the targets of today's raids would severely damage the financial apparatus which bankrolls organized crime," Mitchell said at the time. Numerous big-time gamblers were arrested in the raid. FBI Director J. Edgar Hoover singled out several "national gambling figures" taken into custody, among them Elliott Paul Price and Frank (Lefty) Rosenthal, of Las Vegas; Jerome Zarowitz and Gerald Hay Kilgore, of Los Angeles; Billy Cecil Doolittle of Atlanta; Joseph Lombardo, of Buffalo; and Max Abramson, of Omaha.

Another device for Mafia figures to buy into lucrative Las Vegas gambling houses was revealed in February 1971. They used a large holding company, the Emprise Corporation, as a front, giving loans to gambling houses through the corporation and receiving controlling share of stock in return. A federal grand jury in Los Angeles returned a ten-count indictment charging three mid-western men high in organized crime, a former Michigan municipal Judge, two other individuals, and a corporation, with violating federal and state laws by concealing their ownership in the Frontier Hotel gambling casino in Las Vegas.

It was contended by the government that Anthony Zerilli, president of Hazel Park Racing Association and identified as a *"capodecino"* in the Detroit Mafia, and Michael Polizzi, president of a die-casting firm and also identified with the Detroit organized crime syndicate, had conspired with others to buy a secret interest in the Frontier casino. They had bought the interest through the Emprise Corporation.

Emprise dabbled in holdings in many racetracks, including Zerilli's Hazel Park. Through its subsidiary, Sportservice, Inc., it operated the concessions at tracks and sports stadiums throughout the country.

The indictment charged that when Zerilli and Polizzi were turned down by the Nevada Gaming Commission, they arranged to purchase the stock for control through "a front" by loans from Emprise.

Anthony Giardano, one of the leading organized crime figures in St. Louis, had also used Emprise loans to buy an interest in the Frontier. Giardano maintained that his occupation was that of a member of the board of directors of Banana Distributing Company of St. Louis; but according to articles in *Life* magazine by Denny Walsh, an investigative reporter from St. Louis, Giardano was the leading La Cosa Nostra figure in that city.

When Zerilli and Polizzi sought and were denied a gaming license by the Nevada Gaming Control Board, according to the indictment, they arranged for Jack Shapiro, Arthur Rooks, the former Judge, and Alex Kachinko to become the licensed investors in Vegas Frontier. These individuals secretly acted as nominees for the benefit of Zerilli, Polizzi, and other unknown associates, with Jack Shapiro becoming the managing director of the Frontier Hotel, the indictment charged. It is alleged that Zerilli, Polizzi, and Attorney James Bellanca arranged for Emprise Corporation to make fictitious loans to Rooks and Kachinko for their investment, documenting them in a manner to avoid detection of their true nature. It was also alleged that Emprise Corporation would acquire a hidden interest in the Frontier Hotel by furnishing funds to Philip M. Troy and he would then purchase shares as a secret nominee in Vegas Frontier, Inc.

In July 1971, the federal grand jury in Los Angeles ended a long investigation of the tangled financial affairs of the Beverly Ridge Estates Corporation and the $11 million that group had obtained from the Teamsters Central States Southeast and Southwest Area Pension Fund. The grand jury charged that some of that money was obtained by false pretenses by the promoters of the residential subdivision and golf course in the Santa Monica Mountains.

The project collapsed, and there was a foreclosure and bankruptcy proceedings and a $28 million fraud suit by the trustees of the pension fund. Those indicted on July 3, 1971, were Roy Gene Lewis, 41-year-old former Los Angeles City Building and Safety Commissioner, and Leonard L. Bursten, 41; both were charged with fraudulently obtaining $15,000 in development funds borrowed from the Teamsters Union pension fund. Bursten, manager of the Beverly Ridge Estates, was indicted on another count of fraudulently obtaining $48,000 of the borrowed funds and for alleged failure to include $26,000 of this amount on his 1968 federal income-tax return.

Lewis was charged with perjury on another indictment returned by the Los Angeles grand jury in connection with his denial that he received $25,000 from a corporation associated with the Beverly Ridge project and a $250,000 "finder's fee" paid in connection with another pension-fund loan. Bursten, an expediter, was regarded as a close friend of James R. Hoffa, the former Teamsters president, who for years had been the control man in the multimillion-dollar pension fund.

Bursten had been involved in another development financed through the Teamsters Union pension funds, Honeymoon Isle, in Tampa, Florida. That project also went sour. Bursten was convicted in 1970 in Miami for evading $93,093.40 in federal taxes by creating a "fictitious" stock loss of $140,000.

Lewis, an appointee of Los Angeles Mayor Sam Yorty, was alleged to have lied about his knowledge of a $250,000 finder's fee paid by Beverly Hillcrest Hotel for obtaining a $3.5 million loan from the Teamsters pension fund. Lewis testified he received $50,000 of the fee, but that the remaining $200,000 was to go to Pacific American Investments, Ltd., in Hong Kong. It was claimed that he perjured himself in denying knowledge that the $200,000 was to be returned by Bursten to the United States.

The Los Angeles Strike Force under Al King could have spent most of its time examining the Teamsters involvement with organized crime figures through the investments of more millions in California and Las Vegas gambling joints. After all, it doesn't take much imagination to see the possibility for fast dealing in the handling of about $800 million in Teamsters pension money. All that it is necessary to do is take a look at the track record of some of the characters around the pension funds and on past performance to note the large amount of under-the-table cash that had passed.

15

NEW YORK — FROM COSTELLO TO COLOMBO

"There comes a time when a spade should be called a spade, and there also comes a time when a phony war should be called a phony war. That time has been reached in Lyndon Johnson's much-touted and loudly-heralded 'war on crime.' The sweeping—and they are sweeping—regulations just put out by Attorney General Ramsey Clark restricting the use of wiretaps and electronic listening devices are the last straw. The Attorney General surely would not have sounded this call for retreat without the approval of the President. So one is driven to the conclusion that the war on crime is a phony war, and that all of the President's high-flown speeches, not to mention the Attorney General's rhetorical contributions, have been nothing more than wordy exercises designed to conceal the fact that this Administration's heart is not in its so-called war." *Editorial, July 12, 1967, in the Washington* Star.

THE barrage of criticism that hit the Johnson Administration for the rapidly rising crime rate resulted in the establishment of the first Strike Force in Buffalo, New York, in November of 1966. Ramsey Clark hoped to allay the censure of both Democrats and Republicans, and prove that conviction could be won without resorting to wiretapping which he had already condemned as a questionable infringement on the rights of citizens to communicate and a law-enforcement tool of questionable value. The President had ordered the FBI to shut down all the eavesdropping and wiretapping in Las Vegas, and he was caught with the necessity of making the best of it even if he had been opposed.

Robert Peloquin headed the first Strike Force; but before it had completed its initial assignment it had been taken over by Thomas Kennelly, who had learned something of the technique of that approach from the work with the Hoffa squad and Walter Sheridan.

While Peloquin and Kennelly did not accept the Attorney General's thesis that wiretapping was not worth the trouble, they did tend to agree that better cases could be made if the FBI cooperated just a little more with other agencies of the federal government. Kennelly's views had been solidified by the accomplishments of the Hoffa squad under Attorney General Robert F. Kennedy when there had been reliance on the FBI on routine operations such as the surveillances in the Nashville and Chattanooga areas.

The Strike Force concept was on trial in Buffalo, and was being forced to move without benefit of wiretapping. It was fortunate to make a major case without the necessity of a wiretap, with the cooperation of an informant.

Pascal Calabrese, 28, a professional thief who had been convicted of robbing the Buffalo City Treasurer's office, decided to talk to try to reduce his five-year prison term. He told police and the Strike Force officials of his role in the planning of a robbery of Mrs. Walker McCune, of Rancho Santa Fe in California, and Phoenix, Arizona.

He related that Mafia leaders Frederico G. Randaccio and Pasquale Natarelli had hired him to take part in the theft of $500,000 worth of Mrs. McCune's jewelry. True, Calabrese was a convicted thief in another case, but he was well corroborated on the facts of the McCune conspiracy.

When Randaccio and Natarelli were found guilty, along with Charles Coci Singer (Bobby Milano), Louis Sorgi, and Stephen Cino, Ramsey Clark's contention that convictions could be obtained without wiretapping was proved. The wiretapping advocates had never argued that convictions were not possible with well-corroborated inside informants. However, they had also contended that with witnesses such as a convicted thief, it was essential to have all the corroboration to demonstrate that he was not making up a yarn just to receive consideration for clemency.

By the time the verdict was in on the Randaccio-Natarelli conviction, the Strike Force effort in Buffalo had resulted in indictment of 15 people on conspiracy to rob banks in Buffalo and Weirton, West Virginia, and interstate use of the telephone for gambling, and passing forged money orders.

Sam Pieri, a high-ranking member of the Stefano Maggadino family in Buffalo, was released from prison in May 1963, after serving a nine-year term on a narcotics charge. By 1970, the La Cosa Nostra underboss was again on trial on a charge involving $300,000 in stolen jewelry. Juror Paulette C. Davis became aware that Pieri was winking and blowing kisses to her in the jury box. Later, in the courthouse corridor, Pieri sidled up to her near a candy stand, slipped a $100 bill into her purse and whispered: "There is more where that comes from." There were also more FBI agents in the corridor than Pieri realized.

When Mrs. Davis notified United States Attorney H. Kenneth Schroeder the next day there was plenty of corroboration for her story. The judge immediately declared a mistrial on the jewelry theft conspiracy, and Pieri was charged with bribery and obstruction of justice. With a corridor filled with FBI agents to support the juror's story, Pieri was convicted and sentenced to five more years in the penitentiary.

The fortuitous circumstances of a convicted robber informing on two Cosa Nostra members and the blundering arrogance of Sam Pieri trying to fix a juror in a corridor loaded with witnesses did not invalidate the importance of the proper use of court-approved wiretapping and eavesdropping testimony.

Later, when Strike Force head Tom Kennelly was promoted and returned to Washington, James R. Richards was put in charge of the Buffalo office and Attorney General John Mitchell removed the bars to use of court-approved wiretapping. By this time the wiretapping was being used also by the Brooklyn and New York City Strike Forces headed by Denis E. Dillon and Daniel P. Hollman in the area of New York City where New York City District Attorney Frank Hogan's office had made such an excellent record.

Thanks to the aggressive action by Hogan's office, Hollman found the New York Police Department better than Newark. Because wiretapping had been legal in New York State until the Supreme Court decision in the Benanti case in 1957, Hogan's office was alert to the possibilities of police corruption and policemen were aware of and made wary by the mere knowledge that they might be overheard and that such evidence might be used against them.

Before he left office as United States Attorney, Robert Morgenthau named the "Big Six" in the La Cosa Nostra in the New York and New Jersey area as Joseph Anthony Colombo, Sr., of Brooklyn; Frank LaBruzzo, of Queens; Carlo Gambino, of Brooklyn; Gerardo (Jerry) Catena, of South Orange, New Jersey; Thomas (Three Finger Brown) Luchese, of Lido Beach, Long Island; and Thomas (Tommy Ryan) Eboli, of Englewood, New Jersey. By that time Joe Bonanno and Joe Magliocco had been removed from the scene by a sneaky double-cross. Bonanno and Magliocco approached Joseph Colombo to let a contract to dispose of three of their rivals—Carlo Gambino, Thomas Luchese, and Stefano Magaddino. Colombo saw advantages for himself in tipping off the intended victims, and he touched off the so-called "Bananas war" in which Bonanno disappeared and at least six others were slain.

Elevated to the command of the Profaci family in 1963, success spoiled Joe Colombo. Overconfident with his success in dealing and double-dealing with other mobsters, and made bold by his major public relations success as a civil rights enthusiast, his fleeting fame embittered other Mafia leaders and particularly the renegade Gallo brothers, Larry and Crazy Joe.

It was ironic that the very people who were bringing discredit to Italian-Americans would shout the loudest about the "injustice" of government agencies using the reference "Mafia" and "La Cosa Nostra." Law enforcement officials of Italian extraction were among those who most resented Joe Colombo's establishment of and financing of the Italian-American Civil Rights League Club to protest the use of the terms "Mafia" and "La Cosa Nostra." But on July 21, 1970, Colombo won what appeared to be a major victory when Attorney General John N. Mitchell, on orders directed from the White House, insisted that both "Mafia" and "La Cosa Nostra" be dropped. In fact, Deputy Assistant Attorney General Henry Peterson simply changed the reference to "criminal syndicate organizations" or similar terms; and in some respects it was better, because the major syndicate activities had always been open to all crooks without regard to "ethnic" background. The Mafia and La Cosa Nostra simply restricted the inside group to those of Italian extraction, but were willing to work with Jewish, Irish, Swedish, or French crooks.

In November 1970, it was reported that Frank Costello, at age 79, might be coming out of retirement to assume the role of peacemaker. Vito Genovese had maintained a control of sorts over his family of more than 400 racketeers even while in the federal prison at Atlanta. His death, in February 1969, created a leadership vacuum since his chief *caporegimes,* Jerry Catena and Thomas Eboli, were experiencing difficulties of their own. Catena was jailed in 1970 for contempt of a New Jersey State Commission of Investigation, and Eboli had suffered two heart attacks.

Colombo was making it apparent that he believed he deserved to inherit the Genovese mantle, and regarded his victory in banning the use of the terms "Mafia" and "La Cosa Nostra" as an indication of what power he possessed as a kind of new public-relations-minded mobster who could play a civil rights theme and make it pay.

Italian-American law enforcement officials, including Ralph Salerno, were angered that the Justice Department and the Nixon Administration would make concessions to the IACRL which they knew to be dominated by Mafia money. There was also grousing about yielding to the political pressures of La Cosa Nostra itself by some business interests in connection with the filming and advertising of *The Godfather.* Concessions were made to eliminate use of "Mafia" and "La Cosa Nostra."

The Brooklyn and New York Strike Forces and the grand juries were well on their way to proving that Joe Colombo was indeed the boss of La Cosa Nostra. But they were working quietly and were well aware that this was the best way to prove that Colombo was more than simply a real estate salesman for Cantalup Realty Company, with some small interests in a flower shop and funeral home.

On July 14, 1970, a federal grand jury sitting in the Southern District of New York returned a five-count indictment against Nicholas (Jiggs) Forlano, a *capo* in the Joseph Colombo organized crime family. Indicted with Forlano on the charges of conspiracy to gamble were Charles Rubin Stein, Charles Karp, James DeNegris, Jr., James Conforte, Sr., and Ruby Lazarus.

Court-authorized wiretap surveillances had established that Forlano and Stein were running a large gambling operation in New York City and Mount Vernon, and that DeNegris and Conforte had a gambling operation in West Haven, Connecticut. DeNegris and Conforte used the Forlano-Stein operation to layoff some of the action they had taken. Lazarus and Karp were identified as employees of Forlano and Stein. Stein and Forlano had been identified by a 1965 report of the New York State Commission of Investigation as "the two biggest loan sharks in the five boroughs."

Before Colombo had smilingly accepted IACRL's "Man of the Year" award, the FBI had developed evidence that the club was being used as a rendezvous point for some of the men who formed a part of Colombo's policy racket. During Ramsey Clark's ban on use of the 1968 eavesdropping and wiretapping law, Colombo ran his rackets with confidence that his great American free enterprise operation —gambling—did not fall into the subversive-activities category that would have made it possible to use a wiretap. Colombo occasionally used the telephones, completely assured that any unauthorized wiretap information picked up was not admissible in court.

Colombo carefully avoided any contact with policy runners, and only about once a week saw the woman who kept his books and delivered his money. The way he figured it, the FBI could not tie him to the operation without an inside informant, and in this respect he was fairly well insulated by a few top supervisors—Nicholas Mainello, Peter Candarini, Joseph Candarini, and Joseph (Joe Notch) Iannaci.

When Attorney General Mitchell gave the go-ahead on wiretapping in February 1969, Colombo issued his own orders. No one was to mention his name, or make any reference to him which might lead back to his headquarters. Colombo would deal with only two or three people at the most, and none was to know any more than just what was necessary to run a little segment of the whole policy operation.

Theresa Schettini and her sister-in-law, Phyllis Schettini, were to have the deliveries made to them at 2530 Cropsey Avenue in Brooklyn, between 4:30 P.M. and 5 P.M. every afternoon to be processed for pickup by Colombo once a week. Essentially there was nothing to connect Colombo with the leather shop at 2264 Bath Avenue, which served as his major headquarters. But on December 18, 1970, the FBI followed Mainello from the leather shop and noted that he placed a brown paper bag in the trunk of his car. Accompanied by Peter Candarini, Mainello made several stops before proceeding to the IACRL Club at Bay Forty-third Street and Cropsey Avenue.

The FBI also noted that the trunk was not opened until Mainello had removed the paper bag and gave it to Theresa Schettini as they were parked near the IACRL Club.

On December 21, 1970, during a similar surveillance, a box of records was transferred to Theresa Schettini at the rendezvous point.

It was a real "Guys and Dolls" operation with names like "Charlie 46," "Patty Boxcars," "Tommy Scar," and "Fats Farouk" showing up on the telephone logs. Payoffs to Brooklyn police were necessary for smooth operation and periodically warnings were issued: "Even though we're paying [for] police protection this doesn't allow us to become brazen or open in our operations." Or: "Policy runners are becoming too careless."

The FBI, with the wiretaps and bugs and informants on the inside, had no trouble in identifying the policy rackets as under Joe Colombo's direction. Charlie DeMarco, Frank Ferraro, Pasquale Consolet, Thomas Amato, and Joseph Iannaci were charged with conspiracy to gamble, along with the "dolls," Theresa and Phyllis Schettini, whose complaints about "sloppy records" had been included in the tapes.

Although Colombo had been convicted on a perjury charge involving falsification on his application for a New York State real estate license, he was still riding high and confident in the early spring of 1971 when other gang leaders became irritated with his big public relations drive. Joe Colombo had started believing his own press clippings—a major error for either politicians or gangsters. He started going on television and radio talk-shows, and challenging the FBI to quit harassing him.

Although FBI agents and Strike Force lawyers quietly smouldered with indignation that this Mafia hoodlum seemed to be ending up with too many favorable stories—stories that gave the impression that he was an honest civil rights leader—they knew that the day of reckoning was near.

On March 23, Colombo won an eight-day delay in surrendering to start a one- to two-and-one-half year jail sentence for perjury. His lawyer said he would use the delay to bring an appeal on the conviction that he lied in applying for a real estate broker's license.

On Monday, March 22, Colombo received the "Man of the Year Award," and was pictured as "the guiding spirit of Italian-American unity." Before the 1,400 admirers at a $125-a-plate dinner at Huntington, New York, he pledged that he would build a hospital, a youth center, and a narcotics treatment clinic. On the same day, Natale Marcone, the president of the IACRL Club, was charged with obstructing government business, and a companion, Joseph Candorini, was charged with felonious assault in connection with the picketing of the St ten Island *Advance* newspaper a month earlier. They had picketed the newspaper for reporting that the Italian-American Civil Rights League was under investigation by federal authorities, and in the process Candorini had assaulted a policeman. The newspaper reports were accurate, and neither the picketing of the FBI nor of the newspaper ended the investigation.

Less than two weeks later, on April 2, Colombo and 30 members of his gang were arrested; and on April 23, 1971, they were indicted on charges of running a $10 million-a-year gambling conspiracy. The indictment contained the details of the case as developed by the FBI and the Brooklyn and New York Strike Forces. They had a total of 95 days of court-approved eavesdropping and wiretapping to support the complaint.

At the time that the Strike Forces were working on Colombo's gang, a Senate investigation was moving hard on other aspects of the Colombo enterprises. The Senate Permanent Investigations Subcommittee headed by Chairman John L. McClellan (Dem., Ark.) was in the process of tying major theft rings to various organized crime figures, including men high in the Joe Colombo family. Chief Investigator Phil Manuel had been fortunate to have on the staff a New York detective, William B. Gallinaro, who had known Colombo since their youth in Brooklyn.

For at least a dozen years Gallinaro had been trying to put Colombo in jail, and he knew every turn in Colombo's path that it was possible to get into without wiretapping. Gallinaro found it pure pleasure to be working with a Senate Committee which had the jurisdiction and the will to put together the full story of Joe Colombo, without being hemmed in by an indictment that was confined to only one aspect of the Colombo operation.

The McClellan Subcommittee hearings on the Mafia involvement in loan-sharking rackets, security theft rackets, and hijacking of cargo planes at Kennedy Airport, had spelled out evidence which identified Cosmo (Gus) Cangiano and Anthony Peraino as members of the Joseph Colombo family operation.

One of the most sensational witnesses at the hearing was Robert F. Cudak, a confessed thief who had worked with Cangiano and Peraino prior to conviction in thefts at John F. Kennedy Airport in New York and other airports. He estimated that his stealing had resulted in turning over about $100 million a year to the organized crime rings that worked with certain Teamsters Union officials to keep a monopoly on major airports.

Attorney General John Mitchell had arranged to grant immunity to Cudak to get the inside story on those with whom he dealt in the organized crime rings. Cudak identified Gus Cangiano as a major fence for stolen property, and complained that he did not like to deal with Cangiano because of the low prices. "Cangiano has been identified as a very close associate of a number of members of the Colombo family, " Detective Bill Gallinaro said.

"The same intelligence source states that Cangiano is involved in pornography, stolen and counterfeit credit cards, counterfeit identification, and acts as a fence for stolen securities," Gallinaro said. He explained that Cangiano had ties with the Colombo family organization, and that it was essential for an independent thief to go through the crime network to market stolen property.

Cangiano's criminal record showed that he had been arrested eight times for criminal receiving, possession of stolen mail, and in 1970, for interstate transportation of stolen securities. He had never been convicted, although several of the cases were still pending in mid-June, Gallinaro told the McClellan Subcommittee. He took the Subcommittee members through a trail of thievery and suspected murder in Florida, Brooklyn, Boston, Chicago, and Mexico City.

Gus Cangiano took the Fifth Amendment on questions related to

Cudak's testimony and the corroboration supplied by the McClellan Subcommittee staff. Cudak was only one of half a dozen major witnesses who were granted immunity over the months of the hearings to give the Senate Subcommittee a look at the inside of stolen-security rings and the sophisticated marketing of millions of dollars in securities that took place each year. Colombo was just one of many tied to major theft rings along the New York, New Jersey, and Philadelphia area.

Harry Riccobene, linked with the Angelo Bruno family of La Cosa Nostra by the Pennsylvania Crime Commission, was tried and convicted on charges of interstate transportation of a stolen $500,000 U.S. Treasury bill.

In his report in mid-July 1971, FBI Director J. Edgar Hoover called attention to the increasing number of thefts from big brokerage houses and financial institutions that were causing his organization special concern.

On September 18, 1970, Hoover said that securities valued at approximately $500,000 were taken from a large New York City brokerage firm. FBI investigations indicated that an overseas representative of a small American brokerage firm was attempting to negotiate securities from this theft in Switzerland. The representative of the small American firm was identified as Dinty Warmington Whiting. He was arrested by the FBI in New York, and indicted by a federal grand jury on May 26, 1971, but failed to show in court for a hearing slated for June 7, 1971, and was declared a fugitive.

A total of $2,219,700 in stock certificates were reported missing from another large New York City stock brokerage firm in September 1970. By mid-January 1971, information developed by the New York FBI office indicated that the stocks were being offered for sale. Three men were arrested on January 15, 1971, and stock certificates valued at $1,005,510 were recovered. Prosecution was pending in the United States District Court in New York City.

In May 1971, Victor Habib Moussa was arrested in New York, having come from Lebanon for the purpose of pledging securities on behalf of two Lebanese principals in order to obtain loans. When one brokerage firm contacted made a check, it was determined that the securities in Moussa's possession were those stolen from mail shipments at

Kennedy International Airport during August 1970. Based on a search warrant, FBI agents searched Moussa's luggage at Kennedy International Airport on May 24, 1971, just prior to his departure for Lebanon. Stolen securities worth $1,189,840 were recovered, and Moussa was arrested.

On Monday, June 28, 1971, Joseph Colombo, Sr., was shot twice as he walked through the Columbus Circle crowd at the start of what was to have been a "Unity Day" picnic. Two of the three shots fired by Jerome Johnson, a 25-year-old Negro from New Brunswick, New Jersey, had penetrated Colombo's head and neck and for weeks left him lingering near death. His assailant was shot and killed within a matter of moments, wiping out the only link with those who might have let a contract on Colombo.

No arrests were made at the scene. New York Chief of Detectives Albert Seedman said he did not know who shot Johnson, but that it was not a policeman. Several guns were found in the vicinity of Johnson's body, and police took Carlo Gambino and the Gallo brothers, Crazy Joe and Albert, to the Eighteenth Precinct Stationhouse for questioning.

The Brooklyn Strike Force lawyers had been aware of the demand that the Gallo brothers had made for $100,000 to keep the peace in Brooklyn and the general lack of stability that characterized their crime career. They also were aware that the Gambino mob harbored resentment at all the attention that Colombo had brought to the Italian-American group through his challenge to the federal government.

The Colombo gambling case was an example of those cases that could not have been made without the court-authorized wiretapping and eavesdropping. The confidence Colombo had in operating his $10 million-a-year policy program was so typical of the confidence that the big gamblers, narcotics wholesalers, and theft rings had so long as they could rest assured that there would be no wiretapping in the organized crime field.

Even as the Strike Force operations were registering major blows on organized crime, Justice Department lawyers were sharply aware of a ruling by a federal judge in Washington, D.C., that barred nearly all the eavesdropping evidence in the largest seizure of heroin in Washington history. United States District Judge Joseph C. Waddy ruled that in his view the narcotics agents made no effort "to minimize the interception of communications not otherwise subject to interception" as the law required.

Judge Waddy's challenge to the Administration's wiretapping was a broad one, for he contended that all the wiretapping evidence and all the "fruits" of wiretapping evidence were not admissible. This essentially tossed out all the wiretaps as well as all the evidence seized in connection with search warrants based on those taps. If that ruling stood up, it would virtually destroy the case against 14 defendants.

The ruling was based on Judge Waddy's acceptance of the views of defense lawyers that only about 40 percent of the calls on the two telephones were directly related to operations of the narcotics ring, and that this amounted to "indiscriminate use of wire surveillance." He contended that the Justice Department had taken the order from United States District Judge John Lewis Smith, Jr., and that nearly "all conversations were overheard and recorded, and that approximately 60 percent of the calls were completely unrelated to narcotics."

The government claimed that in narcotics cases it is essential to monitor all conversations to determine if the calls are likely to be related to narcotics. In the government's appeal, Assistant U.S. Attorneys Don T. Bucklin and Phil Kellogg declared that instead of 40 percent being directly related to narcotics as Judge Waddy estimated, that in fact it was more like 98 percent of the calls that related to the narcotics traffic in the junkie jargon.

The coded jargon of the junkies sounded like a harmless conversation about mundane things, but was often relaying information relating to delivery and units of heroin. The question of whether "mother had breakfast ready," followed by the promise to "stop by tonight to pick it up," may have sounded like innocent chitchat to Judge Waddy, but was easily recognized by less naive agents as junkie jargon arranging a delivery.

The arrests made on February 24, 1971, were followed by seizure of about $500,000 worth of heroin found in the possession of the wholesale narcotics ring.

In the appeal on the case, United States District Attorney Thomas Flannery explained to the court that the code included the usual boy-girl reference to heroin and cocaine, but that some callers used terms such as "thing" and "equipment" to refer to narcotics, and that the whole conversation had to be taken into account in determining whether it was related to narcotics or might be related to narcotics trade. Flannery noted that Duke Williams, one of the defendants, used a variation of streets to designate the number of units in ordering narcotics. Thus "put me on Fifth Street," or, "meet me on Fourth Street," indicated an order for five or four units of narcotics.

It was pointed out that frequently it is difficult to determine the difference between an innocent call and one related to narcotics. This is particularly true in the first part of a call that might seem to be so much irrelevant chatter before the pushers get down to business.

Flannery's office suggested some guidelines to determine whether there was undue monitoring of calls and noted that using these guidelines, no more than 1.56 percent of the calls were beyond the scope of the order. He suggested the following:

1. All calls between two known conspirators are permissibly intercepted, absent some clear showing of a withdrawal from narcotics dealings.
2. The first call between a conspirator who has dealt in narcotics over the phone and a new caller is permissible to determine whether the new caller is involved in the narcotics operation.
3. Subsequent calls between a conspirator and a "new caller" are permissibly intercepted until the person's involvement in the narcotics trade may reasonably be excluded.
4. Calls to which an unidentified conspirator is a party are permissibly intercepted as privileged for purposes of aiding in the identification of the conspirator.

The Geneva-Mother calls were cited by Judge Waddy as "the most blatant examples" of a failure by agents to minimize interception of unrelated calls. He also complained about the lack of justification for intercepting some calls to a bank.

In the appeal, the United States Attorney's office noted that the "enormous profits which can be derived from traffic in illicit narcotics" make it only fair to intercept all calls from the sources to the banks. They also noted that it is lawful for officers executing a narcotics search warrant to seize money which appears to be the proceeds of an illegal enterprise.

"We contend that the conversations indicating the existence of a bank account in the name of a conspirator are properly intercepted . . . under an order involving certain persons and others engaged in a narcotics operation," the government stated.

"It is reasonable for the agents to have concluded that seeing [Burnis] Thurmon, and hearing him at varying times throughout several days, appearing not to work at any job, driving a Lincoln automobile, engaging in narcotics dealings virtually every day and often many different times a day, that any money he might have had then was [from] the proceeds of his illicit narcotics business."

Assistant U.S. Attorneys Bucklin and Kellogg expressed their fears that seven major narcotics dealers would go free on technicalities on the ruling by Judge Waddy. They stressed their view that on the "N Street telephone" there were only six calls (1.56 percent) beyond the scope of the order. Unanswered incoming and outgoing calls not counted, 126 (32.8 percent) involved substance of the narcotics enterprise. Seven calls involved narcotics enterprise in part, 21 had evidentiary value, and 142 calls (36.9 percent) were "permissibly intercepted, but ambiguous calls the purpose of which could not be determined." There were 55 calls (14.3 percent) involving conversations unrelated to the narcotics enterprise which were intercepted with the reasonable expectation that narcotics would be involved.

The affidavit in support of the wiretaps indicated a broad interest in the inquiry at such locations as Atlantic City, New Jersey; Philadelphia, Pennsylvania; New York City; and in Ecuador. "Virtually all conversations material to the conspiracy could reasonably be expected to be conducted in coded or cloaked language. . . . As this wiretap developed, in fact, narcotics transactions were conducted in terms which varied as to each conspirator."

Assistant United States Attorney Harold Sullivan, head of the major crimes operations in the District of Columbia, had been under a heavy guard for months in connection with the prosecution of another Mafia-connected narcotics ring. The deaths of nine men and a woman with some connection with the narcotics-peddling conspiracy trials had caused some unusual steps to be taken to protect government attorneys as well as key witnesses.

A total of 56 persons were under indictment for allegedly being a part of the narcotics ring that included Enrico (Harry) Tantillo, a Mafia figure from the New York and New Jersey area, who had been identified as a major source of heroin and convicted on a charge of conspiracy to sell narcotics and possession of cocaine.

Carmine (Chow Mein) Paladino was found guilty of conspiracy and possession of narcotics. Lawrence (Slippery) Jackson, identified as the biggest wholesaler in Washington, was found guilty of conspiracy and on six counts involving the sale of heroin. Robert (Bobby) Verderosa was found guilty of conspiracy and possession of narcotics, as was Leon James. Carl W. Brooks, a former Intelligence Division police officer, was found guilty of conspiracy for his role in alerting the narcotics ring to police information on raids.

That trial started with seven defendants and included Mary P. Davis, who died during the course of the trial. It appeared that she died of natural causes; but the transcript of a telephone conversation taken prior to the trial indicated that she had threatened to become an informer, and that Jackson and his brother, Lester, had discussed "disposing of her."

United States District Judge Aubrey Robinson was placed under tight protection by United States marshals after the trial resulted in the conviction of Tantillo, Paladino, and Slippery Jackson. The massive trial transcript and the issue of wiretapping evidence compounded the problems in connection with the appeal being filed. Some 6,000 pages of trial transcript as well as 14,000 pages of wiretap transcript became a part of the record.

A look at the background of Tantillo gave some indication of why the government was uneasy about the possibility of tampering with witnesses during the appeal process. In the past, Henry Tantillo had been convicted of threatening witnesses; he also had two narcotics convictions upset on technical grounds and sent back for retrial, only to have the key witnesses decline to testify at a second trial.

Government prosecutors related that ten persons who had some connection with the series of indictments on the narcotics ring had died within a few weeks. They declined to discuss the entire list because some were and some were not possible government witnesses. Charles (Popeye) Hailes, an associate of Tantillo in narcotics dealings, was shot and killed in November 1970. There had been some belief that Hailes was going to turn state's evidence, but prosecutors gave no indication publicly as to whether this was true or false. Harry Hawkins, of Washington, was arrested and tried in connection with the murder of Hailes, but the prosecution handled the whole trial without getting into the connections with the narcotics case.

Tantillo was arrested on a counterfeiting charge while out on bail after his initial arrest on the narcotics charge, and he was indicted in New Jersey and facing a trial on charges of possession of two kilograms of cocaine. United States Attorney General John Mitchell and District Attorney Flannery declared that they saw no reason why Judge Robinson should not have kept in jail the six convicted on the narcotics charges.

The Attorney General drew a distinction between holding men in jail in the period prior to trial, and in jailing them during appeal after conviction. "If we want to get these traffickers off the street, there is no reason why judges shouldn't keep them incarcerated," Mitchell declared.

Flannery said that Tantillo and the other defendants represent a serious threat to the entire community. "The defendant Tantillo poses a gross danger to the community. I think it is fair to say, Your Honor, that in the last 20 years no man had caused so much misery in this city."

On July 16, 1971, a federal grand jury in New York indicted eight men for stock fraud and securities manipulation conspiracies including John Lombardozzi, brother of Cosa Nostra boss Carmine Lombardozzi.

The indictments were obtained by the Justice Department's New York Joint Strike Force on Organized Crime after an intensive investigation by the Securities and Exchange Commission of the financial affairs of Picture Island Computer Corporation (PIC) succeeded in interest by Leisuresources, Ltd.

It was charged in the indictment that Lombardozzi and other owners of the Florida-based corporation had filed false and fictitious reports with the Securities and Exchange Commission to give the impression that the firm had assets totaling $50 million, when in fact the assets of the firm were "worth little or nothing."

John Lombardozzi has not been publicly identified with La Cosa Nostra, but was carried in the Organized Crime file of the Justice Department; and a number of those indicted with him have a long history of stock-fraud indictments, convictions, and restraining orders.

The importance of the 37-count indictment in the organized crime field was emphasized by the fact that the announcement was made jointly by Deputy Attorney General Richard G. Kleindienst and Securities and Exchange Commission Chairman William J. Casey.

Daniel P. Hollman, head of the New York Strike Force, said that the scheme involved the widespread distribution of millions of shares of Picture Island Computer Corporation, later known as Leisuresources, Ltd.

In addition to John Lombardozzi, those named in the indictment were:

Francis Peter Crosby, also known as Peter Francis Crosby, 46, of East Orange, New Jersey, who was convicted in 1960 on mail frauds growing out of the sale of Texas Adams Oil Company stock. He served a five-year jail term, and since he was paroled he has been four times enjoined from selling stocks for fraudulent practices.

Dinty W. Whiting, of Louisiana, now living in Geneva, Florida, who has been disbarred from the practice of law in Florida after conviction on charges of mail and wire frauds in 1961.

Morris H. Gotthilf, of North Miami, Florida, a certified public accountant, who in December 1969 was enjoined from selling stock.

Samuel Benton of Nevada and Miami, Florida, who has been indicted in connection with the sale of stolen securities.

Hilmer Burdette Sandine (also known as Harry Sandine), 48, of Miami, who was arrested and convicted in 1966 on charges involving sale of stolen securities.

William F. Hamilton, a New York lawyer, with no known criminal record.

Leslie I. Zacharias, also known as Lee Zacharias, 32, of New Jersey and Miami Beach, Florida, who has been an associate and representative of many members of the Newark organized crime groups. Each of these defendants is charged in all the 37 counts of the indictment on stock fraud, stock manipulation, mail fraud, sale of unregistered securities, and conspiracy.

The indictment charges that PIC and its subsidiaries falsely claimed ownership of a $1 million certificate of deposit in the Bank of Sark, Isle of Guernsey, English Channel Island; had a 20 percent interest in 3.5 million acres of offshore lands north of Alaska worth $31.5 million, and owned 5,000 acres of land in the Imperial Valley of California worth $1.33 million.

16

TEAMSTERS TENTACLES—POWER, POLITICS, AND PENSION FUNDS

"If the security of the national government is a sufficient interest to render eavesdropping reasonable, on what tenable basis can a contrary conclusion be reached when a state asserts a purpose to prevent the corruption of its major officials, to protect the integrity of its fundamental processes, and to maintain itself as a viable institution? The serious threat which organized crime poses to our society has been frequently documented. The interrelation between organized crime and corruption of government officials is likewise well established, and the enormous difficulty of eradicating both forms of social cancer is proved by the persistence of the problem if by nothing else." *Justice Byron White, dissenting on the Berger case and focusing attention on the need for electronic eavesdropping authority.*

MANY fine and hard-working people are among the two million members and officers of the Teamsters Union. Unfortunately it is necessary to begin with an emphasis on that fact, because delving into Teamsters Union workings and discovering its power levers makes one doubt that anything honest or decent survives in this union or the politicians it touches.

James R. Hoffa headed a union with a treasury of more than $40 million. He watched as millions more poured into the welfare and pension funds, and he recognized the power he derived from being able to control the loans and investments to be made with this money.

Hoffa's cynical philosophy—"every man has his price"—taught him that even industrial giants will jump through hoops under the right circumstances. The same code allowed Hoffa and his friends to "accept" a 5 or 10 percent cut from loans made to hotels, gambling casinos, or condominiums. When he was found guilty of mail and wire frauds and conspiracy, $20 million in loans from pension funds was involved and it was alleged that there was more than $1 million in kickbacks to Hoffa associates in "old, small bills."

This was only the tip of the iceberg. There is a tremendous potential for power in the union's overall phases of trucking or docking. Dave Beck, the union's former president, claimed as teamster domain not only trucks but anything that could be hauled on a truck.

This explains how the Teamsters Union was involved in trying to create a monopoly in the garbage collection business in New York and Los Angeles, a monopoly that allowed the union and cooperating industry to "tax" for essential services. It explains how the Teamsters Union became the enforcement arm for racket-laden monopolies involving jukeboxes and pinball machines.

Trucks move nearly everything in America today. Even when railroads or airlines are the major carriers, the local cartage company delivers the product to its final destination. This mighty union became the instrumentality for befouling everything in America that the syndicate believed worth contaminating.

As president of the International Brotherhood of Teamsters, James Hoffa administered the national union treasury. He appointed international officers to manipulate the national convention, which then voted him a salary of $100,000 a year and provided an unlimited expense account. If they did not yield to his orders, he had the authority to place their locals in trusteeship and name the trustees. As president, he automatically became a member of the board of trustees controlling pension and welfare funds. He made his position on the board the equivalent of control.

The Taft-Hartley requirement that such funds have equal representation from labor and management gave Hoffa as union president initial control of half the trustees. In addition, his leverage in matters of union grievances brought truckline executives into conformity. A hard frown from Hoffa meant "I'll remember *you*, brother!" A soft loan implied "It pays to go along."

Jimmy Hoffa had the power and the friends to put up a tough fight against the Justice Department's attempts to imprison him. But the government had probably the only combination that could have done the job—Attorney General Robert Kennedy and his brother, the President, backing him. When Bob Kennedy could not be bought by support from the Teamsters, or pushed around by threats that the union would withdraw political support, James Hoffa, his Teamsters and even their political allies lost all their advantage. The years spent cultivating and corrupting political power in the big states were fruitless when the Democratic leaders and their gangster friends recognized the futility of trying to drive a wedge between the President and the Attorney General.

Hoffa, the direct activist, then turned to his only alternatives—Congress, the courts, and the jury system.

There were indications that he had bought or coerced many of the local judges in the Detroit area, and that he had a few federal judges in his pocket as a result of the days when Teamsters lawyer, George Fitzgerald, was Democratic National Committeeman from Michigan. These indications were strong enough to dissuade the Justice Department from trying to bring Hoffa to trial in that jurisdiction.

In Florida, questions about a couple of District Judges made Kennedy unwilling to attempt any action in that area. Knowledge of the Carmell incident raised doubts as to the wisdom of moving against Hoffa in Chicago.

Therefore Kennedy decided to bring the first action against the Teamsters boss in the Middle District of Tennessee. A former aide, John Siegenthaler, was editor of the Nashville *Tennessean* and politically knowledgeable in that area. Kennedy also felt that the federal judges named under Kefauver's influence were a few cuts above the judiciary in the big cities where the machine's influence often prevailed. Even so, it was important to remain aware that Hoffa might try to buy the jury there.

Kennedy's caution was justified. It became evident that Hoffa and his scouts had been in Tennessee months before the trial. Ewing King, head of Teamsters Local 327, was simply one of many local union officials used by Hoffa in an attempt to buy several of the jurors.

Later it also came out that the huge Teamsters treasury was too much of a temptation for Z. T. Osborn, a prominent Tennessee lawyer. Osborn, who was nationally famous as the victor in a school-desegregation case, was convicted of jury tampering and tampering with prosecution witnesses in another Hoffa trial. He was disbarred, served a prison term, and died a broken man.

A number of other local lawyers, lured by Teamsters money, played suspicious parts in convincing bellhops, prostitutes, and others of questionable credentials to swear out false affidavits. Fortunately the local judiciary sustained its reputation for integrity. The judges were not only honest, but careful that the trial could stand review by a United States Supreme Court suddenly apprehensive about the use of wiretapping or eavesdropping by informants gathering evidence.

When Lee Harvey Oswald shot President Kennedy, Jimmy Hoffa immediately recognized the effect on Robert Kennedy's power. Now, he gloated, Bobby Kennedy was "just another lawyer."

"He is not going to be able to guarantee patronage, or advancement to the Court of Appeals, or the Supreme Court," Hoffa said in an interview taped by WSM-TV in Nashville. "He is not going to be able to promise—as he has many times—promotions if [he] could secure convictions, disregarding all the ethics that normally is practiced in court cases."

Hoffa was particularly bitter at that time because only two days before the assassination the federal court in Nashville had disbarred Z. T. Osborn on grounds of the jury-tampering charge. It was shocking that a man like Osborn would be involved in an attempt to corrupt the federal judicial system, but it was no more shocking than Hoffa's brutal use of power.

Hoffa was outraged that two United States District Judges had authorized FBI agents to conceal a recording device on the body of an informant who had been approached by the Nashville attorney.

"I feel that it's a travesty on justice," Hoffa stormed, "that the government, the local officials, and the judges should have any part of a setup [to] entrap him and take away from me a competent lawyer to represent me. . . . I believe it is the full intention of those who have perpetrated this crime—and it is a crime, and should be treated as such—in entrapping the attorney I had hired."

Determined to avoid imprisonment, Hoffa resorted to attempts to buy or coerce Edward G. Partin to change his story. The Louisiana Teamster official was a key witness in the jury-tampering case. During the next six years, Partin was threatened with physical violence, harassed by local and federal court actions and, through a New Orleans municipal judge, offered $1 million to retract his testimony.

As Special Counsel to President Nixon, I spelled out pertinent parts of the record of pressure on Partin when I opposed clemency for Hoffa in the fall of 1969, and sent copies of *Tentacles of Power,* my book on the Teamsters boss, to the head of the Criminal Division, Will Wilson, to Attorney General John Mitchell, and to other White House aides to give them background.

Teamsters officials and truckline officials beat a path to my door to point out the political realities: the Teamsters were a wealthy and powerful union and could be helpful with money and manpower in a political campaign; George Meany and other AFL-CIO leaders were aligned with the Democratic Party and would remain so; therefore Hoffa was the only force strong enough to assure a Republican counterbalance in the 1972 election; Hoffa was a conservative, and if Meany bowed out, the AFL-CIO presidency would probably go to Walter Reuther, an ultraleft-wing force in labor. (That argument died with Reuther.)

In each succeeding labor stoppage threat, Hoffa was pictured as the one man who could restore stability to the labor movement. They also argued that Jimmy Hoffa had been framed by Robert Kennedy and that unethical methods had been used to persuade Partin, a convicted thief, to testify against Hoffa by offering him forgiveness on some pending federal charges.

I pointed out that there was more to the jury-tampering conviction than just the word of Edward Partin, and that I had been in Nashville during the initial trial and in Chattanooga for the second trial. It was no frameup. There was full corroboration for Partin on every essential point, plus much more evidence indicating that Hoffa had not stopped trying to tamper with the prosecution and the courts even after that conviction.

For many months I argued that political dislike for the late Senator Kennedy should not be carried to the point of believing that the whole case against Hoffa was a fabrication. I knew it was not so. I had spent the better part of 30 years covering the Teamsters Union and its links with local crime and political corruption. I had devoted nearly 20 years to following the career of Jimmy Hoffa, and saw that it was not by accident that he was aligned with the major Mafia hoodlums in nearly every city in the nation.

In Chicago, his closest friend was Joey Glimco of Local 777, often arrested but never convicted. The Chicago Crime Commission reports as well as the McClellan Committee identified Glimco as a top Mafioso in the Middle West.

In New York, Hoffa's closest friends included at least four members of La Cosa Nostra family of Gaetano Luchese, alias Three-Fingers Brown. They were Anthony (Tony Ducks) Corallo; James Plumeri, alias Jimmy Doyle; Carmine Tramunti, alias Mr. Gribs; and John Dioguardi, alias Johnny Dio. In the Vito Genovese family, Hoffa's associates included Michael (Trigger Mike) Coppola and Anthony "Tony Boy" Boiardo.

In Newark, it was not necessary to probe very deeply to find Hoffa's links with union-Mafia corruption there. Anthony (Tony Pro) Provenzano served a term in prison in connection with the Teamsters shakedown of trucklines in New Jersey. When Provenzano bowed out of the International executive board, his place as vice-president in the International Union was taken by his brother Salvatore (Sam) in 1971. Sam Provenzano was later indicted on charges of counterfeiting and trafficking in stolen securities.

In Detroit, the Hoffa links to the Mafia have been detailed in hearings going as far back as the jukebox-racket investigations of 1953, when he was tied up with William Bufalino in what was called "a gigantic, wicked conspiracy to, through the use of force, threats of force and economic pressure, extort and collect millions of dollars" from union members and independent businessmen.

Hoffa had equally close ties in Detroit with several mobsters identified in the Valachi report as part of the Detroit Mafia.

In Cleveland, Hoffa operated through his old friend, N. Louis (Babe) Triscaro, a twice-convicted robber who still managed to be a big man in Teamsters affairs, and William (Big Bill) Presser, Teamsters boss who threw his weight around at union conventions and who had served a number of jail terms for altering financial records of the union and for restraint of trade in establishing a jukebox monopoly.

As late as July 23, 1970, a federal grand jury in Cleveland returned indictments indicating that Babe Triscaro and Big Bill Presser were up to some of their old tricks. Triscaro, president of Teamsters Local 436, was also the link between the Teamsters Union and the building trades. The indictment charged that Triscaro and Ernest M. Green engaged a management representative in a conspiracy to deposit "large sums" of pension-plan money in the Parkview Federal Savings and Loan of Cleveland, and in return solicited and received personal loans from the bank.

On the same day as the Triscaro indictment, Presser was indicted on charges of conspiring to collect $590,000 from employers in violation of the Taft-Hartley labor law. Presser, an international vice-president of the Teamsters Union, had been released from prison only a few years earlier after serving a term for contempt of Congress for destroying records of financial transactions then under subpoena by the McClellan Committee.

Obviously the time in prison had not affected Presser's standing in the Teamsters Union; in fact it may have enhanced it. He was president of the Ohio conference of Teamsters, president of Teamsters Joint Council 41, and president of Cleveland Taxicab Drivers Local 555.

The indictment charged that Presser and James Franks of Chicago conspired to sell advertising in the *Ohio Teamster Journal* to enable employers to buy labor peace. Franks discussed labor problems and troubles in "such a manner so as to create in the mind of said employer the belief that the monies paid would buy freedom from such labor problems and troubles."

Under this scheme, Franks collected more than $590,000 and personally received a 75 percent share which came to over $460,000. The indictment stated that only 500 copies of the *Ohio Teamster Journal* were published and that the *Ohio Teamster Journal* appeared only with supplemental pages in 1968. It was another example of the manner in which racketeers were able to use the funds and power of the Teamsters Union to extort money and keep the victims from complaining by the constant unspoken threat of a strike.

The garbage collection scandals in New York City had involved Bernard Adelstein, boss of Teamsters Local 813 and a Hoffa supporter; and garbage workers' scandals in Los Angeles involved another Hoffa man, Frank Matula, Jr., of Local 396. Vincent (Jimmy) Squillante, described by federal narcotics authorities as a major dealer in illegal narcotics, shifted from docks and policy rackets into the carting business as executive director of the New York Cartmen's Association.

Squillante, identified as a key figure in the Carlo Gambino family, and Anthony (Tough Tony) Anastasia of the International Longshoremen's Association, were both allied with Hoffa, according to testimony and reports of the McClellan Committee.

Whether these alliances were simply a matter of convenience in each individual area or part of a nationwide plan, made little difference. The mob understood the unbridled power of the Teamsters Union over the whole business community and over most of the other unions dealing with them. The International Teamsters Union was an instrument of corruption and racketeering in nearly every community in the country.

The Strike Force has undertaken a tremendous assignment in an effort to demolish this unholy alliance, even with Hoffa in prison. It cannot rely on the prospect of Hoffa's relinquishing control of the union even if he retired from office. After all, he will be receiving $100,000 a year for life from the union; he may rationalize that he has an obligation to give something in return.

As late as May 1971, the Detroit Strike Force found a dramatic example of the legacy that Jimmy Hoffa and the Mafia had left for law enforcement in Detroit—a deep corruption that will take years to eradicate.

One hundred and fifty-one persons, including Detroit Police Inspector Alex Wierzbicki and 15 other Detroit policemen, were arrested in FBI raids in 37 Michigan cities. The police were charged with obstruction of law enforcement in connection with gambling, carrying on illegal gambling activity, and conspiracy to violate federal gambling laws. Included were three lieutenants, six sergeants, one detective, and five patrolmen. It was one of the biggest law-enforcement efforts put together in the history of Michigan, and was significant because the court-authorized wiretapping made it possible. The raids were unusual in that the Strike Force group already had films of some of the police taking payoffs in a downtown bar, the indictments charged.

It was only necessary to go back to the reports of the McClellan Committee of a dozen years earlier to find spelled out in some detail the outline of "Hoffa's hoodlum empire." "James Hoffa, from his early years in the labor movement, has formed an alliance with the kingpins of the Nation's underworld, a partnership which has moved him swiftly up through the ranks of the Teamsters hierarchy to his present powerful post," the McClellan Committee stated in 1958. "Hoffa's first association was with the Detroit mob. He parlayed this into his equally close connections with underworld figures in Illinois, New York, Ohio, Indiana, Nevada, and other parts of the country.

"Hoffa speaks of 'rehabilitation' as the justification for his consorting with criminals and hoodlums. If an occasional law violator had found his way into the Teamsters organization, this might be a noble sentiment. But on the basis of these hearings, it appears to the Committee that a criminal background was a prerequisite for job placement and advancement in the Teamsters firmament."

It is as futile to base any hope on a reformation of James R. Hoffa as it would be to hope for Tony Accardo or Meyer Lansky to give up the brutal power they possess. In prison, Hoffa still tried to manipulate the power levers in the Teamsters Union. Out of jail, Jimmy Hoffa will run the Teamsters Union regardless of who carries the title of "General President."

On July 14, 1971, a federal grand jury in New York returned an indictment charging that Allen Dorfman, a special consultant to the Central States Southeast Southwest Pension Fund, had received a $55,000 kickback on a $1.5 million loan of union pension funds. The

48-year-old Chicago insurance man had been one of Hoffa's closest friends for a period of more than 20 years, and had been considered the man most influential in obtaining loans from the $700 million fund since Hoffa had gone to prison at Lewisburg, Pennsylvania, in March 1967.

Control over the huge pension fund, which before 1972 would be approaching the billion-dollar mark, was one of the major points at issue among the underworld groups in New York and Chicago who had been jockeying for position. Dorfman, son of a Chicago labor-racket figure linked in official hearings with the Capone mob, had been one of the most controversial and influential figures around Hoffa from the time a House Subcommittee started to dig into the first indications of scandal in the fund back in 1953.

The commissions were clearly excessive, and the arrangements were in no sense made at arms' distance, but Hoffa defended it on grounds that business leaders dealt with "friends." The specific two-count indictment was returned in connection with pension fund loans of $1.5 million to Neisco, Inc., a North Carolina textile company. Dorfman was identified as president of the American Overseas Insurance Company of Chicago, and he listed addresses in Riverwood, Illinois, and North Miami, Florida.

Hoffa was convicted of conspiracy and mail and wire frauds in connection with kickbacks of about $1 million on loans totaling more than $20 million from the same Central States Southeast Southwest Pension Fund that he dominated. Dorfman was identified on the fringe of those transactions, but never to the point of involvement in the frauds.

When Hoffa was indicted for jury-tampering in Tennessee, Dorfman was one of those indicted, but was acquitted in a trial that lasted for a month. He has been a constant companion of Hoffa at International Brotherhood of Teamsters conventions over a span of nearly 20 years, and his role as an influential pension-fund "consultant" was not missed by those in need of money who could not get it through conventional banking sources.

The indictment of Dorfman was considered a breakthrough in the Organized Crime Section, for it was the first indictment of Dorfman on the pension funds where he was known to be most active.

17

SOME JUDGMENTS ON RAMSEY CLARK

"We cannot think it to be wise or prudent or necessary to take away from the police any weapon or to weaken any power they now possess in their fight against organized crime. . . . If it be said that the number of these cases where methods of interception are used is small and that an objectionable method could therefore well be abolished we feel that . . . this is not a reason why criminals in a particular class of crime should be encouraged by the knowledge that they have nothing to fear from methods of interception. . . . This, in our opinion, so far from strengthening the liberty of the ordinary citizen, might very well have the opposite effect." *From the report of The Committee of Privy Councilors, appointed to inquire into the interception of communications (1957). It was reprinted in "Wiretapping Eavesdropping and the Bill of Rights Hearing before the Subcommittee on Constitutional Rights, 85th Congress, 2nd Session," pp. 460-499.*

IN the spring of 1971, when FBI director J. Edgar Hoover sought a $4.5 million increase in appropriation he had no trouble justifying it. The Justice Department had the leaders of organized crime on the run. Meyer Lansky, financial wizard for the mob, was under indictment for "skimming" from the Flamingo Hotel and casino in Las Vegas, and for contempt of court for refusing to appear when subpoenaed before a grand jury. It was obvious to the 68-year-old mobster that his troubles were just starting. He fled to Israel.

Salvatore (Momo) Giancana, top dog in the Chicago Cosa Nostra, had left the country after serving a year in federal prison for contempt. Offered immunity if he would answer questions for the Justice Department before a federal grand jury, he refused. During his period in prison he lost control of his mob.

From sanctuary in Mexico and South America, Giancana looked to the United States and saw little choice if he returned. Before a federal grand jury, his alternatives would be to answer the questions or go back to jail. If he answered the questions—he knew what the Cosa Nostra laws decreed for mob leaders who talked.

At that time, Hoover could point to the fact that in Chicago the Strike Force had convicted John Philip (Jackie the Lackey) Cerone, who was the "acting head of the Chicago mob." The Strike Force had systematically gone after every man who became boss in Chicago—Sam (Teets) Battaglia, Joseph Aiuppa, Felix (Milwaukee Phil) Alderisio, Paul (the Waiter) Ricci, James (the Monk) Allegretti, William (Willie Potatoes) Daddano, Sam De Stefano, and Rocco Pranno. The law was after Joseph (Joey) Glimco, Hoffa's pal and boss of Teamsters Local 777 of the Taxicab Drivers Union. Although Glimco had won a reversal of a criminal court conviction, there had been affirmation of a U.S. Tax Court ruling that he owed $94,465 in back taxes.

Fiore (Fifi) Buccieri and his pals were also on the lam, and the indictments included half a dozen of the local and state politicians who worked with the mob.

In New Jersey, gang leader Sam (the Plumber) DeCavalcante was in jail; and other mob leaders and their political friends were convicted, under indictment, or caught in the sights of John Bartells and his Strike Force. In Kansas City, Mafia boss Nicholas Civella was under indictment and scheduled for trial; and Strike Force boss Mike Defeo's troops were rounding up other members of the Civella gang.

There had been more than 400 search and arrest warrants in major interstate gambling raids under the new Organized Crime Control Act of 1970. It seemed likely that the use of court-approved wiretapping and the new immunity statutes would break the back of organized crime's gambling activities, a multibillion-dollar business.

"Among the rings broken up were a number handling between fifty million and one hundred million dollars a year in wagers," Hoover told the House committee. "A coordinated sweep in the Detroit area led to the arrest of some sixty-six individuals, including one syndicate member described as the largest numbers operator in the State of Michigan. Also seized were nearly 60 weapons, approximately sixty-two thousand dollars in cash and negotiables, extensive gambling paraphernalia, and huge quantities of gambling records."

Hoover said that coordinated gambling and narcotics raids had resulted in the arrest of many of the country's top gambling and under-world figures. He noted at the time that two had been convicted, and the others were awaiting trial.

Martin and Jesse Sklaroff and seven members of their multimillion-dollar Latin-American policy ring had been arrested after two years of investigative effort by the FBI and the Strike Force. The Sklaroff case was one of dozens that established the importance of eavesdropping and wiretapping and also demonstrated the great care taken to avoid interference with the general public's conversations on pay telephones.

The New York Strike Force had directed a three-state move in New Jersey, New York, and Connecticut, in November 1970. As a result, the government men arrested more than 50 members of a syndicate-controlled bookmaking ring handling over $35 million a year in wagers.

Raiding parties of over 200 agents swept through the states of Louisiana and Mississippi, seizing more than $6 million in cash and gambling equipment. "Nationwide gambling raids by over four hundred FBI agents operating out of thirteen field offices resulted in the. . .arrest of twenty-nine individuals and the seizure of over two million dollars in cash and property," Hoover said. "Among those taken into custody were national gambling figures Elliott Paul Price and Frank (Lefty) Rosenthal, of Las Vegas; Jerome Zarowitz and Gerald Hay Kilgore, of Los Angeles; Billy Cecil Doolittle, of Atlanta; Joseph A. Lombardo, of Buffalo; and Max Abramson, of Omaha."

Hoover called attention to the undercover work of FBI agents in a "mob-controlled New York casino estimated to have been handling between thirty-five thousand and one hundred thousand dollars a night in wagers as part of the operation of Sam DeCavalcante, from New Jersey."

In these intrastate raids, "which came just two weeks after the enactment of the new law, three massive numbers banks were smashed in the Philadelphia area, resulting in the arrest of six subjects and the seizure of approximately sixteen thousand dollars in cash," Hoover said.

"Because the gambling investigations are directed against well-coordinated hoodlum rings, often involving large numbers of underworld figures, extensive finances, widespread communications networks, and the latest in security devices, it is essential that the government avail itself of every weapon at its disposal in meeting this challenge," Hoover testified. "One such weapon—and an increasingly invaluable one—is the court-approved electronic surveillance technique provided for in the Omnibus Crime Control and Safe Streets Act of 1968.

"Because of the very potency of this weapon, care must be taken to insure that it is utilized only in those cases whose size, complexity and importance warrants it," Hoover said in an answer to the criticism by Ramsey Clark and others. "This the FBI has been most careful to do."

He noted that court-approved wiretaps were directly responsible for the arrest of Sam the Plumber, and more than 50 members of his $20-million-a-year gambling ring. Court-approved installations were responsible for the Detroit area raids in May 1970; the arrest in November 1970 of Nick Civella and three of his associates; the nationwide raids of December 12, 1970; and the February 6, 1971 raids in seven states and the District of Columbia, resulting in 56 arrests and seizure of approximately $60,000 in cash.

Hoover declared that for the first time in history organized crime could not count on the size, wealth, power, and internal security of its own structure to provide immunity from prosecution.

"Now, these are no longer all-encompassing," Hoover testified. "Congress has given the federal government a powerful countermeasure of its own in the court-approved electronic source, and the results of months—and sometimes years—of investigation are beginning to bear fruit in the form of increased arrests, confiscations, and convictions."

Hoover's sentiments were echoed by Secret Service Chief James Rowley; head of the Bureau of Narcotics and Dangerous Drugs John Ingersoll; Commissioner of Internal Revenue Randolph Thrower; Vernon Acree, head of the inspection operation in the Internal Revenue Service; Custom Commissioner Myles Ambrose; and Eugene Rossides, the Assistant Secretary of Treasury most involved with the problem of enforcement of tax laws and control of narcotics.

Hoover gave examples of some gambling that was more than just "a harmless pastime." "In June 1970, a New York City bartender was arrested who reportedly had robbed some twenty banks in a three-month span in order to pay off thousands of dollars in gambling and loan-shark debts," Hoover said. "Seven months earlier, two men entered pleas of guilty to having robbed a Jacksonville, Florida, bank in order to pay off gambling debts."

Hoover also noted that it is expensive for a city to have vice operations, which inevitably result in the corruption of civic and police officials. He could have added that weak courts and court decisions are frequently present where there is vice, and that the truly corrupt city requires 10 percent more in taxes and gives less in services because of kickback arrangements.

"The new Organized Crime Control Act of 1970 makes much local corruption a federal violation, since it provides criminal penalties for conspiracy to obstruct enforcement of local laws with the intent to facilitate an illegal gambling business," Hoover said.

A major source of illicit revenue for the underworld comes from hoodlum loan-sharking. In 1968, this practice was placed within the FBI's jurisdiction. Since that time, there have been numerous prosecutions. The conviction of Gyp DeCarlo, New Jersey Mafioso, is typical of federal success in this area. In October 1970, FBI investigations of loan-sharking in the Chicago area alone culminated in the conviction of 11 hoodlums, including three identified as syndicate members. The ring was conducting a multimillion-dollar operation, according to J. Edgar Hoover.

In February 1970, Ilario Zannino, also known to the underworld as Larry Baione, acting head of a New England mob, was indicted for conspiring to fence $165,000 worth of jewelry taken from a Boston merchant. He was convicted in November, and sentenced to seven years in prison.

Carlo Gambino, one of the top gangland figures in New York, was arrested on a charge of conspiring to commit a $6 million armored-car robbery. The robbery plans were cancelled only because one of the other ringleaders was arrested for similar activity in Boston.

FBI agents arrested 15 underworld figures in the Detroit-Toledo area for their participation in a fraudulent bankruptcy operation involving approximately $100,000 worth of merchandise. "Among those taken into custody were three men described to a Senate Subcommittee in 1969 as 'captains' in the Detroit mob."

Carmine Traumunti, a top New York City mob leader, was arrested along with a number of his associates in connection with a stock-manip-ulation scheme. The principal stockholder of an investment corporation had been held in a Miami hotel room and beaten until he gave the conspirators his stock certificates. Among those arrested and charged in the 72-count securities-fraud indictment were John Dioguardi, also known as Johnny Dio, and Vincent Alo, another Cosa Nostra figure.

As Hoover was testifying before the House Appropriations Com-mittee, the McClellan Subcommittee was putting together a sensational hearing. It revealed accusations of the loose handling of securities by New York stock firms, thefts from the mails at more than a dozen airports across the country, and the use of Mafia money to manipulate huge corporations on an international level.

The hearing pinpointed the halfway measures that had been taken by the Johnson Administration and made a mockery of former Attorney General Ramsey Clark's claim that eavesdropping and wire-tapping were an infringement on the rights of citizens, and a waste of time with regard to law enforcement.

By mid-1970, there was speculation about why Ramsey Clark had made some of his statements on eavesdropping and wiretapping. Some said he was "only doing what the President told him to do," and they excused former Attorney General Nicholas Katzenbach on the same basis.

But Ramsey Clark's comments persisted even after he was out of the Justice Department. His bleeding for the poor criminals was so ex-tensive that some joked that he must be in quest of the Mafia vote. However, his comments won him much praise among the liberal writers, and his book, *Crime in America,* was reviewed with favor by some writers who considered the comments on social problems as "enlight-ened" thinking.

Publication of the book and some criticism of Hoover had drawn the response from the FBI Director that Clark had been "the worst Attorney General," and Hoover referred to him as a "jellyfish."

Hoover commented that when Clark's book, *Crime in America,* came out, "I wasn't too concerned about what he said in his book, but Mr. DeLoach, who was formerly one of my assistants, called me and reminded me that a recording had been made of Clark's speech at the convention of former special agents held here in Washington in 1967 when he was Attorney General. I had attended a convention luncheon at which Clark was also a guest. I made a few remarks, and then Clark got up and spoke in laudatory terms about somebody," Hoover explained. "I didn't realize who he was referring to until the end of his remarks. He praised the Bureau to the skies, and then said the Bureau is merely a reflection of the image of its director.

"When I listened to the recording of that speech and read what Clark had said in his book, I was so outraged it caused me to make the statement that he is a 'jellyfish.' "

Hoover made these remarks at the House Appropriations Subcommittee hearing.

Representative Cederberg then took the occasion to note that only two years earlier Attorney General Clark had said: "The FBI, in my judgment, has done one of the best investigative and enforcement jobs in the country dealing with communism." He said he felt that Ramsey Clark "did, in writing, authorize the use of electronic surveillances by the FBI" in cases involving subversion.

"That is correct," Hoover replied, "and he has since deprecated their value in criminal cases. Yet the record shows in the organized crime field the tremendous successes we have had. A great portion of that success was made with court-authorized wiretapping."

Some said it was significant that Clark took his position on wiretapping and eavesdropping when Robert Kennedy was still alive. Senator Kennedy was firmly committed to legislation to win court-approved wiretapping, but was otherwise on the same side of various issues as the liberal newspapers and political groups. Opposition to wiretapping may have appeared to be the only way for a young man with obvious presidential aspirations, who at that time was backed by everyone from The New York Times to President Johnson, to move to the left of Senator Kennedy.

APPENDIX A

LA COSA NOSTRA – UNITED STATES

Redrawn from a map furnished by the Senate Subcommittee on Criminal Laws and Procedures, chairman John L. McClellan.

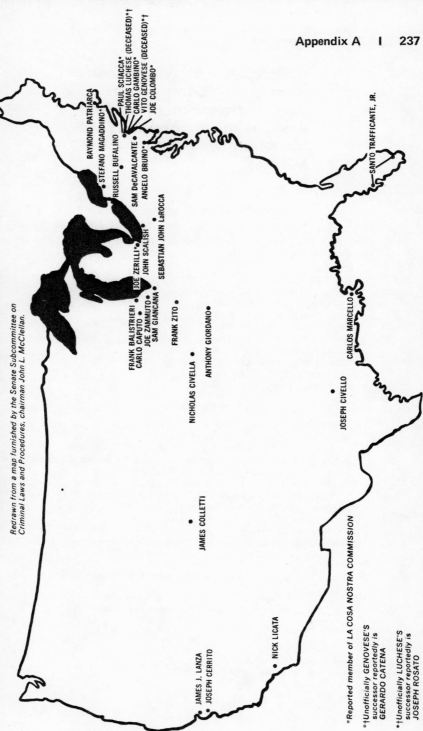

RAYMOND PATRIARCA
STEFANO MAGADDINO
RUSSELL BUFALINO
PAUL SCIACCA*
THOMAS LUCHESE (DECEASED)*†
CARLO GAMBINO*
VITO GENOVESE (DECEASED)*†
JOE COLOMBO*
SAM DeCAVALCANTE
ANGELO BRUNO*
SEBASTIAN JOHN LaROCCA
JOE ZERILLI*
JOHN SCALISH
FRANK BALISTRIERI
CARLO CAPUTO
JOE ZAMMUTO
SAM GIANCANA
FRANK ZITO
NICHOLAS CIVELLA
ANTHONY GIORDANO
SANTO TRAFFICANTE, JR.
CARLOS MARCELLO
JOSEPH CIVELLO
JAMES COLLETTI
NICK LICATA
JAMES J. LANZA
JOSEPH CERRITO

*Reported member of LA COSA NOSTRA COMMISSION

*†Unofficially GENOVESE'S successor reportedly is GERARDO CATENA

*†Unofficially LUCHESE'S successor reportedly is JOSEPH ROSATO

APPENDIX B: La Cosa Nostra "Commissions." Justice Department charts brought up to date in 1969 by Attorney General John Mitchell.

LA COSA NOSTRA: THE "COMMISSION"

Set forth as follows is a schema of the structure of La Cosa Nostra's "Commission" as composed in 1960 as compared to the current make-up and status of this group:

"COMMISSION"–1960

Vito Genovese, New York City.
Carlo Gambino, New York City.
Joseph Profaci, New York City.
Joseph Bonanno, New York City.
Thomas Luchese, New York City.
Stefano Magaddino, Buffalo, New York.
Angelo Bruno, Philadelphia, Pennsylvania.
Joseph Zerilli, Detroit, Michigan.
Salvatore Giancana, Chicago, Illinois.

"COMMISSION"–1969

Carlo Gambino, New York City.
Joseph Colombo, New York City.
Paul Sciacca, New York City.
Open (Carmine Tramunti emerging as successor to the deceased Thomas Luchese. "Commission" status not yet decided.)
Open (Gerardo Catena acting boss following death of Vito Genovese. Successor and "Commission" status not yet decided.)
Stefano Magaddino, Buffalo, New York.
Angelo Bruno, Philadelphia, Pennsylvania.
Joseph Zerilli, Detroit, Michigan.
Open (Anthony Accardo and Paul DeLucia are acting in charge of the Chicago "family" due to Giancana's flight from the United States in 1966.)

LA COSA NOSTRA–BOSTON, MASS.

Set forth as follows is data regarding the leadership of the New England "Family" of La Cosa Nostra as of 1960 and as it is structured in 1969:

IN 1960

Boss: Raymond Patriarca.
Underboss: Anthony Santaniello.

Consigliere: Joseph Lombardo.
Capodecina: Joseph Anselmo, Michael Rocco, John Williams, Henry Tameleo.

IN 1969

Boss: Raymond Patriarca.
Underboss: Gennaro Angiulo.
Consigliere: Joseph Lombardo.
Capodecina: Joseph Anselmo, Ilario Zannino, Edward Romano (acting
   Capodecina).

LA COSA NOSTRA—BUFFALO, N. Y.

The following was the leadership structure of the Buffalo "family" of La Cosa
Nostra as of 1960:
   Boss: Stefano Magaddino.
   Underboss: Fred Randaccio.
   Consigliere: Vincent Scro.
   Capodecina: Jacomino Russolesi, Benjamin Nicoletti, Sr., Roy Carlisi,
      Pasquale Natarelli, Joseph Falcone.
The following is the leadership structure of the Buffalo "family" as of 1969:
   Boss: Stefano Magaddino.
   Underboss: Joseph Fino.
   Consigliere: Vincent Scro.
   Capodecina: Frank Valenti, Benjamin Nicoletti, Sr., Roy Carlisi, Pasquale
      Natarelli, Joseph Falcone.

LA COSA NOSTRA—CHICAGO, ILL.

The following represents the leadership structure of the Chicago "family" of
La Cosa Nostra as of 1960:
   Boss: Salvatore Giancana.
   Underboss: Frank Ferraro.
   Consigliere: Jointly held by Anthony Accardo and Paul DeLucia.
   Capodecina: Ross Prio, Rocco Potenzo, Fiore Buccieri, Joseph Aiuppa,
      Frank LaPorte, William Daddano.
As follows is the leadership make-up of the Chicago "family" as of 1969:
   Boss: Open (Anthony Accardo and Paul DeLucia acting in charge of
      Chicago "family" due to flight of Salvatore Giancana from United
      States in 1966, and incarceration of his interim successor Samuel
      Battaglia).
   Underboss: Open (John Cerone acting Underboss).
   Consigliere: Open (Felix Alderisio possibly acting in this capacity).
   Capodecina: Ross Prio, Fiore Buccieri, John Cerone, Joseph Aiuppa, James
      Catuara, William Daddano.

LA COSA NOSTRA—DETROIT, MICH.

Set forth as follows is pertinent data regarding the leadership structure of the
Detroit La Cosa Nostra "family" as composed in 1960 as compared to 1969:

IN 1960

Boss: Joseph Zerilli.
Underboss: John Priziola.

Consiglieri: Angelo Meli, Peter Licavoli, Joseph Massei.
Capodecina: William Tocco, Giacamo W. Tocco, Joseph Bommarito, Matthew
   Rubino, Raffaele Quasarano, Anthony Giacalone, Dominic Corrado,
   Anthony Zerilli, Michael Polizzi, Anthony Besase.

IN 1969

Boss: Joseph Zerilli.
Underboss: John Priziola.
Consiglieri: Angelo Meli, Peter Licavoli, Joseph Massei.
Capodecina: William Tocco, Mathew Rubino, Raffaele Quasarano, Anthony
Giacalone, Dominic Corrado, Giacamo W. Tocco, Anthony Zerilli, Michael
Polizzi, Anthony Besase.

LA COSA NOSTRA–LOS ANGELES, CALIF.

The following was the leadership of the Los Angeles La Cosa Nostra "family"
in 1960:
   Boss: Frank DeSimone.
   Underboss: Simone Scozzari.
   Consigliere: Charles Dippolito, Joseph Giammona, Joseph Dippolito,
      Joseph Adamo–San Diego.
The leadership of the Los Angeles La Cosa Nostra "family" as of 1969 is as
follows:
   Boss: Nicolo Licata.
   Underboss: Joseph Dippolito.
   Consigliere: Tommy Palermo.
   Capodecina: Dominic Brooklier, Angelo Polizzi, Joseph Adamo–San
      Diego.

LA COSA NOSTRA NEW JERSEY "FAMILY"

The following represents the leadership structure of the New Jersey "family"
of La Cosa Nostra as of 1960 and 1969:

IN 1960

Boss: Nicholas Delmore.
Underboss: Frank Majuri.

IN 1969

Boss: Samuel DeCavalcante.
Underboss: Frank Majuri (Joseph LaSelva reported to operate as DeCavalcante's Underboss for Connecticut membership).

LA COSA NOSTRA–NEW YORK, N. Y.

Set forth as follows is the leadership of New York City's five La Cosa Nostra
"families" as composed in 1960 compared to their current structure as in 1969:

JOSEPH PROFACI "FAMILY"

In 1960:
   Boss: Joseph Profaci.
   Underboss: Joseph Magliocco.

Consigliere: Charles LoCicero.
Capodecina: Harry Fontana, John Oddo, Salvatore Mussachio, Salvatore
Badalamente, John Misuraca, Ambrose Magliocco, Nicoline Sorrentino,
Simone Andolino, John Franzese, Joseph Colombo.

In 1969:
Boss: Joseph Colombo.
Underboss: Salvatore Mineo.
Consigliere: Benedetto D'Alessandro.
Capodecina: Vincent Alo, Simone Andolino, Harry Fontana, Nicholas
Forlano, John Franzese, Frank Richard Fusco, John Misuraca, Salva-
tore Mussachio, John Oddo, Carmine Persico, Nicholas Sorrentino,
Joseph Yacovelli.

CARLO GAMBINO "FAMILY"

In 1960:
Boss: Carlo Gambino.
Underboss: Joseph Biondo.
Consigliere: Joseph Riccobono.
Capodecina: Anthony Anastasio, Domenico Arcuri, Paul Castellano,
Joseph Colozzo, Pasquale Conte, Aniello Dellacroce, David Amodeo,
Charles Dongarra, Alfred Eppolito, Peter Ferrara, Arthur Leo, Carmine
Lombardozzi, Rocco Mazzie, Joseph Paterno, Joseph Silesi, Peter
Stincone, Joseph Traina, Ettore Zapi, Joseph Zingaro.

In 1969:
Boss: Carlo Gambino
Underboss: Aniello Dellacroce.
Consigliere: Joseph Riccobono.
Capodecina: David Amodeo, Domenico Arcuri, Joseph Colozzo, Vincent
Corrao, Pasquale Conte, Charles Dongarra, James Failla, Peter Ferrara,
Joseph Gambino (brother of Carlo Gambino), Anthony Napolitano,
Gaetano Russo, Giacomo Scarpula, Paul Castellano, Anthony Scotto,
Anthony Sedotto, Peter Stincone, Guiseppi Traina, Mario Traina,
Ettore Zappi, Joseph Zingaro, Olympio Garofalo, Frank Corbi, Frank
Perrone, Joseph Paterno, Joseph Silesi, James Eppolito, Frank Rizzo.

VITO GENOVESE "FAMILY"

In 1960:
Boss: Vito Genovese.
Underboss: Gerardo Catena.
Consigliere: Michele Miranda.
Capodecina: Anthony Strollo, Angelo DeCarlo, Eugene Catena, Michael
Coppola, Peter DeFeo, Frank Tieri, Antonio Carillo, Cosmo Frasca,
Rocco Pellegrino, Vincenzo Generoso, Salvatore Celembrino, Vincent
Alo, Ruggiero Boiardo, John Biele, Thomas Greco, James Angelino,
Frank Celano.

In 1969:
Boss: Open (Gerardo Catena acting in view of death of Vito Genovese).
Underboss: Gerardo Catena (Thomas Eboli, acting).
Consigliere: Michele Miranda.
Capodecina: Vincent Alo, Ruggiero Boiardo, Angelo DeCarlo, Antonio
Carillo, Salvatore Celembrino, Frank Celano, Peter DeFeo, Cosmo

Frasca, Vincenzo Generoso, Michael Generoso (acting), Thomas Greco, Philip Lombardo, Rosario Mogavero, Frank Tieri, Harry Lanza, Rocco Pellegrino, Salvatore Cufari.

THOMAS LUCHESE "FAMILY"

In 1960:
  Boss: Thomas Luchese.
  Underboss: Steve LaSalla.
  Consigliere: Vincent Rao.
  Capodecina: Antonio Corallo, Joseph Laratro, Joseph Luchese, John Ormento, James Plumeri, Joseph Rosato, Salvatore Santora, Carmine Tramunti, Paul Correale.
In 1969:
  Boss: Open (Carmen Tramunti, acting boss).
  Underboss: Steve LaSalla.
  Consigliere: Vincent Rao.
  Capodecina: Antonio Corallo, Joseph Lagano, Joseph Laratro, Joseph Luchese, John Ormento, Joseph Rosato, Chris Funari, Paul Vario.

JOSEPH BONANNO "FAMILY"

In 1960:
  Boss: Joseph Bonanno.
  Underboss: Frank Garofalo.
  Consigliere: John Tartamella.
  Capodecina: Carmine Galante, Natale Evola, Matteo Valvo, Frank La-Bruzzo, Thomas DeAngelo, Joseph Notaro, Nicholas Marangello.
In 1969:
  Boss: Paul Sciacca.
  Underboss: Frank Mari.
  Consigliere: Michael Adamo.
  Capodecina: Philip Rastelli, Nicholas Marangello, Armando Pollastrino, Nicholas Alfano, Joseph DiFilippi, Giovanni Fiordilino, Pasquale Gigante, John Morale, Dominick Sabella, Michael Sabella, Sereno Tartanella, Joseph Zicarelli, Louis Greco.

LA COSA NOSTRA–PHILADELPHIA, PA.

The following is a scheme setting forth the leadership of the Philadelphia "family" of La Cosa Nostra as it is currently composed and as it was structured in 1960:
  In 1960:
  Boss: Angelo Bruno Annaloro.
  Underboss: Ignazio Denaro.
  Consigliere: Joseph Rugnetta.
  Capodecina: Philip Testa, John Cappello, Pasquale Massi, Joseph Sciglitano, Peter J. Maggio, Nicholas Piccolo, Joseph Scafidi, John Simone.
  In 1969:
  Boss: Angelo Bruno Annaloro.
  Underboss: Ignazio Denaro.
  Consigliere: Joseph Rugnetta.
  Capodecina: Philip Testa, John Cappello, Joseph Lanciano, Joseph

Sciglitano, Peter J. Maggio, Nicholas Piccolo, Joseph Scafidi, John Simone.

LA COSA NOSTRA–SAN FRANCISCO AREA

Set forth as follows is pertinent data regarding the leadership structure of the San Francisco, and San Jose, California, La Cosa Nostra "families" as composed in 1960 as compared to 1969:

SAN FRANCISCO–1960

Boss: James Lanza.
Underboss: Gaspare Sciortino.

SAN FRANCISCO–1969

Boss: James Lanza.
Underboss: Gaspare Sciortino.
Capodecina: Vincenzo Infusino.

SAN JOSE–1960

Boss: Joseph Cerrito.
Underboss: Charles Carbone.
Consigliere: Steve Zoccoli.
Capodecina: Angelo Marino, Emanuel Figlia, Philip Morici, Joe Cusenza.

SAN JOSE–1969

Boss: Joseph Cerrito.
Underboss: (Charles Carbone deceased and no known replacement).
Consigliere: Steve Zoccoli.
Capodecina: Emanuel Figlia, Philip Morici.

LA COSA NOSTRA INDICTMENTS AND CONVICTIONS–1960 TO MARCH 1969

235 Indictments involving 328 Defendants.
137 Cases resulted in Conviction of 182 Defendants.
32 Defendants were Acquitted.
Indictments against 31 Defendants were Dismissed.
Conviction of 22 Defendants was Reversed.
257 Known or suspected Members of Cosa Nostra were indicted and/or convicted between 1960 and March 1969.

APPENDIX C: La Cosa Nostra "Families." Charts furnished by the Government Operations Committee.

THE VITO GENOVESE FAMILY

Vito Genovese *Boss*

Thomas Eboli *Acting Boss*   Gerardo Catena *Underboss*   Michael Genovese *Messenger*   Michele Miranda *Consigliere*

Caporegime

| Vincent Alo / James Angelina | Michael Coppola / Pasquale Eboli | Thomas Greco / Richard Boiardi | Michele Miranda |

Vincent Alo Regime	James Angelina Regime	Michael Coppola Regime	Pasquale Eboli Regime		Richard Boiardi Regime	Michele Miranda Regime
Soldiers–Buttons	*Soldiers–Buttons*	*Soldiers–Buttons*	*Soldiers–Buttons*	*Soldiers–Buttons*	*Soldiers–Buttons*	*Soldiers–Buttons*
Nicholas Belangi	Louis Barbella	Charles Albero	Dominic Alongi	Joseph Agone	Settimo Accardi	John Gregory Ardito
Lawrence Centore	Joseph Barra	Alfred Cupola	Edward Capobianco	Philip Albanese	Albert Barrasso	Lorenzo Brescia
Francesco Cucola	Morris Barra	Anthony DeMartino	Joseph DeNegris	Ottilio Caruso	Anthony Boiardi	Anthony Carillo
Aniello Ercole	Earl Coralluzzo	Benjamin DeMartino	Cosmo DiPietro	Mike Clemente	Paul Bonadio	Frank Celano
Frank Galluccio	Tobias DeMiccio	Theodore DeMartino	Alfred Faicco	George Filippone	Thomas Campisi	Salvatore Celembrino
August Laietta	Mattew Fortunato	Pasquale Erra	Anthony Florio	Joseph Lapi	Antonio Caponigro	Alfred Criscuolo
Gaetano Martino	Paul Marchione	Anthony Ferro	Mario Gigante	George Nobile	Charles Tourine, Sr.	Pete DeFeo
Aldo Mazzarati	John Savino	Joseph Lanza	Vincent Gigante	Michael Spinella	Peter LaPlaca	Joseph Lanza
Sabato Milo		Frank Livorsi	Michael Maione		Ernest Lazzara	Alfonso Marzano
Rocco Perrotta		Philip Lombardo	Vincent Mauro		Andrew Lombardino	Barney Miranda
James Picarelli		Felix Monaco	Gerardo Mosciello		Paul Lombardino	Carmine Persico, Jr.
Louis Prado		Louis Pacella	Sebastian Ofrica		Anthony Marchitto	David Petillo
Rudolph Prisco		Joseph Patera	Joseph Pagano		Anthony Peter Riela	Mathew Principe
Nicholas Ratenni		Al Rosato	Pasquale Pagano		Salvatore Chiri	Frank Tieri
Batisto Salvo		Anthony Salerno	Armando Perillo			Eli Zaccardi
George Smurra		Ferdinand Salerno	Girolamo Santuccio			
Gaetano Somma		Angelo Salerno	Fiore Siano			
		Dan Scargiatta	John Stopelli			
		Giovanni Schillaci	Joseph Valachi			
		Frank Serpico				
		Joseph Stracci				
		Joseph Tortorici				

Michael Coppola / Pasquale Eboli *Caporegime*

THE CARLO GAMBINO FAMILY

Carlo Gambino *Boss*

Joseph Riccobono Consigliere

Joseph Biondo *Underboss*

Caporegime

Anthony Sedotto
Anthony Zangarra
Joseph Colazzo
Aniello Dellacroce

Charles Dongarro
Peter Ferrara
Carmine Lombardozzi
Ettore Zappi

Paul Castellano
Paolo Gambino
Arthur Leo
Rocco Mazzie

Soldiers—Buttons

Andrew Alberti
Germanio Anaclerio
Joseph Armone
Eduardo Aronica
Peter Baratta
Charles Barcellona
Frank Barranca
Ernesto Barese
Sebastiano Bellanca
Salvatore Bonfrisco
Michael Bove
Anthony Carminati
James Casablanca
Matthew Cuomo

Alex D'Allesio
John D'Allesio
Mike D'Allesio
Charles DeLutro
Nicholas DiBene
Alex DeBrizzi
Charles Gagliodotto
Frank Gagliardi
Michael Galgano
Pasquale Genese
Anthony Granza
Frank Guglieimini
Sally Guglieimini
Joseph Indelicato

Giuseppe LoPiccolo
Frank Luciano
Aniello Mancuso
Genaro Mancuso
Joseph Manfredi
James Massi
Frank Moccardi
Sabato Muro
Frank Pasqua
Michael Pecoraro
Dominick Petito
Larry Pistone
Anthony Plate
Hugo Rossi

Giacomo Scalici
Joseph Scalici
Salvatore Scalici
Giacomo Scarpulla
Mike Scandifia
Al Seru
James Stassi
Joseph Stassi
Felice Teti
Arthur Tortorella
Peter Tortorella
Paul Zaccaria

THE GAETANO LUCCHESE FAMILY

Gaetano Lucchese *Boss*

Vincent John Rao *Consigliere*

Stefano LaSalle *Underboss*

Caporegime

Joseph Lucchese	Salvatore Santoro
John Ormento	Carmine Tramunti
James Plumeri	Natale Evola
Joseph Rosato	

Ettore Coco
Anthony Corallo
Joseph Laratro

Soldiers—Buttons

John Dioguardi	Neil Migliore	Joseph Silesi
Charles DiPalermo	Vic Panica	Nicholas Tolentino
Vincent Corrao	Andinno Pappadia	Angelo Tuminaro
Joseph DePalermo	Anthony LoPinto	Joseph Vento
Salvatore Granello	Vincent Potenza	Anthony Vadala
Anthony Lisi	Calogero Rao	Sam Valente
Salvatore LoProto	Charles Scoperto	Tom Valente
Salvatore Maneri	Salvatore Shillitani	James Vintaloro

Frank Arra
Nicholas Bonina
Frank Campanello
Paul John Carbo
Sam Cavalieri
Donato Laietta
Edward D'Argenio
John Di Carlo
Thomas Dioguardi

THE GIUSEPPE MAGLIOCCO FAMILY

Giuseppe Magliocco *Boss*

Salvatore Mussachio *Underboss*

Caporegime

Sebastiano Aloi   Harry Fontana
Simone Andolino   John Franzese
Salvatore Badalamenti   Ambrose Magliocco
Leo Carlino   Nicholas Forlano
Joseph Colombo   John Oddo

Soldiers—Buttons

Anthony Abbattemarco   Albert Gallo, Jr.   Frank Profaci
Cassandros Bonasera   Joseph Gallo   James Sabella
Alphonse D'Ambrosio   Lawrence Gallo   Modesto Santora
Salvatore D'Ambrosio   Philip Gambino   Joseph Schipani
Bartolo Ferrigno   Gaetano Marino   Giuseppe Tipa
Cosmo Frasca   Sebastiano Nani   Joseph Yacovelli

THE JOSEPH BONANNO FAMILY

Joseph Bonanno *Boss*
Carmine Galante *Underboss*
Frank Garafolo *Consigliere*
Joseph Nataro *Caporegime*

Soldiers—Buttons

James Colletti
Michael Consolo
Rosario Dionosio
Nicholas Marangello
Frank Mari
John Petrone
Angelo Presinzano
Frank Presinzano
Philip Rastelli
George Rizzo
Michael Sabella
Joseph Spadaro
Costenze Valente
Frank Valente
Nicholas Zapprana

other caporegime unidentified

APPENDIX D: La Cosa Nostra "Areas." Identified in the Valachi Hearings.

BUFFALO, NEW YORK, ORGANIZATION

Stefano Magaddino *Boss*
Fredrico Randaccio *Underboss*

Lieutenants

John Cammillieri
Pascal Natarelli
Roy Carlisi
Steven Cannarozzo

Section Leaders

Salvatore Brocato
Joseph Fino
Salvatore Bonito
Daniel Sansanese
Paul Briandi
Anthony Perna
Salvatore Rizzo
Pascal Politano
Sam Lagattuta
Salvatore Miano
Michael Tascarella

Relatives of Boss

Antonio Magaddino
James LaDuca

RHODE ISLAND AND
BOSTON, MASSACHUSETTS, ORGANIZATION

Philip Bruccola *Former Boss*
Raymond Patriarca *Boss* Genaro J. Angiulo

Rhode Island	*Boston, Mass.*
Henry Tamello	Frank Cucchiara
Antonio Lopreato	Anthony Sandrelli
Americo Bucci	Larry A. Zannino
Louis J. Taglinetti	Joseph Lombardi
Frank Morrelli	Francesco P. Intiso
John Candelmo	Leo Santaniello
Dominic J. Biafore	Peter J. Limone
Francis Joseph Patriarca	Michael Rocke
Alphonse Capalbo	Joseph Anselmo
Albert Le Pore	Santo Rizzo
Santino Ruggerio	John Gugliemo
Giuseppe Simonelli	Ralph Lamattina
Frank Forti	Theodore Fuccillo
Richard Ruggerio	Henry Selvitelli
Frank Ferrara	Nicholas A. Giso
Albert Joseph Vitali	Samuel Granito
Alfredo Rossi	

THE MAFIA ORGANIZATION IN THE DETROIT AREA

Ruling Council

Joseph Zerilli   John Priziola   Angelo Meli   William Tocco   Peter Licavoli

Administrators and Heirs Apparent

Michael Rubino	Joseph Massei	Joseph Bommarito	Raffaele Quasarano	Anthony Giacalone
Salvatore Lucido	Dominic P. Corrado	Santo Perrone	Michael Polizzi	Vincent A. Meli

Chiefs / Lieutenants

Chiefs	Chiefs	Chiefs	Lieutenants	Lieutenants
Dominic Corrado	Peter Vitale	Nick Ditta	Julian Cavataio	Frank Randazzo
Joseph Triglia	Paul Vitale	Vincent Finazzo	Peter Cavataio	Joe Brooklier
Tony Teramine	Joseph Barbara, Jr.	Michael Bartalotta	Salvatore Serra	Ricco Priziola
Anthony Cimini	Joseph Bommarito	Sam Lobaido	Sam Caruso	Tony Randazzo
	Frank Meli			
	Benedict Bommarito			
	Sam Finazzo			
	Dominic Cavataio			
	Eddie Guarella			

Section Leaders

Peter Maniaci	Angelo Lombardi	James Macagnone	Mario Agosta	Dominic Allevato
Dominic Bommarito	Anthony Imburnone	James Galici	Sam Giordano	Paul Cimino
Joe Coppola	Danny Bruno	Joseph Lobaido	Arthur Gallo	
Pete Lombardo	Pete Trupiano	Leonardo Monteleone	Frank Mudaro	

Windsor, Canada, Segment

Onofrio Minaudo (Lieutenant)   Joe Catalanotte (Lieutenant)   Nicolas Cicchini (Section Leader)

CHICAGO-ITALIAN ORGANIZATION

Overall Chicago Area, Bosses and Lieutenants

Salvatore Giancana	Dominic Brancato	John Cerone
Sam Battaglia	Felix Anthony Alderisio	Giuseppe Glielmi
Anthony Accardo	Rocco Fischetti	Rocco DeStefano
Paul Ricca	Ross Prio	Frank Caruso
Dominic Nuccio	Frank Ferrera	Fiore Buccieri
Dominic DiBella	Marshall Caifano	William Aloisio
	Francesco Cironato	

West Side

William Daddano	Leonard Gianola	Mario A. DeStefano	Ned Bakes	Joseph A. Ferriola	Rocco Potenza	Frank Fratto
Charles English	James Mirro	Sam DeStefano	Dominic Blasi	Ernest Infelice	Louis Rosanova	Frank Eulo
Frank Buccieri	Charles Nicoletti	Vito DeStefano	Samuel Cesario	Vincent J. Inserro	Rocco Salvatore	James Torello
Joseph Aiuppa	Anthony Pitello	John DeBiase	Eco James Coli	John Lardino	Joseph Siciliano	Phillip Mesi
Albert Capone	Louis Briatta	Rocco DeGrazia	Dominic Cortina	John L. Manzella	Tarquin Simonelli	Frank Manno
John Capone	Albert Frabotta	Charles Tourino, Jr.	Joseph Colucci	Sam Mesi	Frank Teutonico	Nick Manno, Jr.
Matthew Capone	Joseph Gagliano	Dominic Volpe	Americo DePietto	William Messino	Nick Visco	Sam Manno
Ralph Capone	Joseph Fusco	Sam Ariola	Anthony Eldorado	Rocco Paternoster	Joseph A. Accardo	Thomas Manno

North Side

Placideo Divarco	Frank Orlando	James Policheri	Anthony DeMonte	Michael Glitta	L. Buonaguidi	Joseph LaBarbara
	Joseph Liscandrella	Samuel Liscandrella	Frank Liscandrella	Cosmo Orlando	Ben J. Policheri	

South Side

George Tuffanelli	James Roti	James Catura	James R. Cordovano	Anthony DeLordo	Charles B. DiCaro	Joseph N. DiCaro
	Anthony Panzica	Louis Tornabene	Frank C. Tornabene	Joseph Caruso	Anthony DeRosa	

TAMPA, FLORIDA, AREA

Alfonso Diecidue (deceased), 1947
Santo Trafficante, Sr. (deceased), 1964

Top Man

Santo Trafficante, Jr., alias "Louis Santos"

Elders

Salvatore Scaglione, alias "Sam"   Gaetano Mistretta, alias "Joe"

Members

Frank Diecidue	Joe Bedami	Philip Plazza	Alphonso Scaglione
James Costa Longo	Augustine Primo Lazzara	Angelo Lo Scalzo	Henry Trafficante
Angelo Bedami	Domenick Furci	Stefano Scaglione	Salvatore Joe Lorenzo
Ciro Bedami	Sam Cacciatore Trafficante	Nick Scaglione	James Guida Bruno

Central and East Florida Coastal Area

Samuel Cacciatore

Nonmember Associates and Employees Associates

Harlan Blackburn

Rudy Mach	Joe Wheeler	Mathew Smith	"Sonny" Brown
Don Mach	Max Reid	Macon Tribue	George Solomon
Dan Fussel	Mary Chardan	Julia Ciphon	Ralph Strawder
Buddy Parron	Phil Riffe	Hoy Anderson	Benny White
Glen Brechen	Clyde P. Lee	Kat Bradshaw	William Harrell
Tommy Berry	Jesse Joyner	Cecil Merritt	Elvin Carroll
Clifford Bell	Vasco Joyner	Clayton Thomas	

NONMEMBER ASSOCIATES OF
CHICAGO-ITALIAN ORGANIZATION

Overall Chicago Area

Murray Humphreys
Ralph Pierce
Gus Alex
Lester Kruse
Fred Thomas Smith
Leonard Patrick
David Yaras

West Side

Joseph Corngold
Elias Argyropoulos
August Dierolf Liebe
Edward Vogel
Leo Rugendorf
John Wolek
William Block
Nick Bravos
George J. Bravos
Maish Baer
Frank Zimmerman
Gus Spiro Zapas
Jack Patrick

North Side

William Goldstein
Joseph Arnold
Robert Furey
Phillip Katz
Irving Dworetzky

South Side

Bernard Posner
Arthur Markovitz
Michael Markovitz
Hyman Gottfried

APPENDIX E: Strike Force Chain of Command in the Organized Crime and Racketeering Section of the Justice Department

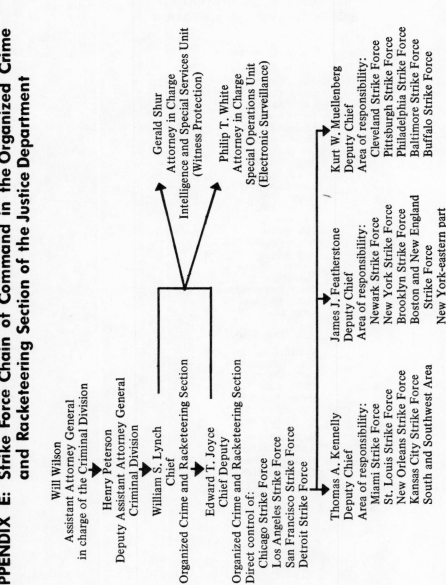

Will Wilson
Assistant Attorney General
in charge of the Criminal Division

Henry Peterson
Deputy Assistant Attorney General
Criminal Division

William S. Lynch
Chief
Organized Crime and Racketeering Section

Edward T. Joyce
Chief Deputy
Organized Crime and Racketeering Section
Direct control of:
Chicago Strike Force
Los Angeles Strike Force
San Francisco Strike Force
Detroit Strike Force

Gerald Shur
Attorney in Charge
Intelligence and Special Services Unit
(Witness Protection)

Philip T. White
Attorney in Charge
Special Operations Unit
(Electronic Surveillance)

Thomas A. Kennelly
Deputy Chief
Area of responsibility:
Miami Strike Force
St. Louis Strike Force
New Orleans Strike Force
Kansas City Strike Force
South and Southwest Area

James J. Featherstone
Deputy Chief
Area of responsibility:
Newark Strike Force
New York Strike Force
Brooklyn Strike Force
Boston and New England
Strike Force
New York-eastern part

Kurt W. Muellenberg
Deputy Chief
Area of responsibility:
Cleveland Strike Force
Pittsburgh Strike Force
Philadelphia Strike Force
Baltimore Strike Force
Buffalo Strike Force

BRIEF BIOGRAPHIES OF STRIKE FORCE PERSONNEL

WILLIAM S. LYNCH
Chief
Organized Crime and Racketeering Section, May 1969

Mr. Lynch was born in New York City on December 5, 1926. He received his B.S. degree from Fordham University in 1950, and his LL.B. from Harvard Law School in 1953. He served as an Assistant United States Attorney in Southern District of New York from 1955 to 1959, returning to private practice from 1959 to 1961, and has been with the Justice Department since 1961. From 1961 to 1966 he was assigned to the Organized Crime and Racketeering Section on trial and appellate work. From 1966 to May 1969, he served as Deputy Chief of the Organized Crime and Racketeering Section under Henry Peterson.

EDWARD T. JOYCE
Chief Deputy
Organized Crime and Racketeering Section

Mr. Joyce was born May 23, 1920, in New York City. He received his LL.B. degree from St. John's University in 1949. He was in private practice from 1949 to 1952, and joined the Justice Department in 1958 upon discharge from the United States Navy as Commander. He has been in the Organized Crime and Racketeering Section conducting trials on a wide range of racketeering matters. He became Chief Deputy of the Organized Crime and Racketeering Section in June of 1969.

JAMES J. FEATHERSTONE
Deputy Chief

Mr. Featherstone was born November 14, 1926, in Wilkes-Barre, Pennsylvania. He received an A.B. in 1950 from St. Peter's College, and an LL.B. in 1953 from Fordham University Law School. He joined the Department of Justice in October 1955.

KURT W. MUELLENBERG
Deputy Chief

Mr. Muellenberg was born January 6, 1932, in Jena, Germany. He received a B.A. from the University of Maryland in 1958, and an LL.B. from the University of Maryland Law School in 1961. He joined the Department of Justice in December 1966.

THOMAS A. KENNELLY
Deputy Chief

Mr. Kennelly was born February 11, 1930, in Dubuque, Iowa. He received a B.A. in 1951 from St. Thomas College, and an LL.B. in 1954 from Santa Clara University Law School. He joined the Department of Justice as an Assistant United States Attorney in San Francisco in 1958, and was transferred to Washington in May 1962.

GERALD SHUR
Attorney in Charge
Intelligence and Special Services Unit

Mr. Shur was born in New York City in 1933.

He was graduated from the University of Texas with a degree of Bachelor of Business Administration and was awarded the degree of Doctor of Jurisprudence in 1957.

Mr. Shur entered the private practice of law in Corpus Christi, Texas. He was appointed to the position of trial attorney in the Organized Crime and Racketeering Section of the Department of Justice in 1961, and served as area coordinator of federal investigations involving organized crime in the New York City area. Subsequent to service as an area coordinator, Mr. Shur was appointed Staff Assistant to the Section Chief. In the summer of 1969 he was appointed Attorney-in-Charge of the Intelligence and Special Services Unit which is charged with the responsibility of coordinating all intelligence activities of the Organized Crime and Racketeering Section.

PHILIP T. WHITE
Attorney in Charge
Special Operations Unit

Mr. White was born in Lynn, Massachusetts, November 27, 1924. He is a native of Massachusetts, and received his A.B. degree from Boston College in 1949, and his LL.B. degree from Georgetown University in 1951.

He served as law clerk to United States District Judge Edward M. Curran, District of Columbia, from 1951 to 1952, and since 1952 has been employed as an attorney in the Department of Justice, serving in the Office of Legal Counsel and the Internal Security and Criminal Divisions. Since 1958, Mr. White has served as a trial attorney in the Organized Crime and Racketeering Section of the Criminal Division, and for the past two and one-half years has been Attorney-in-Charge of the Special Operations Unit of this Section which supervises, inter alia, all federal applications for court-authorized electronic surveillance pursuant to Title III of the Omnibus Crime Control and Safe Streets Act of 1967.

APPENDIX F: Strike Forces and Personnel

Strike Force No. 1—Buffalo, New York
Organized November, 1966

JAMES R. RICHARDS, *Chief*

Mr. Richards was born November 21, 1933, in Kinderpost, Missouri. He received a B.A. in 1955 from Western State College, and an LL.B. in 1960 from the University of Colorado Law School. He joined the Department of Justice in February 1969.

Others in the unit are:

Dennis P. O'Keefe
Robert G. Ryan
Robert C. Stewart

Strike Force No. 2—Detroit, Michigan
Organized December, 1967

LAURENCE LEFF, *Chief*

Mr. Leff was born January 26, 1934, in New York, New York. He was educated at City College of New York, receiving a B.B.A. in 1958, and at Fordham University Law School, with an LL.B. in 1962. He joined the Department of Justice in July 1969.

Others in the unit are:

George G. Newman
Clyde B. Pritchard
Alfred G. Kaufman
Haskell H. Shelton
Arnold G. Shulman

Strike Force No. 3—Brooklyn, New York
Organized April, 1968

DENIS E. DILLON, *Chief*

Mr. Dillon was born December 21, 1933, in New York, New York. He graduated from Fordham University in 1955 with a B.S., and from

Fordham University Law School in 1962 with an LL.D. He joined the Department of Justice in 1962.

Others in the unit are:

Joseph F. Lynch
Michael B. Pollack
William T. Murphy
James O. Druker
Liam S. Connan

Strike Force No. 4—Philadelphia, Pennsylvania
Organized July, 1968

RICHARD T. SPRIGGS, *Chief*

Mr. Spriggs was born March 29, 1935, in Rome, New York. He received a B.A. in 1958 from Colgate University, and an LL.B. in 1961 from Cornell University. He joined the Department of Justice in December 1968.

Others in the unit are:

Robert C. Ozer
Raymond E. Makowski
Joel H. Slomsky

Strike Force No. 5—Chicago, Illinois
Organized October, 1968

SHELDON DAVIDSON, *Chief*

Mr. Davidson was born February 13, 1938, in Chicago, Illinois. He graduated from De Paul University in 1959 with a B.S.C., and from De Paul Law School in 1962 with a J.D. He joined the Department of Justice in September 1962.

Others in the unit are:

Peter R. Viara
Douglas P. Roller
David M. Quinn
Michael H. King
Terry R. Lord
Lee A. Hawke
Herbert Beigel
James R. Hastings

Strike Force No. 6—Newark, New Jersey
Organized December, 1968

JOHN R. BARTELS, *Chief*

Mr. Bartels was born November 27, 1934, in Brooklyn, New York. He studied at Harvard College, where he was awarded a B.A. in 1956; the University of Munich in 1956 and 1957; and Harvard Law School, receiving an LL.B. in 1960. He joined the Department of Justice in April 1969.

Others in the unit are:

Robert T. Richardson
Herbert T. Posner
Frederick P. Hafetz
Joseph L. Cranwell
Roy B. Beene
John L. Kase

Strike Force No. 7—Miami, Florida
Organized December, 1968

DOUGALD D. McMILLAN, *Chief*

Mr. McMillan was born September 8, 1930, in Malone, Florida. He was awarded a B.S. in 1953 from Florida State University and an LL.B. in 1958 from the University of Florida. He joined the Department of Justice in August 1961.

Others in the unit are:

William L. McCulley
Gary L. Betz
Marilu Marshall
William P. Cagney III

Strike Force No. 8—Boston, Massachusetts
Organized May, 1969

EDWARD F. HARRINGTON, *Chief*

Mr. Harrington was born September 16, 1933, in Fall River, Massachusetts. He received a B.A. in 1955 from Holy Cross College, and an LL.B. in 1960 from Boston College Law School. He joined the Department of Justice in November 1961.

Others in the unit are:

Albert F. Cullen, Jr.
John R. Tarrant
Fred T. Bennett

Strike Force No. 9—New York, New York
Organized July, 1969

DANIEL P. HOLLMAN, *Chief*

Mr. Hollman was born August 10, 1930, in New York, New York. He was awarded a B.S. from Fordham University in 1942, and an LL.B. from Fordham University Law School in 1957. He joined the Department of Justice in September 1957.

Others in the unit are:

Gerald T. McGuire
Milton J. Carp
Patrick T. Burke
Joel M. Friedman
Patrick T. Philbin
Michael L. Sterrett
Patric F. Broderick

Strike Force No. 10—Cleveland, Ohio
Organized November, 1969

Strike Force Chief position vacant
William Tomlinson resigned July, 1971

ROBERT D. GARY, *Acting Chief*

Mr. Gary was born June 4, 1941, in Lorain, Ohio. He was awarded a B.A. in 1963 from Western Reserve University, a J.D. in 1966 from Western Reserve University School of Law, and an LL.M. in Criminal Justice in 1967 from New York University School of Law. He joined the Department of Justice in September 1967.

Others in the unit are:

Roger L. McRoberts
Steven R. Olah

Strike Force No. 11—Los Angeles, California
Organized January, 1970

ALFRED N. KING, *Chief*

Mr. King was born October 24, 1931, in Des Moines, Iowa. He graduated from William and Mary College with a B.A. in 1953, and from Georgetown University Law School in 1961 with an LL.B. He joined the Department of Justice in October 1961.

Others in the unit are:

Richard P. Crane, Jr.
Allan B. Streller
Robert S. Thaller

Strike Force No. 12—St. Louis, Missouri
Organized May, 1970

GERALD E. McDOWELL, *Chief*

Mr. McDowell was born April 20, 1942, in Norwich, Connecticut. He received an A.B. from the University of Rhode Island in 1964, and an LL.B. from the University of Virginia Law School in 1967. He joined the Department of Justice in July 1967.

Others in the unit are:

Thomas M. Vockrodt
Harry L. Strachan, III
J. Kenneth Lowrie

Strike Force No. 13—New Orleans, Louisiana
Organized June, 1970

JOHN E. WALL, *Chief*

Mr. Wall was born October 4, 1931, in Lynn, Massachusetts. He graduated from Boston College in 1954 with a B.S.; from Columbia University Law School in 1960 with an LL.B.; and Georgetown University Law School in 1965 with an LL.M. He joined the Department of Justice in September 1963.

Others in the unit are:
John L. Smith
Jimmy L. Tallant
K. Eric Gisleson
Michael P. Carnes

Strike Force No. 14—Pittsburgh, Pennsylvania
Organized October, 1970

JULES T. BRUNNER, *Chief*

Mr. Brunner was born July 24, 1937, in Chicago, Illinois. He was awarded a B.S. from the University of Wisconsin in 1960, and a J.D. from Loyola University in 1964. He joined the Department of Justice in November 1969.

Others in the unit are:

Kenneth A. Bravo
Terrance A. Norton
John M. Elias
Thomas A. Bergstrom

Strike Force No. 15—Baltimore, Maryland
Organized November, 1970

WALTER T. BARNES, *Chief*

Mr. Barnes was born December 30, 1925, in Lynn, Massachusetts. He graduated from Fordham University in 1949 with a B.S. degree, and from Georgetown University Law School in 1952 with an LL.B. He joined the Department of Justice in November 1952.

Others in the unit are:

William S. Kenney
Joseph Kiel
James H. Jeffries, III
David E. Holt

Strike Force No. 16—San Francisco, California
Organized December, 1970

JAMES E. RITCHIE, *Chief*

Mr. Ritchie was born September 16, 1936, in Lordsburg, New
Mexico. He graduated from Oklahoma State University in 1958 with a
B.S., and from the University of Tulsa Law School in 1961 with a J.D.
He joined the Department of Justice in December 1968.

Others in the unit are:

Philip R. Michael
Maurice K. Merten
Jack O'Donnell
Stephen H. Scott

Strike Force No. 17—Kansas City, Missouri
Organized February, 1971

MICHAEL A. DeFEO, *Chief*

Mr. DeFeo was born October 17, 1938, in Kansas City, Missouri. He
received a B.S. in 1959 from Rockhurst College; an LL.B. in 1962 from
the University of Missouri School of Law; and an LL.M. in 1963 from
Northwestern University. He joined the Department of Justice in
August 1963.

Others in the unit are:

Gary Cornwell
James A. Twitty
John C. Emerson

Strike Force No. 18
Organized February, 1971

ROBERT J. CAMPBELL, *Chief*

Mr. Campbell was born March 25, 1939, in Elmira, New York. He
was awarded an A.B. by the University of Notre Dame in 1961, and an

LL.B. by Harvard University Law School in 1964. He joined the Department of Justice in September 1966.

Others in the unit are:

William (Bill) McCulley
Harold (Hal) Webb
W. Boone Vastine

APPENDIX G: Strike Force Report on Court-Authorized Electronic Surveillance

During the years 1969, 1970, and 1971 to date, a total of 387 court orders (including 65 extensions) have been obtained and executed in connection with federal organized crime investigations. During this same period only one application for a court order was denied.

The categories of offenses in which the 387 orders have been obtained and executed are as follows:

Gambling	279
Narcotics	74
Extortionate Credit Transactions	23
Counterfeiting	4
Interstate Transportation of Stolen Property	3
Theft from Commerce and Robbery	2
Kidnapping	1
Obstruction of Justice	1
	387

All but 15 of the executed interception orders have been productive.

As a result of these interceptions, over 1,200 arrests have been made and more than 100 convictions obtained.

Examples of several recent successful intercepts, where normal investigative procedures could not be utilized, are as follows:

In May of this year (1971), agents of the U.S. Customs Agency Service seized five tons of marihuana attempted to be smuggled into the United States at San Francisco, California, by boat from Mexico, and arrested Richard Michael King of San Diego, leader of this narcotics smuggling conspiracy and other members of his group. King and 13 others have been indicted by a federal grand jury in San Diego for conspiracy to violate the federal narcotics laws.

On May 28 and 29 of this year, agents of the U.S. Customs Agency Service at Los Angeles arrested Alfred Salas and eight other Los-Angeles-area residents on charges of importing heroin and cocaine into the United States from Mexico. Ten pounds of high-grade cocaine and heroin were seized, and indictments are expected to be returned.

On May 6 of this year, federal grand juries in the Eastern and Western Districts of Michigan returned 16 indictments charging 153 persons on federal gambling charges including violation of the Syndicated Gambling provisions of the Organized Crime Control Act of 1970. In one indictment, 16 members of the Detroit Police

Department, including one Inspector, three Lieutenants and seven Sergeants, as well as a number of high-echelon Detroit area gamblers, were charged with conspiracy to obstruct the criminal laws of the state of Michigan with intent to facilitate an illegal gambling business. This indictment marks the first employment of Section 1511 of Title 18, United States Code. The return of the indictments was coordinated with the arrests of the defendants and the execution of more than 100 search warrants.

On April 21 of this year a special federal grand jury in Brooklyn, New York, returned indictments against Joseph Colombo, head of a La Cosa Nostra family in New York City, and 30 other defendants for violation of the prohibited illegal gambling business provisions of Section 1955 of Title 18, United States Code. The interceptions disclosed a large-scale race-horse policy operation with an estimated gross revenue of approximately $10 million a year.

In June of this year a U.S. District Court jury in Miami, Florida, returned guilty verdicts against two major Miami bookmakers, Martin and Jesse Sklaroff, on federal gambling charges in violation of Section 1084 of Title 18, United States Code (Transmission of wagering information by use of a wire communication facility by persons engaged in the business of betting or wagering).

INDEX